How
to be
Heard

Secrets for Powerful
Speaking and Listening

by
Julian Treasure

Cover Design: Roberto Núñez
Layout & Design: Roberto Núñez

For permission requests, please contact the publisher at:
Mango Publishing Group
2850 Douglas Road, 3rd Floor
Coral Gables, FL 33134 USA
info@mango.bz

For special orders, quantity sales, course adoptions and corporate sales, please email the publisher at sales@mango.bz. For trade and wholesale sales, please contact Ingram Publisher Services at customer.service@ingramcontent.com or +1.800.509.4887.

How to be Heard: Secrets for Powerful Speaking and Listening

Library of Congress Cataloging-in-Publication number: 2017953621
ISBN: (paperback) 978-1-63353-671-5, (ebook) 978-1-63353-672-2

BISAC category code:
SEL040000 SELF-HELP / Communication & Social Skills
BUS007010 BUSINESS & ECONOMICS / Business Communication / Meetings & Presentations

Printed in the United States of America

For Jane and Holly, who missed me, supported me, and loved me throughout the writing of this book.

The website

This book has a companion website at www.howtobeheardbook.com, with a special area for you as a bookowner, protected by the password **conscious**. Once you've entered the password you'll have access to a treasure trove (pun intended) of valuable assets that will help you on your journey to conscious speaking and listening. You'll be able to access the fascinating interviews conducted for this book in full: you can listen to them in streaming audio, or read the complete transcripts. There are also audio blogs from me, covering many of the topics in the book, often with extra detail or information.

Introduction

S ound has always been my primary connection with the world. In my childhood in South West London we lived by parks and later a river, and I remember listening with wonder at night to the sound of gentle summer rain outside my window, or looking up in woodland walks and being transported by the sound of wind rustling lush Spring leaves together in rich, fascinating waves. It was inevitable that music became a passion from the start; I spent many hours in darkened rooms listening studiously through cherished headphones to a fast-growing collection of precious vinyl. Becoming a musician was the natural next step, and my parents were tolerant enough to buy my first drum kit and bear the pounding from my bedroom as I tried to emulate heroes like John Bonham and Bill Bruford.

Many paradiddles and many bands later, I sold my magazine publishing business and at last had the chance to unify my work with my passion for sound. I had spent more than fifteen years helping brands to create written content that would engage, enlighten and entertain their customers—all the while continuing to play and make music in my spare time. Now I wanted to help those same organisations to make sound that was appropriate, effective and beautiful, both in their marketing and in the spaces they managed, from offices to banks, shops, malls and airports. And so The Sound Agency was born in 2003, its mission to prove that good sound was good business.

The Sound Agency was always about sound, not just music; in fact, we have spent a lot of time removing mindless music from places where it was playing inappropriately and upsetting people. To develop a robust *modus operandi* that applied not only art and aesthetics but also science and technology, I read papers, journals and books, initially about the psychology of music, and then about the greater subject of sound and how it affects human beings. We started to ask the question "How does your brand sound?" with increasing understanding and experience, and then I created a set of models and tools that allowed us to map the effects of all sorts of sound on employees, customers and prospects.

In 2007 I pulled all this thinking together into a book, inevitably entitled *Sound Business*, which became a respected textbook for audio branding agencies and their clients alike, helping them to explore this exciting new territory of intentional, designed sound. Two years later, I got the chance to speak at the TEDGlobal conference in Oxford, England, albeit with the challenge of condensing everything I'd learned about sound into six minutes! That talk led to four more in successive years, all of them subsequently published as videos on the TED website. As I created them, my focus shifted from sound in business to sound in human interaction—in other words, to listening and speaking.

For many years, I had known that very few people listened well. This was clear from the blank faces we usually met when trying to sell The Sound Agency's services: every major brand has a book defining it, many of them as thick as a Bible and even referred to as 'brand bibles'—and none of them contain any pages at all about sound. Our society is crashingly ocular. The business managers we met didn't think at all about the sound their organisations made, so each time before we could start selling our wares, we had to have a short, transformative conversation, explaining how sound affects people and why the management need to be listening. This conversation is what eventually formed the core of my first TED talk, and it usually resulted in an astonished expression and the phrase: "Now you say it, this is so obvious, but we've never thought about it before!" You may well encounter that little paradox yourself at points in this book, and you will be in good company. Most of the top managers I've met at major companies have had exactly this experience. I remember presenting to the CEO of British Airports Authority when London Heathrow's beautiful Terminal 5 was in the early stages of construction. Like many successful senior managers, he was open to challenge and grasped big ideas fast. About five minutes into my passionate description of how sound affects people, he stopped me and said: "I cannot believe we're about to spend four billion pounds on a new building, and we have never asked: 'How will it sound?'"

I gradually realised that what's true for people running brands is just as true of all of us in every aspect of our lives. Most people do not listen much at all. And when I started thinking about human communication I saw the full extent of the tyranny of the eyes: not only do we not listen well, we don't speak well either. Somewhere along the way, our oldest, most natural, powerful and effective mode of communication got taken for granted, devalued and then left behind as the world became ever-noisier and technology beguiled our eyes and appropriated our fingers too.

People have always been scared of public speaking, but now it seems we have a generation scared of private speaking too. Research shows that youngsters would rather text or instant message than talk to ask someone out, or to break up with someone. The next oldest generation loves the big social media platforms, and the one above that is lost in email overload. When we want to communicate, our first instinct is to reach for a piece of technology and type.

This is about to change, even for the most tech-savvy. Billions have been invested in speech recognition and voice synthesis, and more importantly in artificial intelligence (AI). Scary as this development may be (check TED to understand why), it does mean that within the next five years we will be having meaningful, natural conversations with machines. When each of us has our own AI assistant, we will have no need to deal with dozens of apps and our umbilical connection with screens will be broken. Unless we want to look at something, we will simply ask. Voice communication will be back, as we query the Internet, make travel reservations, carry out financial transactions, manage our houses and cars, send messages and even (whisper it) communicate with other human beings by speaking and listening.

In parallel, we saw in the year 2016 what happens in politics if people can't or won't listen. Democracy depends on civilised disagreement, which requires listening to people with whom we disagree and understanding and respecting their perspective. It also requires the skill of oratory, the elegant and skillful exposition of an argument in a debate in order to persuade others or explain complex issues. Increasingly, political discourse is being carried out in soundbites to journalists or even in 140 bombastic characters. People seek out proof that they are right on the Internet, collecting views that support theirs and ignoring antithetical ones. This is a recipe for polarisation. The only antidote is skilled conversation: conscious listening and powerful speaking working together.

These two crucial abilities affect one another in a circular relationship: it's hard to be a great, powerful speaker if you don't listen, or to be a great listener if you can't articulate your own thoughts. This is the central subject matter of this book.

Technology is unstoppable, so time is short. We urgently need to reclaim the art of conversation. However, if we look to traditional education, there is little or no infrastructure to help us. Very few schools teach speaking or listening in any serious way, and no countries that I know of have national curricula with exams in these vital life skills. This is the gap that this book is designed to fill: we urgently need to educate ourselves if we are to master sound communication, pun intended. My TED talk on powerful speaking is the sixth most-viewed of all time, with around 50 million views on the Internet at the time of this writing. It's wonderful that so many people have taken this in—but the talk is only a few minutes long, and necessarily passes over much of the depth and breadth of the topic. It's also worth noting that my TED talk on conscious listening has only one quarter as many views, which says something about our communication. We prioritise sending over receiving, which is itself a dangerous mistake.

For all these reasons, I was delighted when Mango offered me the opportunity to write a whole book about the skills of speaking and listening. At last, I can make publicly available the content and the lessons I've learned from seminars and workshops on conscious communication that I've given to thousands of people over the last few years. I hope the result will be interesting, engaging, transformative—and most of all a practical resource you can pick up and refer to again and again.

If you want to make a difference in the world, or to be a great parent, or to have a brilliant relationship, or to lead and inspire people, or to be someone that people stop to listen to, or to be a real friend, or to be a star salesperson, or even to stand on the TED stage and change the way people think forever... this book is for you.

Table of Contents

Introduction   6

Chapter One
Why this matters   14

Chapter Two
The dark side   50

Chapter Three
Exploring listening and speaking   96

Chapter Four
How to listen consciously   132

Chapter Five
How to achieve perfect content   186

Chapter Six
Your vocal toolbox   236

Chapter Seven
Stagecraft   264

In closing   304

Author Bio   306

Chapter One

Why this matters

This book contains many exercises and suggestions that will help you to become a conscious, attentive listener, and a powerful, effective speaker when you practice them. That's a lot of potential work, so we start in this chapter with the *why*... revealing the four effects of sound; the power of conscious listening and speaking and what you can gain by improving these skills; and the issue that almost everyone suffers from.

What's at stake for you?

Working in four powerful but largely unnoticed ways, sound (especially how we speak and how we listen) affects almost everything we feel, think and do. Inevitably this process shapes the full panoply of our results in life, both today and in the long term.

Over the years, I have distilled this process down to three core outcomes: happiness, effectiveness and wellbeing. If none of these are important to you, you need read no further! However, I suspect they do matter a lot to you, so let me promise you that the information, exercises and revelations in this book do, when practiced, have the power to transform your outcomes in all three of these critical areas.

Let's look at what you stand to gain from taking this path.

HAPPINESS

We all know what happiness is, but achieving it remains the eternal human challenge. It certainly isn't about material possessions or financial wealth: once people are above the poverty level and not stressing about where their next meal is coming from, psychologists find that there is no correlation at all between money and happiness. Nor do fame, respect or reputation create happiness: famous or gifted people are just as prone to misery as the rest of us (maybe more so if you believe the gossip pages).

The only factors that do seem to correlate with happiness are connectedness and service. People who have strong family and social connections, or who serve others in meaningful ways, tend to be happier than average.

Both traits require well-developed speaking and listening skills. Service can only be effective if you listen well so that you understand what someone really needs; good functional relationships are built on clear, compassionate two-way communication. You'll be learning skills throughout this book that will enhance your relationships at work, at home and in your community, and that will generate greater happiness for you as a result.

The sound around you also has an impact on your happiness. Noise creates stress, and often real pain and misery. Pleasing sounds that mean something to you may instantly make you feel good. We'll be learning how to manage sound for greater happiness throughout the book.

EFFECTIVENESS

Many of the people who have come to my trainings say that they are there because they have the feeling nobody listens to them, or that they can't seem to get their passion or their views across to others. Without good communication, it really is hard to have an impact in life. We can't all develop the potent listening of a Mahatma Gandhi or the persuasive eloquence of a Martin Luther King—but we can all make the most of the gifts we've been given by learning how to use our voice and our ears to maximum effect.

Speaking and listening are critical skills if you want to make a difference in the world, to lead and inspire people or to be a great parent. These things all rely on the power and effectiveness of your speaking and your listening. Everything in this book is aimed at giving you mastery of these vital skills.

We'll also be considering the context for communication throughout the book. Ambient sound has a real impact on how well we can connect, so we'll be exploring how this works and discovering ways to deal with destructive sound throughout this book.

Ambient sound also has a powerful impact on how well we process information, so it can dramatically alter how efficient you are in your work. Simply by listening to your environment and paying attention to its effects on your communication and thinking, you become able to take steps to optimise your working conditions and transform your productivity. This might mean moving away from, or blocking out, unhelpful, distracting or debilitating sound; or, if you have control over your space, it might mean identifying the sound that is most productive for you to work in—something that most people never consider.

Tip: I can't predict what sound might be best for you to use in working, because we are all different and your personal associations will be very significant in this process. Nevertheless, I suggest that you start experimenting with nature sound that is stochastic, which means composed of many small, random events that combine to create a pleasing wash with no significant individual events to grab your attention. Examples are moderate birdsong, gentle rainfall, gentle running water like babbling streams and small waterfalls or fountains, mild wind in leaves or grass. Probably best to avoid the soporific sound of soothing surf! If you try music, then you may find the most productive genres are those with low density, which means not too many changes in melody, rhythm or dynamics and no significant major events. Those guidelines may lead you towards reflective styles like ambient or gentle chamber music, or repetitive styles like trance, techno, chant or modal music. Styles with strong dynamics and frequent changes are probably more distracting; these might include full-blown orchestral music, jazz, pop, rock, dance or urban. Many people, especially youngsters, think they are more productive with loud, high-density music playing, but in most cases that is true only in that they are doing the work at all or that they continue to do it for longer: in terms of output per minute, high-density sound is generally distracting. I do want to emphasise that we are all different, and I expect that there are some for whom thrash metal is a very productive backdrop, so please do experiment for yourself and be open-minded and creative!

WELLBEING

In 1859, Florence Nightingale wrote: "Unnecessary noise is the most cruel absence of care that can be inflicted on sick or well." Recent research has shown how right she was. Sound can powerfully affect our health and wellbeing, for good or for ill—and sadly in most cases it's the latter. Listening consciously is the key to transforming what in many cases is a negative effect into a positive one in your life.

There are three levels to the impact of sound on our wellbeing.

Level 1

Loud sounds can damage your hearing. If we're not listening consciously, it's all too easy to be exposed and damaged without becoming aware of it. For many years noise induced hearing loss (NIHL) has been a major issue for people whose jobs expose them to loud sounds, from soldiers in battle to those working in manufacturing and construction. Now it's a recreational hazard as well as an occupational one as a result of headphone abuse—something that barely existed before the invention of mobile sound with the Walkman in 1979. Delivering music at high volume deep into the ear for hours a day is a recipe for hearing damage, and possibly severe hearing loss later in life. A 1998 scientific paper found that almost 15 per cent of American teenagers have permanent hearing damage, while a 2010 survey in London found that two thirds of the people interviewed were exceeding the recommended safe listening level, some of them by massive amounts.

Of course, headphones can be a joyful and productive experience. Noise cancelling headphones are excellent on flights, and headphones can also mask unpleasant or distracting sounds when we are trying to work. The trick is using them healthily, and not being tempted to keep turning the volume up.

Tip: If you or any of your family use headphones, here are three ways of making sure that you don't damage your hearing. First, invest in the best headphones you can afford. Cheap, low performance headphones tempt people to turn up the volume in search of the detail and bandwidth they miss at moderate listening levels due to the poor quality of the components. Second, make sure the volume is not so loud that you can't hear someone speaking loudly to you from a metre (roughly three feet) away. Third, do not listen for hours every day, especially at a level above the one suggested here. Expert advice on safe listening times depends on volume so it's hard to give unequivocal guidance, but please be aware that most mobile devices are capable of maximum volumes with recommended daily exposure times of just a few minutes!

Level 2

Sound directly affects your overall health as well as your hearing. Long term exposure to noise has been shown to increase the risk of heart disease and stroke, largely because it increases blood pressure and creates stress. This is not restricted to industrial-scale noise: with group work in class, teachers are regularly exposed to enough noise to activate this effect. It is probable that many teachers are shortening their lives by working in noisy classrooms day after day.

Noise also results in massive global health issues by causing sleep deprivation. The World Health Organisation estimates that around eight million people in Western Europe are suffering nightly sleep interruptions due to traffic noise that's way above its recommended maximum level; many more are affected in the same way by nearby airports or railways. Long term sleep deprivation has many serious health effects, from stress and depression to impaired immune systems; it also leads to accidents, impatience, irritability and violence. This problem has not been quantified in other territories, but I have no doubt that it exists all over the world, especially in the fast-growing cities where more than half the world's population live.

On a more positive note, sound can also heal and restore. There is a large and well established tradition of music therapy, now supported in the USA by learned journals, a mass of scientific evidence and a major organisation in the American Music Therapists Association. Carefully chosen music has been shown to aid recovery from strokes and heart attacks, as well as being powerfully effective for many with severe autism, dementia and many other conditions. Recent UK research has shown that birdsong can also be therapeutic, which backs up my long-held belief that the sounds of gentle wind, water and birds are healthy for us.

Level 3

Our focus in this book is speaking and listening. Wellbeing is enhanced by being able to express oneself clearly and effectively, but it can be compromised by the frustrations that arise when we feel we are not listened to in life. At the same time, conscious listening is the key that unlocks wellbeing from all sound. If we become conscious of the sound we make and the sound we consume, we can start to manage our environment to avoid unhealthy sound and surround ourselves with sound that works for, not against, our wellbeing.

Context is key

In this chapter, we spend some time investigating sound in general before we dive deep into the secrets of powerful speaking and conscious listening. We do this because speaking and listening always happen in a *context*. This context is often unhelpful: noisy offices, badly designed meeting rooms, poor phone or VoIP connections, low quality or badly adjusted public address systems, street corners with loud traffic noise, an elevator full of people listening... the list goes on. When you remember to consider the context for your communication, you can take measures to improve it, maybe moving an important conversation in time or in space to create a more appropriate and supportive context that will help it to work better.

So... let's explore sound!

Sound affects!

The first step on our journey to master speaking and listening is to become conscious about the power of sound.

Since before you were born, sound has been affecting you in four powerful ways, all explained and explored in this chapter. Every day, sound impacts your wellbeing, effectiveness and happiness—and yet I doubt you often think about it.

Let's define sound as 'vibration that humans can hear'. That's a very small subset of all vibration. Everything in the universe is vibrating, from the tiny strings that comprise subatomic particles right up to huge astronomical objects; as you read this, your entire body is vibrating!

We measure the frequency of vibrations in cycles per second, known as Hertz (Hz). For human beings, the audible range is from around 20 Hz to 20,000 Hz (20 kHz). Animals have different ranges; for example, cats can detect far higher frequencies than we can, right up to about 85 kHz, allowing them to hear the high-pitched squeaks of mice, which are inaudible to us.

We hear a doubling of frequency as an octave, so our 20-20,000 Hz audible range spans just under 10 octaves. By contrast, the entire visible light spectrum is just one octave. Hearing degrades with age and gets damaged by exposure to loud noise, so many people can no longer hear the full audible spectrum. I know this all too well: after years of drumming in bands, I can't hear anything above 12 kHz and I have tinnitus, a ringing sound in the ears that becomes quite evident if I sit in very quiet places. We'll look at hearing in more detail in Chapter Three.

Sound always requires a medium to carry it. In most cases the medium is air, though you may be surprised to learn that sound travels almost five times as fast, and much further, in water. To understand how sound works in a medium, imagine a densely-packed crowd standing in a room. If you were to barge into someone on one side, the domino effect will end with someone on the other side of the crowd falling over. This is exactly how air carries sound waves; the air molecules bump into one another, and the wave propagates. Without a medium, sound simply can't travel, so it was perfectly accurate for the promoters of the film *Alien* to say "In space no-one can hear you scream."

Most sounds we hear are composites of many frequencies. Usually there is a fundamental, which in music we hear as the pitch, plus overtones, which are what give the sound its particular timbre or colour. Overtones create timbre: they are how we distinguish a flute from a trumpet playing the same note, or how we instantly recognise a familiar voice. Tuneful overtones with frequencies that are perfect multiples of the fundamental are known as harmonics.

Harmonics exist in many of the sounds we encounter, even though we are largely unaware of them. I once had a revelatory experience with harmonics during a week-long workshop with the great American overtone singer and teacher David Hykes. The practice of modulating and filtering the harmonics of my own singing voice (which is how overtone singers are able to sing two notes at once) had an effect on my ears, sensitising them to harmonics in general. I got into the car at the end of the third day of the workshop and turned the ignition key—and was astounded to hear all the harmonics of the engine noise. This was the auditory equivalent of seeing a rainbow, where all the constituent colours of light become visible, and it was just as beautiful. Sadly, as the weeks passed, the ability faded and now I no longer hear those harmonics, though I know they are all there. This experience is what gave rise to my listening exercise of savouring, which you will learn in Chapter Four.

Many physical objects have a property called resonance, which means they are particularly responsive at one or more frequencies. You may have experienced something similar in some badly designed rooms, where there's a booming effect at particular frequencies when people speak. A bell is a perfect example: when struck, its resonance emphasises a certain set of frequencies, which we hear as the note of the bell and its harmonics, while it effectively filters out all the other possible pitches. Most musical instruments make use of this property to create notes, and this natural physical effect may well have been what led ancient humans to create music in the first place. Resonance can be destructive too: soldiers break step when crossing bridges in case the tempo of their marching matches the resonant frequency of the bridge, which can create oscillations powerful enough to destroy the structure completely. When the beautiful Millennium Bridge in London opened in 2000 it had an effect nobody had forecasted: its resonance created little vibrations that entrained the people walking across to fall in step, setting up a feedback loop that ended up with the whole structure wobbling alarmingly. The bridge had to be closed and £5 million of special damping equipment installed before it could be reopened.

Some sounds also have rhythm and tempo. Music is the most obvious example, but it's also true of many electromechanical sounds, from manufacturing machinery and pile drivers to air conditioning units and photocopiers. Sounds with rhythm and tempo can exert influence through entrainment, which is the tendency of oscillating bodies to fall into synchrony, with the most powerful oscillators establishing the tempo. The Dutch scientist Huygens was the first to notice that pendulum clocks hanging closer to one another always end up in synchrony, with pendulums swinging exactly together. This entrainment effect works on us humans too, as we'll see shortly.

All the effects of sound tend to increase with its intensity. We measure sound in decibels (dB), which are logarithmic. This means that we perceive an increase of 10 dB as a doubling of the volume level—so 80 dB of noise is not double the intensity of 40 dB; it's 16 times as loud!

Before we move on, let's define noise as 'unwanted sound'. This is inevitably a moving target because it's personal: my music might be your noise, and vice versa. Nevertheless, we can all agree on some sounds being noise: the sounds of road traffic, aircraft, construction and heavy industry are not going to top anyone's list of favourites.

I hope you're starting to see how rich, complex and fascinating sound is. Now let's investigate the four powerful ways in which it affects you every day of your life.

PHYSIOLOGICAL

The human body is 70 per cent water, which makes us rather good conductors of sound. It's not surprising, then, that sound can powerfully affect us physiologically, changing our heart rate, breathing, hormone secretions and even our brain waves. All our bodily rhythms can be affected by sound.

An age-old example of this is the fight/flight reflex. Many thousands of years of sharing caves with bears or tigers sharpened this instinctual response to any sudden or unexplained sound, and it still operates in you today. You may know intellectually that a dropped plate or backfiring car is not actually a threat—but long before you've processed that thought or any visual input, your autonomic nervous system, using much more primitive parts of your brain and working far faster than your conscious cortex ever can, has already acted, releasing hormones that accelerate your heart rate and increase blood pressure and blood sugar levels so that you're ready for vigorous activity. Any sudden, loud or unexplained sound will have this effect.

Your heart rate and breathing can both be entrained by any loud external rhythm. The typical resting human heart rate is between 50 and 80 beats per minute (bpm), so it's no surprise that loud dance music at 140 bpm will tend to accelerate your heart, even if you don't take that sound as a threat! Your breathing will tend to follow suit. The opposite effect pertains in a spa or a meditation session, where slow-paced, gentle sound is often used to slow your heart and your breathing, and create physiological calmness.

> TIP: If you ever have problems sleeping, I suggest playing the sound of gentle surf with about 6-10 cycles per minute in your bedroom. This rhythm and tempo is very like the sound of the breathing of a sleeping person and will entrain your breathing and promote rest; also, we tend to associate this sound with being carefree and relaxed and with natural tranquility, so it works on many levels.

From the moment you wake (preferably to something much gentler than the traditional startling alarm clock bell or beep) to the moment you retire, sound plays a significant role in your physiology, affecting your heart, your breathing, your hormone secretions and even your brain waves.

PSYCHOLOGICAL

The second way sound affects us is by changing our feelings, moods and emotions.

The clearest example of this is music. Take a moment to think of your favourite song. I'm joining you by thinking of mine, which is *River Man* by Nick Drake. As your song plays in your mind and you listen with imaginary ears, you may notice a shift in your mood. Music is a very powerful conveyor of emotion, and most people know how to use it deliberately either to counteract a feeling they would rather not have, or to enhance one they are enjoying. The process may be intuitive, but it's also complex because music involves many factors: tempo and rhythm; timbre and dynamics; melody and harmony; and for vocal music lyrics and singing style too. Some of these are cultural; for example, the melancholic association of minor keys is strong in the classic European and American tradition, but far weaker in the Middle East, where some very happy music uses the minor mode.

On top of this, like all sound, music works powerfully by association. These associations may be global, like those evinced by the first two notes of John Williams's famous theme from the film *Jaws* (I bet you just imagined them and thought of a shark!); they may be local, like the social relevance of most folk music; or they may be entirely individual, created by personal emotional experiences that are powerfully tied to a piece of music and rekindled if it is heard again, even years later. Thus, predicting the exact emotional impact of a piece of music on any person or group is very difficult.

What we do know is that human beings have used music for thousands of years to create shared emotional experiences, from tribal rites of passage to religious worship or the modern dance scene. We even use it in war, to give our troops bravery or to intimidate the enemy; that's what bagpipes were invented for. Never has a human society been discovered, no matter how remote, that did not have music, so it clearly is part of our nature, not spread or learned—though of course styles and songs travel, coalesce and collide constantly, especially in the modern, connected world of YouTube, streaming, downloads and public playlists.

While music is the most obvious type of sound that affects us psychologically, it's not the only one. My company, The Sound Agency, often installs birdsong-based soundscapes, and for good reason. The birds have been singing for millions of years, and we have learned through the ages that normal birdsong means all is well. We can tell if something alarms the birds, or, even worse, causes them to stop singing altogether—a phenomenon that has often been reported before volcanic eruptions or tsunamis. That's why normal birdsong makes most people feel safe, even if they are not conscious of this effect. Birdsong is also nature's alarm clock, telling us that it's time to be awake and thus promoting alertness, so this combination of security and wakefulness makes birdsong a very useful sound for working, along with many other activities. Just recently, research has shown that it's also effective in aiding recovery from illness, so it seems that we instinctively like birdsong for some very good reasons.

The latest thinking about the multi-layered process of sound affecting emotions comes from academics in a paper from Lund University in Sweden. It proposes six component pathways in the process. In ascending order of complexity and subtlety, here they are.

Brain stem reflex is the physiological effect discussed above, most importantly the fight/flight reflex. Sounds that are sudden, loud, dissonant, or feature fast patterns tend to induce emotional arousal.

Evaluative conditioning is the associative response we considered above. You associate a sound or song with something, maybe a person or event, and that thing creates the emotion.

Emotional contagion is where we receive the emotion the composer poured into a song because we perceive it—in just the same way that seeing someone crying may make us sad. This puts me in mind of the hilarious scene in the film *Bridget Jones,* where Bridget is wallowing in self-pity and singing along with Jamie O'Neal's version of Eric Carmen's classic *All By Myself.*

Visual imagery involves conjuring up visual images while listening to the sound, so that emotions arise from the combination of the sound and the imagined scene. This is at least partly the process in play if you use gentle surf to relax or lull yourself to sleep.

Episodic memory is where the sound evokes a memory of a particular event in the listener's life and the event creates the emotion (sometimes referred to as the "Darling, they're playing our tune" phenomenon). Post-traumatic stress disorder sufferers may react strongly to the sound of thunder or any sudden bang for this reason.

Music expectancy happens where a feature of the musical structure violates, delays, or confirms the listener's expectations based on previous experiences of the same style of music. Composers have used this for hundreds of years, playfully taking us down a path and then catching us out with an unexpected twist that causes surprise or delight.

Remember, all sound can affect your feelings, not just music.

COGNITIVE

The third effect of sound is on our ability to think, with dramatic effects on our productivity or effectiveness. This mainly because we have quite limited neural bandwidth when it comes to processing sound.

I have never met anyone who can understand two people speaking at the same time. Scouring the available scientific evidence, I have calculated that we have auditory bandwidth for around 1.6 human conversations. This feels about right intuitively; most of us know the feelings of overwhelm, frustration and maybe irritation that arise when two people are talking at us simultaneously, or when we're trying to work on a deadline and someone near us is talking loudly.

Unless you don headphones or wear earplugs there is no way of shutting out distracting sound. In addition, we are programmed to decode language so a nearby conversation takes up one of our precious 1.6 bandwidth, leaving us only 0.6 to listen to the internal voice we use when we're trying to work with words, symbols or numbers. That's why another person's conversation is the most distracting sound of all.

Research on people working in modern open-plan offices has revealed that variable or unpredictable sounds are the most distracting, especially when we have no control over them. After unwanted conversation, the most commonly cited nuisances are ringing phones and office machinery like printers or other people's computers. This kind of noise degrades our ability to think, often dramatically: productivity can be reduced by two thirds in noisy open-plan offices! One survey of 1,800 home and office workers in the UK found that they were losing up to two hours a day to interruptions from noise, mainly from loud colleagues and ringing phones. The estimated cost to the UK economy was £139 billion a year!

Office expert Professor Jeremy Myerson has written extensively on this issue. He points out that we have different work modes, and that open-plan suits only one of them—collaboration, or team-based working, where the main objective is fast communication so it's acceptable to interrupt neighbours without warning. When I interviewed him for a BBC Radio documentary on this topic, Myerson noted that this kind of open-plan working is like frontier territory in its lack of social rules. As he said: "The postman doesn't enter your house unannounced and dump the post on your living room floor, but that's exactly what happens in open-plan offices."

Alert sounds in any environment are particularly disturbing—after all, beeps and buzzes were designed to grab our attention. If an alert sounds in communal space, it alarms not only the person it was intended for, but also everyone else in earshot. This is a major problem in hospitals, where the constant racket coming from beeping machinery has created a phenomenon called 'alarm fatigue': staff become habituated to the noise and cease to register the alarms. This doesn't mean the noise has no effect: the unfortunate patients are also subjected to all these warning sounds, with serious consequences for sleep and stress levels, as we'll see later in this chapter.

So, noise can interrupt collaborative working, as well as being bad for the health. A more profound issue, though, is that four critical work modes are simply not catered to at all in many open-plan offices.

The first is concentration, or individual working, which requires a space more like a library. Noise distraction and lack of quiet working space are among the top complaints on the Leesman Index, which has surveyed hundreds of thousands of office workers about what factors affect their productivity.

Tip: If you have an alert sound set for incoming email, your concentration will be broken every time it chimes, which may be many times an hour. Try instead turning off the alert sound and checking your email in batches at defined times, maybe on the hour every hour for five or ten minutes, or first and last thing each day. You may find you become up to three times as productive!

The second is contemplation, or not working, which might be decompressing after some intense work or maybe gently sharing ideas in a social setting. The first of these is best done in a calming, Zen-type room, while the second requires informal, social spaces (isolated, of course from quiet working areas!).

The third is communication over distance, which often requires privacy. I have come across offices so quiet that the turning of a piece of paper is a major event. In these places there is no privacy at all, so one person making a call disturbs everyone else in the room—not to mention the uncomfortable, intimidated feeling that arises when you realise everyone is listening to your call!

The fourth is conferencing, or structured meetings in groups. Again, privacy is a major issue here: I have experienced many offices where meeting spaces have no walls, or maybe a token fabric partition, which means the sound of the meeting distracts the people working nearby, who can hear every word - and of course the sound of a lively open-plan office makes the meeting more challenging to hear. Meeting rooms need good acoustics and effective attenuation to stop sound travelling out to and in from adjoining spaces.

You have probably had many of these experiences yourself in offices that were designed purely for the eyes. Now that you know the importance of sound, you can take care to move to the most appropriate environment for the kind of work you want to do.

BEHAVIOURAL

Noise has been shown to make people less sociable, and less helpful to others. Loud, fast-paced music will affect the speed and driving style of a car. Powerful oratory can dramatically affect behaviour, inspiring teams to produce great work, converting people to religious faith, radically changing political and social landscapes or inciting mobs to violence. Roaring crowds can inspire sports teams to stellar performances. In martial arts, special words shouted with a strike increase focus and power. Soothing words, mantras and gentle sounds can induce peacefulness or even trance states.

This fourth effect of sound, changing human behaviour, is the most important one in the work of The Sound Agency, and we've proved its efficacy many times. One of the most dramatic examples was in the town of Lancaster, California, where the mayor, R. Rex Parris, wanted to generate positive vibes among downtown pedestrians in the town's signature BLVD area, in order to enhance the city's top priority—safety. We installed a soundscape incorporating birdsong, lapping water and carefully-chosen musical elements, all designed to entrain heart rates downwards and produce calming moods. The sound plays from more than 70 weatherproof loudspeakers along the BLVD. Shopkeepers and restaurant owners in the BLVD were delighted with the sound. More significantly, the Lancaster Sheriff noted a 15% drop in crime after installation, which generated global media interest including the front page of the *Wall Street Journal*, the *Los Angeles Daily News*, the UK's *Daily Mail*, KTLA and KQED radio and NBC Network News.

Research has consistently revealed that the tempo of a soundscape entrains the pace of our behaviour. Multiple studies have shown that fast-paced music causes people to walk faster, which has a significant effect in shops: if we speed up like that we generally spend less time and less money in a shop. The jolly, up-tempo music that most shops play may well be costing them money! We also chew and eat faster in high-tempo sound, so it's no surprise that fast food restaurants usually play fast music to increase table turnaround.

We tend to move away from unpleasant sound if we can, albeit often unconsciously. If you draw a parallel with fragrance this becomes obvious: you would naturally avoid a bad smell, moving away if possible, and you might gravitate towards a wonderful fragrance. The same happens with sound. Unpleasant noise is the auditory equivalent of a bad odour, and it causes avoidance behaviours or, if we can't get away, stress reactions. That's why context is so important for communication, as we'll see towards the end of this chapter and the next.

The circle

Most people I meet visualise spoken communication as a simple linear relationship between speaking and listening rather like this:

Somebody sends; somebody else receives. But is it really that simple?

Of course, the answer is no. First, we're missing an important element. In the last few pages we've discovered that the sound around us directly affects all our significant outcomes in life, and that it forms a powerful context for all our speaking and listening. Sadly, this context is predominantly negative: all too often it damages our best efforts to communicate by drowning our signal in noise. Only rarely are we in a space that's thoughtfully designed to help communication or listening, for example a concert hall or theatre.

So, because all our spoken communication exists in a context, we need a third element in our diagram:

Context

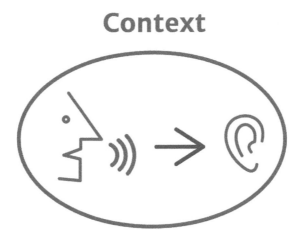

That's better, but it's not right yet. We need to include one more aspect of communication that not many people appreciate—something that can be transformative if fully internalised.

Speaking and listening are not linear, but *circular*: they interact.

The way you listen affects the way I speak. And just as powerfully, the way I speak affects the way you listen. This is very far from one way traffic, and some of the most profound lessons you may learn on this journey derive from this one, powerful realisation. Let's try the illustration again, this time with the circular relationship between speaking and listening.

Context

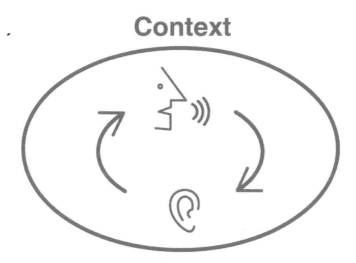

This is the model that underpins the rest of this book. It shows how dynamic and interactive speaking and listening are, and explains why being heard paradoxically requires working on listening!

Let's take a look at the power of skilful listening and speaking.

The power of listening

Listening may be a silent skill, but it has enormous power, as we'll see in the next few pages. The quality of our listening affects our relationships, health, influence, productivity and growth, but in our ocular society we virtually ignore this crucial skill—which is why there's a need for this book.

So, what is the power of listening?

LISTENING CREATES UNDERSTANDING

In 2014, I gave a TEDx talk in Athens (the cradle of democracy) and also at London's Houses of Parliament entitled 'The Sound of Democracy'. I started the talk by walking on stage and saying one word: "Listen!". Silence fell in those two impressive theatres full of hundreds of people. After a while I said: "That is the wonderful sound of several hundred people consciously listening. It's also the sound of democracy, because democracy depends on civilised disagreement—and that is only possible if we understand other people's points of view, even if we disagree with them. *Conscious listening always creates understanding.*"

This is a crucial point, and one that is increasingly threatened in the world we are creating. Post-truth politics, fake news, selective web browsing that only confirms our preconceptions, attack journalism that constantly interrupts or mingles opinion with fact, sound bites, personal broadcasting on social media platforms, 140-character diplomacy... these are all undermining the quality of our listening and eroding our ability to coexist in peace even when we disagree. Not listening makes it possible to caricature, depersonalise and demonise people, and that is a long, dark, slippery slope that leads to horrors that we see all too often in totalitarian societies.

I passionately believe that listening is necessary for peace, and for civil society to exist. That alone is a good enough reason to teach listening in our schools, and to defend it as a crucial bastion of the free world. Politicians always meet for talks: I suspect it might be better if they met for listens instead.

After all, what use is free speech if nobody is listening?

LISTENING PROMOTES INTIMACY

Truly listening to someone requires *all* of your attention. Ask yourself now, when is the last time you truly listened to someone? This is a rare and most generous gift and one that, in our intense, connected, multimedia existence, we are becoming unwilling or even unable to give. What, stop checking my email, Twitter, Facebook and go offline? You may be familiar with FOMO—fear of missing out—which tempts us to live a multi-stream, always-on existence, checking email whilst lying in bed and not talking to our partner, or having conversations with one eye on a screen and the other on a phone. In that twilight world of semi-attention, listening is a tattered vestige of its full self.

Even before technology intervened, true listening was the exception, not the rule. I believe that there are literally billions of people on this planet who have never known what it is to be truly listened to, so scarce is that experience.

Intimacy requires honesty and deep knowledge of another, which can only come through listening. I have heard it said that we seek three things in a relationship: to be heard, to be understood, and to be valued. It's tragic then that one of the most common complaints in relationships is: "He / she never listens to me!", because not listening eroded all three of those needs.

Listening is an act of love, and like all acts of love it requires some work or it can succumb to atrophy.

In this book you'll be learning some structures and exercises to help revitalise your listening in relationships, rebuilding and renewing intimacy.

LISTENING PERSUADES AND INSPIRES

Ask any top-class salesperson what the most important part of a sales call is and they will almost certainly say: "Listening!". We all know how irritating it is to have someone sell without listening. We feel disrespected because our needs are not being discovered or met. Listening is how a good seller can identify the problem, and tailor a solution to match it exactly; a call like that can come across as caring, helpful and kind, to the point where we feel grateful after buying whatever it is. That is a recipe for long term repeat business.

As any parent knows, the need for persuasion is not restricted to selling. Whether the issue is a tantrum-throwing toddler or a recalcitrant teenager experimenting with booze or drugs, listening can be a transformative first step in persuading a child towards more productive behaviours. If we want our children to listen, we need to show them how, by listening to them.

Listening is the oil in the engine of inspiration. We can inspire people only when we know what they want—which means listening.

LISTENING IMPROVES HEALTH

We've seen how dramatically sound can affect our health and wellbeing. Developing a practice of consciously listening to the world around us is the only way to discern which sounds are health-giving, and which will make us sick. If we are conscious, we are in a position to take action, whether that's moving our location or blocking the noise. Some of the exercises later in this book will help you to develop exactly these skills.

LISTENING EDUCATES

It's said that the Greek philosopher and mathematician Pythagoras erected a screen in front of the teacher so that first-year students were not distracted by visual input and could listen properly to what they were being taught. Gradually over the years, the tables have been turned, and the written word has replaced aural teaching at the top of the table, to the point where we now speak of 'book learning'.

Conscious listening is a wonderful tool for learning and for growth. As you'll discover, we listen through a set of filters. Once you gain mastery of that process and control of your filters, you too can empty yourself of what you know (or perhaps what you think you know) and make room for plenty of fresh lessons!

The power of speaking

The human voice is the instrument we all play, but very few people have ever had any training in how to use it effectively. This is a complex, versatile and powerful skill and it is extraordinary that we don't teach or test it in schools.

To paraphrase the old song, it is what you say *and* the way that you say it. Your voice is your breath projected into the world; it's the only part of you that you can send forth outside of your own body

SPEAKING AND INSPIRATION

I live in Orkney, a set of islands off the north coast of Scotland that are liberally scattered with antiquities from prehistory. Possibly the most famous is Ring of Brodgar, a stone circle dating back to around 3,000

BC. Each of the 60 huge stones that originally formed the ring (27 are still standing) had to be dragged miles to the site before being erected, which must have taken incredible organisation and determination, not to mention teamwork, for these Neolithic people. Even with modern equipment this would be a major operation. These people had no power other than their own muscles; they worked of their own volition, unlike the slave labourers who built the pyramids. They must have been very highly motivated.

I often wonder who had the idea to create this seminal structure, which some scientists believe inspired all the stone circles in the UK, culminating in Stonehenge. Whoever it was must have been a potent speaker indeed, to inspire thousands to commit so much time and energy over many years to such a huge project.

Throughout human history, powerful speakers have inspired people to change their beliefs, create or destroy social systems, adopt personal lifestyles, follow religious or philosophical paths, take up arms and fight, form movements, work in teams—and build monuments. Innumerable great sporting performances have been triggered by an inspirational talk from a coach or captain.

If you want to make a difference in the world, you will most likely need to inspire others, and you may need to be a leader. Your voice is the most powerful tool you have for these things.

SPEAKING AND PERSUASION

Possibly the most famous and strongest form of vocal persuasion is hypnosis. You may have seen high-speed onstage hypnotism, where the hypnotist instantly induces trance states and the uses spoken suggestions to have people change their behaviour even after the trance ends. Strong suggestions made to the subconscious are not confined to the entertainment industry; hypnosis is now a widely acknowledged and relatively mainstream therapeutic tool, able (subject to an individual's level of suggestibility) to reduce pain, help stop smoking and clear skin complaints, among other uses.

Persuasion in its widest context is critical in life. Many achievements are beyond the scope of one person acting alone, which means we very often need to persuade others to help us or join our team in order to achieve our goals.

The voice plays a key role in the process of persuasion—not only what we say but also how we say it. Some people struggle to have their voice heard, while others seem to carry natural authority. Stature and body language play a role, but the largest part of this authority derives from speaking, in which both content and delivery play their parts. We will cover both of these aspects of speaking intensively in this book with exercises and tips to help you gain power and authority in your speaking, allowing you to be more persuasive and achieve more of your goals by enrolling people in your passions.

SPEAKING AND HEALTH

If you've ever had the experience of not being listened to, not being able to make a dent in an argument, being disrespected, feeling invisible in a group, not being taken seriously, being talked over, being continually interrupted, or secretly crying out to be heard, then you know that the inability to express oneself clearly and powerfully is bad for you. It's debilitating and frustrating to be ignored. It creates stress and anxiety if it continues or repeats in relationships—and it can eventually cause sickness or even violence. I suspect that at least some of the antisocial behaviour from young people in urban environments arises from this feeling of frustration: "Nobody's listening to me, nobody cares, so why should I?"

If only we taught our children how to express themselves clearly and powerfully, how much less ill health, stress and violence would we see in the world?

SPEAKING STORIES

One of the most potent styles of speaking is storytelling. We all love a story: as soon as we hear the words, "Once upon a time…" our inner child wakes up; we metaphorically curl up and look forward to the wonders to come. For as long as language has existed, I'm willing to bet that people have told stories to share their day, keep alive the exploits of legendary heroes, pass on cultural traditions, or simply to soothe their children to sleep.

For many millennia, stories have been among the most powerful tools in the essential task of passing knowledge and history on from one generation to the next, or from one group to another. From the development of complex language all human knowledge was spread simply by speaking and listening. Throughout those many years, countless groups of humans have sat around fires at night listening with wonder and rapt attention to a local sage or storyteller pass on tales that carried wisdom from the past.

In some societies, this powerful oral tradition still exists. Indian classical music has no written form at all: all the complex, lengthy ragas are learned by rote, transmitted from guru to shishya by word of mouth and demonstration. The same applies in many surviving folk music cultures, including that of Orkney, my home, where it seems almost every child plays an instrument, but not many play from sheet music. Traditional folk music often encapsulates old stories in its lyrics, even if we don't understand the references now; the same is true of many nursery rhymes. The indigenous peoples of Australia can safely navigate the vast expanses of the outback on 'song lines', paths that they follow by reciting the words of songs that list landmarks, waterholes and other way finders. Even in the text-obsessed West, there are still many professional storytellers plying their trade, and storytelling festivals exist in the US, UK, India, Dubai and many other countries. Stories still have power!

The problem

Speaking and listening are natural, fast, efficient, powerful, nuanced and rich ways to communicate, and yet we barely give them a thought; we certainly don't generally teach them with the same devotion we award to reading, writing, mathematics or motor skills. Yes, we joyfully celebrate our child's first words, but as soon as conversation is flowing we take it for granted—meanwhile, we have many milestones spread over years in reading, writing and mathematics (we call them exams) and in motor skills (from walking to riding a bike to driving a car to athletic or sporting achievements).

Wondering why this was so was the reason I got into the sound business in the first place: it seemed so clear to me that we were missing out on something really important by taking for granted listening and speaking. I have thought a lot about this and over the next few pages I will try to unpack the key forces that are working against the ears.

SPEAKING VERSUS WRITING

Speaking is ancient: expert opinion on the dawn of complex language varies from 60,000 to 100,000 years ago. Writing is much more recent, developing around 4,000 years ago. For most of human history, all knowledge has been handed down orally—but writing has sprinted past speaking in its short existence and it now dominates communication in our ocular world.

I absolutely accept the benefits of writing. It can be propagated, copied and published, and many of the world's greatest revolutions in thought or belief result from this. It is fixed and can be referred to, as with a contract. It can be asynchronous, so I can email you while you sleep in another time zone and you can read my message the next day when you wake.

However, I do believe the pendulum has swung too far, which is why many organisations are now training people in listening and speaking skills—though mainly the second. It's interesting to note that my TED talk on speaking has been viewed around four times as many times as the one on listening. We prioritise sending over receiving, just as we prioritise written communication over spoken.

I think there are several reasons for the dominance of the eyes over the ears in the modern world.

NOISE

The world is noisy, and getting noisier. Since the Industrial Revolution, we've been surrounding ourselves with mechanical, and now electronic, noises, some of them very loud indeed. Transport has always been noisy—the Romans had to introduce ordnances to control the clatter of carts in the streets of their capital 2,000 years ago—but now we have pervasive jet engines and tyre noise to contend with. My friend Bernie Krause, the world's most eminent nature sound recordist, relates that it once took 20 hours to get 15 minutes of usable recorded material. "Now it takes 200 hours," he says.

Once we needed to listen carefully, because sound was meaningful: if you were sharing a cave with some bears or tigers, you'd better be listening carefully! Now most noise is meaningless, so we have developed the habit of suppressing it, and we move around the world simply not listening.

The result of this of course is more noise, to the point where the World Health Organisation (WHO) rates noise pollution as the second-largest global threat to health, just behind air pollution. The WHO estimates that in Europe over one million years of healthy life are lost every to traffic noise pollution. As we've seen, eight million Europeans are having their sleep disrupted night after night by traffic noise, with drastic effects on their health, as well as huge resulting costs—up to 2 percent of GDP according to official estimates, which amounts to over 300 billion euros a year.

Noise pervades many vital spaces because we design them with eyes, not ears. Architects train for up to five years, but most of them spend as little as one day studying acoustics and the effects of sound on the people who have to live, work and study in the buildings they will be designing. Ask an architect to show you his or her work and you will look at pictures and models. No wonder many spaces sound so bad.

In classrooms, acoustics are often so poor that speech intelligibility is less than 50 percent for pupils more than a few feet from the teacher, while noise levels during groupwork reach levels that are dangerous for the health of teachers and children.

In hospitals, noise levels are up to 12 times the WHO recommended maximum, which means patients struggle to sleep—and sleeping is how we get well. It's no surprise that noise is the number one complaint of patients in US hospitals. Studies have shown that simply sensitising staff to the sounds they are making can cut noise levels by up to three quarters, so just listening can make a massive difference.

In offices, noise is again the number one complaint, with millions feeling the frustration of trying to concentrate in open-plan spaces that are designed to support only one kind of work: collaboration. We clearly need much more quiet working space.

The story goes on, in hotels, in shops, in restaurants, in airports and train stations, and even in our homes. Noise is all around us. We need to start listening in order to control it and stop these negative effects on health, effectiveness and happiness.

TECHNOLOGY

The breakthroughs in communication of the last several decades have almost all been text-based: email, SMS, instant messaging and social media all rely on eyes and fingers. The result is that millions of people would rather have a conversation in writing than in sound.

The Sound Agency did some research with our friends at Edinburgh Sterling University into preferred channels and messages and it yielded some fascinating insights. Older people were wedded to email, while the middle generations loved SMS and the youngest preferred IM or social media platforms. This brings a whole new dimension to the generation gap: not only do the generations have different attitudes and vocabularies, but also entirely different channels of communication. All the samples agreed on one thing: they preferred to ask someone out, or break up with someone, in writing—possibly because in a scary conversation like that, it's safer not to be around to experience the response in person!

MIT professor and TED speaker Sherry Turkle wrote an excellent book called *Alone Together* on the effects of technology on our relationships. She suggested that, far from bringing us together in a global village, technology is increasing alienation and pushing people apart as we move from a few deep relationships to many shallow ones. I agree with her. In my workshops, I sometimes ask for a show of hands if people do email in bed at night while lying next to their loved one. Increasingly the majority of the people in the room own up to this very destructive behaviour, which I see as another nail in the coffin of spoken communication, driven in by the irresistible hammer of technology. Professor Turkle's follow-up book, *Reclaiming Conversation*, is a wonderful, passionate plea, based on five years of research, for us all to rediscover the critical humanizing art of conversation. Highly recommended, and absolutely in tune with everything you will read in this book.

EDUCATION

We have four communication channels: reading, writing, speaking and listening. Two send; two receive. Two are for the eyes; two for the ears. Reading and writing are considered core skills in every curriculum in the world, while speaking is barely taught in schools—listening, even less so, maybe because it's a silent skill. Sadly, millions of children leave school every year having never been taught how to use their voice to its full, to speak powerfully and well, to look after their precious hearing, or to listen consciously.

Tip: Take some time now to ask yourself, what sounds stop you from working? From resting? From relating to your family, friends and colleagues? From exercising? From sleeping? From enjoying yourself?

Once you have that list, repeat the exercise but this time ask yourself, what sounds do/could help you in all these things?

Listening is the doorway to understanding, and speaking is the strongest expression of ourselves in the world. We need to re-learn how to speak and how to listen. Helping you to achieve that is the mission of this book.

Chapter Two

The dark side

I n this chapter, we start the healing process by revealing some habits that rob power from speaking and listening, and some forces in the modern world that are undermining or even threatening our spoken communication.

THE FOUR LEECHES

Over the years, I've identified a set of very common emotional drivers that tend to suck power out of communication. I call them the four leeches. Most people (me included!) have most, or all, of them in some form. I'm not suggesting they are bad, wrong or to be condemned outright; whilst it may never be possible to surgically remove them, the trick is to be conscious of them and not let them run the show. That, sadly, is what happens much of the time for many people. The result is simply loss of power and effectiveness. The degree of loss depends on the power these leeches have over you. If they remain in the dark, operating below the level of consciousness, they can become dominant character traits, severely compromising the ability to listen well and speak effectively.

The main reason for the negative impact of the leeches is that the underlying emotion giving rise to all four of them is *fear*.

Over the next few pages we'll get to know all four leeches. Some may be minor or even non-existent for you, but I'm willing to bet you'll identify at least one that has affected (or is currently affecting) your outcomes in life. As you consider the leeches and become conscious of their existence within you, their power will be lessened. Simply shining the light of mindfulness on them causes them to wither and lose their power. They grow and strengthen in the dark, and they hate that light!

LOOKING GOOD

We all like to look good. However, this basic human desire can often get in the way of our listening and our speaking.

"I know."

Sometimes, looking good evinces itself in two simple words. The very first story in Paul Reps's *Zen Flesh, Zen Bones* (a great compendium of Zen tales) is a salutary one for anyone who tends to use those words overmuch. Here it is as recounted in that book:

> Nan-in, a Japanese master during the Meiji era (1868–1912), received a university professor who came to inquire about Zen. Nan-in served tea. He poured his visitor's cup full, and then kept on pouring.
>
> The professor watched the overflow until he no longer could restrain himself. "It is overfull. No more will go in!"
>
> "Like this cup," Nan-in said, "you are full of your own opinions and speculations. How can I show you Zen unless you first empty your cup?"

If I know everything, what can I learn? Absolutely nothing. A Zen proverb sums up this proposition nicely: "Knowledge is learning something every day. Wisdom is letting go of something every day."

Even without the use of the actual words, it can be very deflating to be around someone who is professionally impossible to impress. I remember a conversation at TEDGlobal in 2012 with communication expert Trisha Bauman that illustrates this very well. She moved to Paris and for a while thought that she had become inept at communicating her excitement at the sights she was encountering all over the city: every time she extolled the beauty of some landmark, her new friends responded with a shrug and words to the effect of "Of course." It took some time for her to realise the issue was not with her; in that circle of people, if not in Paris generally, it was considered a loss of face to be seen to be impressed by anything at all. Being insouciant was being cool. That's all very well, but it does dampen the fire of childlike excitement, so it clearly acts as a joy-kill. Joy is such a rare commodity in this world that it seems tragic to go around killing it.

Maybe you can relate to this aspect of looking good: stomping, or even delicately treading, on the naive delight of others in order to appear wiser, cooler or more experienced than they are.

Speechwriting

We may have other, more subtle ways of looking good that tarnish communication. In his book *The 7 Habits of Highly Effective People: Powerful Lessons in Personal Change*, Stephen R. Covey wrote: "Most people do not listen with the intent to understand; they listen with the intent to reply." I call this 'speechwriting': while that irrelevant noise (you speaking) is going on in front of me, I'm concentrating on composing my next brilliant monologue. This practice often produces the "anyway..." non-sequitur that blatantly ignores what was just said (but not heard) and moves the topic to a completely different place. This is a trait that often afflicts people in power, even though it is definitely not a good style of leadership: it demoralises the ignored party and can even be humiliating if others are present.

If you tend to do this, try devoting yourself to really listening, and trust that your voice will find the right response without you needing to compose, edit and approve your script in advance.

Competitive speaking

One step up from speechwriting is competitive speaking. You may know someone who practices this very potent form of joy-killing that's all about looking good. I might enthuse: "We're so excited to be going to Greece on holiday this year," and the competitive speaker will jump in with: "Oh yes, I've been to Greece six times and I love it!" My feeling? Deflation. My little piece of joy has been made to look second-rate.

If you ever feel the temptation to indulge in speaking as a competitive event, remember the words of Lao Tzu, the author of the *Tao Te Ching*: "Avoid putting yourself before others and you can become a leader among men."

Embellishment

The word hyperbole comes from ancient Greek, combining two words: *hyper* (beyond) and *bole* (a throw). We 'throw beyond' reality to exaggerate for effect, as in "I've been waiting ages for you!" In the main, this is benign and both parties know what's being done, but the habit of hyperbole can take hold of us and make right-sized words feel insufficient; this can in turn lead to a habit of exaggerating, which can itself be progressive and turn into lying (about which we will be talking more later in this chapter).

Language gets degraded if we frequently use words that are over-strong in order to impress. 'Fantastic' once meant strange or exotic, related to fantasy. 'Amazing' once meant causing wonder or astonishment. These words have long since been downgraded and are now almost exclusively used as synonyms for 'excellent'; their differentiated meanings have all but disappeared. I often speak in the USA, where the habit of describing everything from a pair of trainers to a hamburger as 'awesome' is very widespread. But if a pizza is awesome, how do you describe a stunning sunset? The word has been devalued and its power lost. In another example, the prefix 'super' has started cropping up everywhere: it seems that being excited is no longer sufficient: we must be 'super-excited' now.

This diluting of perfectly appropriate words is a tendency to be resisted, I think; it's a kind of verbal inflation that leaves us all impoverished as words lose their power and their meaning. Perhaps the fast-cut, multi-channel world is creating an addiction to intensity that drives us to use ever-more hyperbolic language. The cost is that many perfectly effective words are being diluted and our ability to express ourselves with precision is being diminished.

Exercise: Say what you mean

This is a tough one. Take on the challenge of saying exactly what you mean and no more—no hyperbole, which means cutting out the intensifiers like 'really', 'very', 'super' unless they are genuinely required, and right-sizing your adjectives. You may want to give yourself a short time limit on this at first, maybe an hour or at most a day. It's a challenging discipline, but its benefit is a degree of recalibration: you may find you have more capacity to express strong feelings by giving back the strength to extreme words.

BEING RIGHT

Most of our censure of others is only oblique praise of self, uttered to show the wisdom and superiority of the speaker.

– Tyron Edwards

If there is one thing we like more than looking good, it's being right, usually in a conversational zero-sum game—in other words, I am right and you are wrong, which makes me feel I am better than you. The desire to be right often drives us to *make* other people wrong, which can be very destructive in relationships. As the American author, educator and therapist Harville Hendrix said: "Do you want to be right, or do you want to be in a relationship? Because you can't always have both. You can't cuddle up and relax with 'being right' after a long day."

The need to be right arises from a fear of being disrespected, or simply of being seen as we really are—flawed human beings, perfectly imperfect, full of contradictions and confusions. We yearn to feel justified and respected, and being right (or making others wrong) is the route we often choose to achieve these desires, because it sets us above other people.

It's not easy to be around someone who has to be right the whole time.

Interrupting

One common habit that springs from the desire to be right is interrupting. This may result from speechwriting, as described earlier, but it can, and often does, arise with no planning at all—simply an overbearing desire to disagree, demand an answer or make a point *now*, without waiting for the other person to finish.

This is becoming more common in our impatient world, particularly in the media, where 'attack journalism' is rife: politicians have learned that they do not get time to develop arguments or to give nuanced answers before they are interrupted, a trait that has accelerated the descent of political debate into soundbites, as well as being a very poor role model for debate in general.

It's not just media interviewers who interrupt: the habit is widespread even in situations where listening can mean the difference between life and death. A survey of physicians in the US and Canada found that patients were interrupted an average of 18 seconds into their opening statements; less than a quarter were allowed to complete what they wanted to say.

Interrupting has two unfortunate consequences. First, we don't get to hear what the other person was going to say, which might have been useful or enlightening, and not what we expected. Second, it most likely damages the rest of the conversation by changing the dynamics—no longer equal, as the interrupter has exercised dominance—as well as the emotional context; the interrupted person may well feel belittled and offended, giving rise to anger, resentment and unwillingness to be open from that point.

Remember, as with all these observations, I am not saying the thing is always bad and wrong. Sometimes we do have to interrupt people! We may be wildly excited; they may have misunderstood; there may be time pressure or even danger; some people are just very long-winded. What am I saying is that, if it becomes a habit, it will reduce the power and effectiveness of your communication.

Exercise: Breathe!

Are you an interrupter? Do you know someone who is? If so, here's a simple exercise to try.

Breathe.

Before you speak, develop the habit of taking a deep breath. This is much easier and more natural than the old-fashioned advice to count to three (or even 10!) before speaking, which itself distracts you from listening to the other person.

As you take your lovely big in-breath, you may just notice that the other person is still speaking!

PEOPLE PLEASING

Most people like to be liked, but when that turns into a great fear of being rejected or of failing, the result can be people pleasing, a behaviour pattern that equates one's own worth with the perceived happiness or approval of others. This is often (though not always) due to experiences of wounding rejection or harsh criticism early in life.

People pleasers may say yes when they mean no, for example going out when they would much rather stay in. They may agree in conversation with opinions that they fundamentally disagree with internally. They may deny their own truth in how they dress, behave and interact with others in order to be liked.

We all have this in us to some degree, especially in the formative and emotionally vulnerable teenage years when we try on identities, join tribes and even adopt uniforms to feel 'part of'. Who wants to be a social reject? Also in totalitarian societies people pleasing can be a life or death affair: not many people in North Korea are interested in standing in their own truth and fearlessly expressing their real opinions, and quite understandably so when the consequence is almost certain death. The same forces can be in play in any social group founded on bullying and intimidation, and when such a group dominates a country the resulting people-pleasing behaviour from millions has devastating consequences, as the Nazis demonstrated in the 1930s and 40s.

In free societies, we do have a choice, and as with all the leeches, it's a question of degree. If someone is (and is perceived to be) very driven by people pleasing, it will rob their communication of power. Agreeing with people all the time can be perceived as weakness, invalidating the views expressed. Honesty and authenticity are absent, and as we'll see later, they are key foundations of powerful communication.

Exercise: Values

If you find yourself people pleasing overmuch, try taking some time to think about your own values. These are probably best expressed as single nouns, for example loyalty, passion, generosity, curiosity or fairness. Ask yourself: what do I stand for? What is important in life? What are my principles? What's not negotiable? Write down everything that comes to you... take your time, come back from time to time until you are sure you've captured every possibility. Then whittle them down to a manageable number, maybe four or five at most. If you can make a mnemonic out of them that helps to make them more memorable! (As an example, my values are faith, love, acceptance and gratitude, which spell FLAG—easy for me to hold on to even with my patchy memory!)

When you have your core values clear, it becomes much easier to stand in them and not be blown around by other people's opinions or needs. You also gain a litmus test you can use from now on to make decisions easier: is this course of action in line with my values?

FIXING

For some people, it's not acceptable for others to be upset. This may derive from people pleasing, or it may be that strong negative emotion is itself something to be feared, either because of too much of it in a violent or explosive family of origin, or perhaps because of complete lack of experience of it, with a cool, reserved family of origin where emotional expression was unacceptable.

Either way, fixing is trying to make it all right. "Don't cry" or "Don't be upset" will be the primary response to pain.

Sometimes people need to be upset, and to express that in grief, sadness, anger or other strong negative emotions. If repressed instead of expressed, these emotions can go deep and dark and corrupt people as they fester.

My aunt told me a story that illustrated how even well-intentioned fixing can cause damage. She was born in Cardiff, Wales in the 1920s. When she was a little girl, her parents told her that she was going to have a baby brother or sister. She was so excited! The spare room was decorated as a nursery and as she watched her mother's bump grow she imagined playing with her new sibling. Eventually the day came and her parents went off to hospital. She waited at home with a neighbour, watching through the net curtains... but when her parents returned, they were alone. Nothing was said; she was sent to stay with relatives. When she returned, the nursery had been redecorated. She did eventually get two little brothers, and much, much later she learned that her first brother had been stillborn—but she never forgot the confusion and loneliness she felt that day. Doubtless my grandparents decided not to discuss it so as not to upset her, but the effect on her was that a bond was broken and she found it harder to trust people from that day on.

Fixing, whether by withholding like that or by distracting or obscuring with extravagant affection, can deny people the feelings they need to feel and thus obstruct healing. Not only that, but many fixers habitually deny *themselves* strong feelings.

When communication is driven by the need to fix, it will lose power and effectiveness because there is a hidden agenda at work—one that is all about the fixer's needs, even though it may be disguised as love.

Exercise: Expressing

Many fixers grew up in reserved families and learned that it is not ok to express, so if you are generally very reserved and avoid strong emotion, a great first step to allowing other people to express strong emotions is to practice doing it yourself. The best access to letting go like this may vary widely from person to person. Some might try watching a few very emotional films and letting themselves have a good cry! More direct and beneficial for others might be to take up a martial art, as long as the teaching emphasises the spiritual aspects of the art and not just the physical: paradoxically, punching things in a spiritual way can put you in touch with the gentler, feeling side of yourself. For yet others, strong experiences like bungee jumping or parachuting or even extreme sports might be very liberating. At the very extreme, there's primal therapy!

Try a few tentative steps and see what works for you. This is all about balance: we are not our feelings, and we don't have to express every emotion to the max—but equally it is not healthy to repress our own strong feelings, or to stop others from having theirs.

The seven deadly sins

In my fifth TED talk, I listed seven deadly sins of speaking. Of course, this is an arbitrary list, but since the talk went up on TED.com in 2015 I haven't had anyone suggest anything major that's missing, and many people have communicated how useful they find it.

Again, I want to stress that I am not saying these seven things are inherently wrong, and to be banned or deplored. Most of them can be useful or enjoyable in moderation, even if as guilty pleasures. However, as with the four leeches, I *am* suggesting that people who habitually (often unconsciously) indulge in any of these traits become harder to listen to, as well as less good at listening.

People sometimes ask me to explain the relationship between the four leeches and the seven deadly sins. The answer is that the leeches lurk behind and generate all seven sins—and behind all of the leeches, as we know, is fear.

Let's meet the seven deadly sins.

1. GOSSIP

Non male loquare absenti amico
(Speak no evil of an absent friend).

Titus Maccius Plautus, Trinummus IV, c. 190 BC

My definition of gossip is speaking ill of someone who's not present. It's not gossip to praise someone who's not there, nor is it gossip to criticise someone to their face.

Gossip is probably the most common form of triangulated communication, which is usually a recipe for trouble. In triangulated communication, person A speaks to person C about an issue he or she has with person B instead of trying to solve the matter directly with person B, thus creating a triangle. Usually person A is seeking validation and/or sympathy. You can hear this going on any day if you sit on a bus or train and listen to the phone conversations around you: in my experience, the vast majority involve gossip in this fashion.

Gossip is seductive, and so common that we tend to become desensitised to it; it has become normal and acceptable. It's a multi-million-dollar business too, from the obvious specialists like celebrity magazines, TV shows, blogs and YouTube channels to the subtler instances in many quality media.

Gossips are superficially popular and it's tempting to listen in, especially if we're in a group who are all indulging. Nevertheless, everyone knows that the moment we leave, a gossip is likely to be speaking about us in exactly the same lurid, critical terms that were just being applied to someone else. Gossips are not credible; much of what they say is unsubstantiated and even malicious; often it is twisted or exaggerated for greater effect, producing a 'Chinese whispers' effect that amplifies stories whilst insisting that every detail is true.

Exercise: Gossip abstinence

If you indulge in gossiping, try abstaining, initially for a short period. It may be that you can commit to do this for a day, or even a week, to start with. Be conscientious: this may involve not reading magazines, watching your usual TV, accessing your favourite blogs or website, and even not seeing certain friends or colleagues or walking away from some conversations. You can usually make an excuse to do so without letting people know what you're doing—or you could enrol some of your associates in the game and make it easier by holding one another accountable.

This is non-trivial and may even be impossible for you, but even if you don't achieve 100 percent abstinence you will give yourself a chance to break the habit and set a new baseline.

2. CONDEMNING

There are no two words in the English language more harmful than 'good job.'

Terence Fletcher in Whiplash

Do you know anyone who habitually condemns or finds fault, for whom nothing is ever good enough, like the monstrous character Terence Fletcher as brilliantly portrayed by JK Simmons in the film *Whiplash*?

I feel for anyone who grew up with such a parent—the kind who, when their child scores 95 per cent in a test, demands to know what happened to the other five. It becomes wearing to be around someone whose listening is always for defects and failure, and whose speaking is endless castigation and condemnation.

Of course, we must condemn evil. As John Stuart Mill said in 1867: "Bad men need nothing more to compass their ends, than that good men should look on and do nothing."

However, like the other six sins, this is a habit we can fall into if our default position becomes critical and condemnatory. It pays to check in and ask the question: am I over-critical? Do I give praise where it's due? Do I naturally give compliments? When is the last time I praised my family? My team or direct reports at work? My friends?

If your honest check-in reveals that you tend to be critical rather than encouraging by default, try this exercise.

Exercise: Praising

Buy a notebook or use a spreadsheet or notes app. Make a page or sheet for each of the people closest to you—family, friends and workmates could all be included—and then set a routine at the end of each day to log in one column instances when you condemn or criticise them and in another column instances when you praise, encourage or compliment them.

After a few weeks, your behaviour will change as this feedback reveals the weight of your interactions. You may then wish to set yourself targets for praising until it becomes more and more natural and the condemning habit has been replaced by a more neutral stance where you give praise and criticism when they are appropriate, rather than condemning by rote.

3. NEGATIVITY

Next door to habitual condemnation is constant negativity. I told a true personal story to illustrate this in my TED talk. My mother suffered from dementia in the last years of her life, and this intensified an already somewhat pessimistic outlook. Her world view became entirely negative, even on days when she was completely lucid. I went to visit her in hospital one day when she was recovering from a small fracture, bringing with me her favourite newspaper. As I handed it to her, I said "Oh look, it's October the first today." She replied: "I know, isn't it awful?" If the date is awful, what hope is there? I tried to make a joke of it, but I knew inside that she was serious; as time passed, it became harder and harder to bring her out of the dark into any sort of light, and it made being in her company emotionally draining.

It is simply debilitating to stay around someone who is highly negative. We might say brightly: "What a lovely morning!" only to be dampened with "It's going to rain later." When this dynamic is repeated endlessly, it's like trying to push water uphill: our positive energy becomes sapped and we end up feeling low as well. The only solution is to leave for a while to recharge.

Exercise: watch NOT

Check in and ask yourself if the word NOT crops up regularly in your speaking. Any sentence including that word is likely to be negative: some people I have met unconsciously inject the word in almost every utterance. If in doubt, ask a friend or record some of your conversations to check. Encouraging people are easier to listen to!

4. COMPLAINING

Do not listen to those who weep and complain, for their disease is contagious.

Og Mandino

I'm a Brit so I know this one very well! Complaining is our national pastime, although fairness compels me to add that this habit does generally overlay a bulldog spirit that still exists today: we may complain, but we do tend to knuckle down when required.

Not all complaining is a sin. If a restaurant serves you a bad dish or if a person or institution fails to deliver on a promise, complain! If you can change anything you don't like, it's right and proper to take action and that often starts with complaining.

The kind of complaining I'm suggesting you pay attention to is the useless kind: complaining about the weather, the government, your neighbour, your sports team... anything that's beyond your capacity or your willingness to change. If you can change it, act. If you can't change it or you won't act, complaining is simply viral misery, infecting the person you are complaining to with your own negative emotion.

This kind of complaining can become an unconscious habit. Do you know an inveterate complainer—someone who moans about just about everything; someone for whom nothing seems to be right? It's hard to be around such a person, and hard to listen to them for any extended period.

Exercise: Gratitude

If you have fallen into the habit of complaining, sit down with a piece of paper and write a gratitude list. Write down everything you can think of that you can be grateful for. This may include any positive aspects of your health, your relationships, your possessions, your achievements, your service for others, your legacy, your surroundings, your experiences. Write until you can't think of anything else. Keep the list by you and reflect on it for a few minutes every day. Add to it every time you think of something new to be grateful for. Gratitude is the most powerful antidote to self-pity and a complaining habit.

5. EXCUSES

An inverse expression of the Looking Good leech is desperately trying to avoid looking bad. We all make mistakes, and sometimes those mistakes upset others by creating cost or other negative consequences for them. In the face of anger or pain, it's tempting to remove ourselves from the line of fire by blaming something or someone else for what happened. "It wasn't my fault—what could I do?" Sometimes that really is true, but very often if we look closely, we will find that we did have a major part to play in what happened.

I'm sure you've made excuses at some point in your life, and you've probably had it done to you many times. It is common human behaviour, but as with the other deadly sins of communication, the problem arises if it becomes a habit. Some people are blame-throwers, casting themselves as eternal victims with the fault being everywhere but here. This kind of behaviour creates two costs.

First, it's dishonest, or at best dissembling, so it undermines trust. People don't give credence to someone who blithely bends or breaks the truth simply to look good or justify themselves.

Second, it obstructs growth. If we refuse to take responsibility for an error or failing, it is very likely to recur: you can't fix something that you swear is not broken. This kind of denial can be very destructive, obscuring self-awareness to the point where we think we are other than what we really are. *The first step in transforming anything is to become aware of it.* Repeated excuses deny us the chance to improve, because we believe there's nothing wrong with us.

6. EXAGGERATION AND LYING

We talked about embellishment earlier in the context of the Looking Good leech. However, embellishment is not restricted to hyperbole; it can express itself in embroidery of the truth. I wonder if you've ever claimed to have read a book you haven't read, or to have watched a movie you've never seen, or to have known someone you really don't know? I suspect we've all done this kind of thing at some point. Mild embroidery like this is relatively harmless, and sometimes it can be a form of rapport-building to warp our reality just a little to fit more comfortably with someone else's—but beware, lying is just around the corner.

As with all the seven sins, this behaviour can become habitual and progressive: lies tend to beget more lies, which can lead to embarrassment, pain and even tragedy. This is a common theme in fiction, from Shakespeare's plays, many of which revolve around lies resulting in either laughter or tears, to the disturbing book and film *The Talented Mr. Ripley* which brilliantly depicts how lies can escalate and trap the perpetrator in pain. There are reasons for this literary fascination with lying: it is very common, and it can be dramatically destructive.

The effect of lying on communication effectiveness can be seismic. If anyone is recognised as a habitual liar, their words are at best suspect, and at worst completely disregarded.

Exercise: Rigorous honesty

Pay attention for a few days to your honesty level. We all like to think we're totally honest, but few people are: white lies pop out to make people feel better or avoid criticism or punishment; maybe exaggerations become habitual to curry favour and be more respected. If you spot any pattern, take stock and consider instituting a rule of absolute honesty in the area of concern. In my experience, settling for near-honesty is not as effective as an absolute commitment where the line is clear and you do not cross it. Be careful not to hurt people around you with rigorous honesty: it is always possible to say nothing, or if compliments are demanded and you cannot honestly give one, you can use double-edged praise, like one actor passionately (and honestly) telling another that his performance was 'unforgettable'!

7. DOGMATISM

I will listen to you, especially when we disagree.

– Barack Obama

The Being Right leech is foursquare behind this sin. Most of the time, the shells fired in the conversational battle to be right are opinions. I grew up in a household where opinions and facts were rarely differentiated, which gave rise to a lot of table thumping and raised voices. These days, I believe this distinction is critical for harmony so I offer a gentle suggestion in my talks and I'll make it to you now. Try using the phrase: "Would you like my opinion about that?" You do have to be ready for the answer no! Sadly, all over the world in billions of conversations every day, opinions are given without seeking any permission, often forcefully or even violently.

Internalising this distinction between opinions and facts is a crucial foundation of humility, and a necessary condition for peaceful coexistence. It's Wednesday. The sun will rise tomorrow morning. My name is Julian. This book is called *How To Be Heard*. These are facts and there is no point disputing them. However, much of daily conversation involves opinions—about sport, politics, society, other people's behaviour, the best course of action in a business or in a team, likely outcomes in the future, or effects of past actions (even historians love to disagree!). The problem lies in attachment. When we identify our own worth with our opinions, we become upset or angry when they are challenged; this is the fear-based energy that drives many arguments and confrontations.

Of course, we need to stay true to our values and our beliefs without being blown about by everyone else's, but we also need to have the capacity to learn and grow. We are not our opinions: we create or collect them.

If you can practice being conscious of the difference between you and your opinions, you may find life becoming much more serene—and more interesting too, as you may be more open to new thoughts and perspectives.

Technology

Most people view technology as inherently benign, which is a rather dangerous generalisation. Certainly, nobody in the world can stop the march of technology, and its benefits are clear: we augment our own capabilities (or even our reality) with a tidal wave of devices and apps; we enjoy cheap food, clothes and energy; we move around the world on faster cheaper, more powerful transport systems. It's seductive and even addictive, which makes it easy to be oblivious to what economists call the externalities—the costs we don't explicitly pay. Pollution, climate change and degenerative diseases like cancer and dementia may be the most widely reported consequences of our technological lifestyle, but I believe communication is another significant casualty. Let's look at how.

RECORDING

Somewhere around 4,000 years ago, complex writing was invented. This was transformative: for the first time, it was possible to record human discourse and thought—or maybe just a shopping list! Initially hand-crafted and slow to reproduce, this invention nevertheless shaped the world as books like the Bible, the Koran, the I Ching and Plato's *The Republic* (all hand-copied at first) influenced millions. The ability to publish the written word accelerated by orders of magnitude with Gutenberg's invention of the printing press in 1440. A little over 400 years later, Thomas Edison patented the phonograph and we became able to record sound as well as words. Within 40 years, the movie camera existed and the toolkit was complete. Now, millions of people consult YouTube by default to find instructions for anything from baking a cake to building a house. As TED's Curator Chris Anderson said in his TED talk on this subject, online video is the new *de facto* educational system for many millions, especially in places that don't have traditional educational infrastructure.

Once, all human knowledge was handed down aurally. You sat at the feet of your teacher and if you missed it, you missed it. Pythagoras considered listening to be so much more important than looking that his probationary pupils, or *akousmatikoi*, were required to sit silently and listen to their teacher deliver the lectures from behind a screen so that their eyes did not distract them from the most fundamental channel of communication: sound.

But today, the premium on careful listening is greatly diminished. We can check the book, listen to the recording or watch the video. There is growing debate about the value of teaching any facts at all to children, since almost anything can be discovered or checked on the Internet. We simply don't have to listen as carefully as we once did, because the cost of *not* listening is far less than it once was.

As we discussed in Chapter One, writing is the hare to the tortoise of spoken communication: this relative newcomer has quickly overtaken speaking, to the point that millions prefer to text, email or message than to speak. As the skills of speaking and listening are undervalued, they are not taught or tested in school; as they are underused in social, business and political interaction, they fall into disrepair. The result is the erosion of accurate expression and reasoned debate, and the rise of soundbites, bombast and polarisation.

HEADPHONES

Like most pieces of technology, headphones can be used for good or for ill. Let's consider the upsides first, of which I think there are four.

I use noise-cancelling headphones on flights and they do an excellent job of eliminating the debilitating sound of wind rushing over the fuselage at 600 mph.

At home, I very much enjoy listening to music through high quality headphones, which do give wonderful value: you have to spend somewhere between 20 and 100 times as much to achieve the same quality of sound through a physical hi-fi system, so audiophiles with a limited budget are well advised to choose headphones, as long as their listening is always individual.

In places with negative or distracting sound, headphones can be the only way to get some peace if you are trying to concentrate or relax. The Sound Agency and Ecophon released a free app called Study some years ago for exactly this purpose, and it has proved very popular. It plays a soundscape specifically designed to help you work and mask any irritating noise without itself distracting you. It stops after 45 minutes to remind you to take a short break.

Finally, there is the thesis of Professor Michael Bull, aka "Professor iPod", that many people wear headphones when moving around in order to gain more control over their personal environment. There is so much intrusion in the modern world, whether from pointless noise, from other people or from marketers, that it's a natural and understandable response to disconnect by setting an aural no-go zone with headphones—the grown-up equivalent of putting your fingers in your ears and humming loudly in order not to hear someone.

However, there are two major downsides with headphone use and they both affect communication negatively.

First, millions of people are permanently damaging their hearing by listening too loud, for too long. Most mobiles are capable of delivering at least 100 dB through typical headphones; even where mandatory default volume limits are in force, users can and often do override them. The recommended maximum daily exposure time to 100 dB of sound is just 15 minutes. It breaks my heart to think of the millions of young people who are listening at this level for hours a day. Noise induced hearing loss (NIHL) is set to become an epidemic; a 1998 study found that already around 15 per cent of American teenagers had permanent hearing damage, and I have no doubt the situation is much worse today. Hearing degrades with age, so we are storing up a massive issue where in a decade or two large portions of the population will be at best hard of hearing, and at worst profoundly deaf.

> TIP: A simple rule of thumb for safe listening is: if you can't hear someone speaking loudly to you from three feet away, it's too loud. Also, buy the best headphones you can possibly afford. Poor quality headphones tempt you to turn up the volume in order to get that visceral buzz from the music.

Second, schizophonia. This is a term coined by the Canadian composer and writer Murray Schafer, who also invented the word 'soundscape'. Schizophonia refers to a disconnect between what we're seeing and what we're hearing, which is absolutely what happens when you put on headphones for commuting, shopping or working. We've noted the beneficial, noise-blocking aspect of this above, but there are two common costs.

First, hearing is our primary warning sense and when we disconnect it we can put ourselves in harm's way. There is a new breed walking the streets that insurance companies are calling 'podestrians', and it seems they are causing numerous accidents by stepping out in front of cars they don't hear, which causes the driver to brake suddenly and get hit by the car behind.

Second, schizophonia destroys social interaction. Board any bus, subway or train and you will see a good proportion, possibly the majority, of the passengers wearing headphones. We may not speak much when commuting but we are at least sharing an experience and conscious of one another. With headphones on, that link is broken and our social spaces are fractured into millions of individual sound bubbles. In that situation, nobody is listening to anybody.

Think about your own headphone use. Make sure you are listening safely and that you have the very best headphones you can afford, especially if you listen for long periods or frequently. And be conscious also of the effects on your connections with humanity and especially your family, friends and workmates.

ALONE TOGETHER

This section is named after an excellent book by MIT's Professor Sherry Turkle, a fellow TED speaker whom I met when she gave her TED talk on this topic. Sherry was originally a major proponent of technology, and in particular its capacity to bring us together in the fabled global village, where all of humanity is connected and understanding is naturally enhanced. However, her research has caused a complete shift in her perspective and she now believes that technology is disconnecting us and loosening traditional social ties, a position elegantly expressed in this book and her more recent one, *Reclaiming Conversation*.

Seduced by technology and especially social media, we have moved from a few deep face-to-face relationships to a large number of shallow, distant ones: the words 'friend' and 'like' have a rather different meaning today compared to 20 years ago. Much of our interaction has become text-based, and youngsters are clearly not developing the social skills to manage face to face communication well, or to develop the empathy that arises from practicing being receptive to the subtleties of voice and body language. Much of the time we are now distracted, our attention and consciousness somewhere else. I am often struck on train journeys by the paradox of a carriage that at first seems full of convivial conversation—until it becomes clear that all the conversation is with people who are not in the carriage at all. There is a covert rudeness, I think, in someone turning fellow travellers into non-people so that he or she can have an intimate phone conversation without any sense of embarrassment or awkwardness.

I call the syndrome of constant text-based communication through mobile devices and social media 'personal broadcasting'. Twitter, Facebook and the rest are entrancing millions of people to believe that the world constantly needs to know their 'status'. The balance between sending and receiving is tipping further away from listening, and it's a vicious circle as the skills of face to face conversation wither, making it ever-more challenging to actually speak to someone and ever-more tempting to send them a text.

We may even become driven by a new social fear called FoMO, or fear of missing out a desperate urge to check and recheck social media in case someone has tagged or messaged us, or tweeted about us. FoMO can become obsessive and even pathological, and it probably plays a role in the depressing picture of a family sitting around the dinner table, all looking at their phones. Research among teens indicates that much of their conversation (when it occurs in person) is about what they are seeing on their phones. This level of connectedness paradoxically weakens our links with those around us.

Exercise: Tech check

This is an extensive enquiry that I ask people to start in my workshops on communication. Take a few minutes to start yours now: consider carefully how technology affects your communication—both speaking and listening, at home, at work and with your friends or important social groups. Keep this one at the front of your consciousness, because technology changes fast, and its effects are not immediately obvious as we rush to adopt the latest gadget. Before TV, families used to talk, read, make music together, eat at the table, play games... aim to look afresh at least once a year at your use of tech and its effects on your social behavior.

IMPATIENCE

How poor are they that have not patience! What wound did ever heal but by degrees?

– William Shakespeare, Othello

There is little doubt that technology is eroding our ability to focus and concentrate for an extended time on one task or object, be it a book, a piece of music or a conversation. A 2015 study of more than 2,000 people by Microsoft found that the average attention span had fallen from 12 seconds in the year 2000 to just eight seconds, which is less than the estimated attention span of a goldfish. The study also found that people were better at multi-tasking than previously, but the influence of technology was clearly dividing the generations: 77 per cent of people aged 18 to 24 responded "yes" when asked, "When nothing is occupying my attention, the first thing I do is reach for my phone," compared with only 10 per cent of those over the age of 65. Increasingly, we listen to tracks, not albums; we channel-hop rather than watching entire shows; we browse the web, spending on average less than a minute on any page; and many young people feel under-stimulated if they are not consuming two or even three streams of input at the same time.

Impatience has had a major effect in political discourse, where we have little time for oratory. The advent of instant, 24-hour news means that most political expression happens not in debating chambers but in front of TV cameras or even on social media. Fuelled by the need to create something to say all day, even in the absence of any real events, a mainstay of the media response has become 'attack journalism', which is obsessed with scandal. Demanding an answer to the question "Who is to blame?" has become the primary purpose of much interviewing and editorial decision-making. This springs from the Being Right leech, of course: we all feel a little better if we can be outraged and judgmental about someone or some organisation doing terrible things, so we implicitly encourage this kind of media sensationalism and witch-hunting. The same leech, expressed in constant impatience, fuels an epidemic of interrupting in media debate (and in millions of private conversations too).

The result is that the soundbite has become the prime vehicle for explaining political policy or opinion; get your proposition across in 20 seconds, or you will be interrupted. Politicians have learned to be 'on-message' at all times, employing large media teams to brief them and buffer them from aggressive questioning; they now avoid expressing strong opinions if at all possible, in case they are called to account later for changing their mind (which is now a heinous crime for some reason).

The conversation that arises in this fast-cut, short attention span, confrontational, blaming world is inevitably impoverished. This is true not only for politics but also for day-to-day discourse. Real listening takes time and effort; it is not compatible with multi-tasking or an eight-second attention span. Effective speaking requires being fully present and conscious. It's not surprising that so many conversations end with a dismissive "whatever!"

DESENSITISATION AND POLARISATION

Impatience has a close relative that's equally dramatically affecting our ability to communicate: it's desensitisation, which results from sensationalism and the pursuit of intensity. Desensitisation powers polarisation in society.

Sensationalism is the large, public version of the hyperbole we discussed in our dissection of the Looking Good leech. For example, in the UK, it seems that there are only two emotional states the popular media are interested in: people are either fine or they are furious. Any time someone is upset in any way, especially celebrities, the headline is: XYZ FURY AT... When the media constantly dumb language down like this, exaggerating emotions to make things seem more dramatic and collapsing a whole range of emotions into one catch-all state, the effect is that we lose the subtleties; shades of grey disappear and we end up with black and white. You are probably already thinking that this kind of reporting combines just about all the deadly sins in one, and you are right.

Sadly, though the temperature of news reporting and political debate has gradually risen we, like the proverbial frog in the cooking pot, have not noticed; we have become desensitised to the point where more accurate, temperate language would seem weak and lame. We are becoming addicted to intensity and numb to nicety and nuance. The creep is visible across traditional media, where news is laced with opinion, broadcast interviews are confrontational, interrupting kills dialectic and the game is to be outraged and find the guilty party. Extreme news media outlets are way more overt in peddling undiluted journalism of hate. We saw the results of this in referenda and elections in 2015 and 2016: anger and accusation displaced reason and compromise, with clearly divisive consequences.

Of course, all these things require the consent of all of us, because if we don't buy, watch or vote then the polarisers are marginalised and powerless. But the desire to be right is so strong that we are easily seduced to move down a long and slippery slope. First comes caricature, which makes it easier to dismiss those we disagree with. Next is condemnation, prejudice and bigotry. Ultimately the slope leads to hatred or difference, which has no place in democracy, which relies entirely on tolerance and civilised disagreement.

We need more listening in politics, and we need it urgently.

Exercise: Engage

Think about your levels of tolerance for people whose views are not your own. If they have been affected by the trend towards polarisation in the recent past, set yourself a goal of reading things you are going to disagree with. We tend to surf the web to validate our point of view. Do the opposite: seek challenge and see if there is something to learn from those who disagree with you.

VOCABULARY

It's hard to be expressive if you can't find the right words. English is very rich in its vocabulary: there are over 470,000 words in Webster's and the Oxford English Dictionary, though the real total is probably over a million according to Internet scans by Google and Harvard University. Of these, something around 170,000 are in current use, and the average person uses between 20,000 and 50,000 of them.

Recent research has shown that we may have a problem brewing: according to a survey in the UK in 2010, teenagers are using only about 800 words a day, and the top 20 words account for one third of their speech. I would guess that 'like' is very high up that list!

Inarticulacy leads to frustration. If we can't accurately describe what we want, what we need or what's wrong, we can feel disconnected and misunderstood. This, surely, is at the root of many confrontations and violent acts. Education is a high priority partly for this reason: to help people to understand and express themselves.

DANGER WORDS

While we're on the dark side and talking about vocabulary, I want to suggest five words or word groups that you might like to watch out for. They can have significant negative effects on the way your speaking is received, especially if they become habits for you.

As with the leeches and sins, I am not saying these things are always bad (though in some cases it's hard to see the positives!). I am saying that it's well worth analysing your own speaking and asking yourself if you use these words often. If so, it may serve you to set up a little internal alarm bell to alert you when you deploy them, to make sure you are not letting them leak power and authority from your speaking.

Let's take a look at the five danger words.

SHOULD

I have banned this word altogether from my vocabulary because I can't think of a single positive use for it. It generally delivers implicit judgment, guilt or regret. When we tell ourselves that we 'should' be doing something, we're acknowledging that the thing would be beneficial and implicitly beating ourselves up for not doing it. "I shouldn't get so upset when people criticise me." "I should have closed that sale." "I should have gone to the gym this week."

When we use it on other people, it can be judgmental, resentful and even confrontational, because it sets us up as superior and often involves unsolicited advice—back to the Being Right leech again. "He should have given me that promotion." "You should lose some weight." "They should never have married."

JUST

As an adjective, this is a good and often noble word, as in "He was a just man" or "It's a just society". As an adverb when used as a minimiser, it can be a major hole in the bucket when it comes to powerful speaking, and also a pernicious little blighter that can get us into trouble by making consequences seem manageable. Have you ever regretted agreeing or deciding to "just have one"? Many regrettable actions have started with the word just!

Also, the word can be demeaning, as in "she's just a secretary" or "he's just a kid," and it can trivialise real issues, as with the "Just say no" anti-drug campaign in the 1980s.

However, it's the apologetic use of the word in speaking that we can monitor for great gain. Consider these common statements and imagine someone saying them:

"I just want to say…"

"I'd just like to start with some housekeeping announcements."

"I just want you to know that…"

Now try these:

"I want to say…"

"I'd like to start with some housekeeping announcements."

"I want you to know that…"

Do you hear how the minimiser is a hidden apology, almost begging for the listener to allow this small, insignificant thing to be said, and how much more direct and assertive the second batch are than the first?

In my experience this word can be a little like bindweed, very hard to remove and very persistent in reasserting itself, but the gardener's job is patiently to continue with the simple practice of spotting the invader and removing it. I hope this practice serves you as well as it has me.

BUT

This word often acts as a road block, for example: "I like you, but…" Are you going to pay any attention at all to what comes before the 'but' in that sentence?

It is almost always possible to replace 'but' with 'and' to the benefit of your spoken or written communication. Sentences flow better, difficult ideas present themselves without appearing as major stumbling blocks, and the whole tone becomes more positive. Try it and see!

YOU MADE ME...

This formulation tends to come out when we're feeling sorry for ourselves. "You made me angry/sad/upset" gives all the power away to someone else. It puts us in the position of a victim, powerless and of course justified in being upset. Again, the Being Right leech is lurking in the background. This is not often a successful formulation, because it casts us as helpless to do anything about the issue, which is often (although of course not always) incorrect.

Who makes your emotions? You do. Other people do things; you have feelings about them. It can often be very powerful to recognise this distinction and take responsibility for the feeling part, replacing the "you made me" formulation with something like: "When you did x, I felt angry/sad/upset." In that version, the two elements are clearly separated along with the roles and responsibilities.

I am not suggesting that we are responsible for all our own pain, or that it's simple to generate positive emotions in the face of tragedy or cruel mistreatment. The world is unfortunately full of examples of disaster, barbarism and inhumanity, and those suffering these things naturally feel pain, fear, grief and even hate. However, in less extreme situations it can be enormously empowering to avoid giving our power away, especially if it's a habit we have fallen into.

MAXIMISERS

These are the words that immediately escalate an argument, like throwing gasoline on a fire. I expect you have used them in anger yourself—almost everyone has. In speaking, they are usually exaggerations that can alienate the listener.

Here they are:

- Always
- Never
- Everyone
- Nobody

In arguments, these words are usually inflammatory, either because they over-accuse, as in "You never listen to me!" or "You always leave your dishes in the sink!", or because they allow us to wallow in self-pity, as in "Nobody cares about me!" or "Everybody hates me!"

Really?

In speaking, they undermine potency because they are usually untrue, as in "Everyone wants a better car" or "We never get our marketing right." They can also leave you looking a little foolish, like the British Minister of War, Lord Haldane, who said in 1907: "The aeroplane will never fly."

THE AGENTS OF MISCOMMUNICATION

You will realise as we work together in this book that I love acronyms, perhaps because my memory is far from flawless. Here's the first, covering six common adversaries of effective speaking and listening and spelling out the word AGENTS. These six enemies of effective communication are:

- Assumptions
- Generalisations
- Emotions

- Noise

- Time

- Semantics

By becoming aware of them, and by spending some time asking if they exist and have any effects in your life, you can manage them, often with dramatic effects on your power and effectiveness in communication.

ASSUMPTIONS

As we'll see in the chapters on listening, our experiences shape our perceptions, and one of the ways that happens is when we form assumptions about the way the world works and especially the way people relate to us.

An example is the best way to explain the way assumptions change communication. Let's start with a simple scenario: a person enters a hotel with a heavy bag and the bellman says: "Let me help you with that."

We'll consider two cases. In the first, the person has formed an assumption based on a tough childhood and many failures in life. The assumption is 'People think I'm weak'. Given this assumption, the bellman's offer is tantamount to an insult, and the response is an irritated: "No thank you I'm perfectly capable of carrying my own bag!"

In the second case, based on a very different life experience, the person has formed the assumption that 'People are kind'. As a result, the bellman's offer is graciously accepted with a smile.

One input; two completely different outcomes, all because of assumptions. We all have assumptions about the world: it's far too complex to understand fully, and so are the people around us. We create models, theorise motivations, predict reactions and create meanings endlessly, and the underlying assumptions fashion our responses to the world and the people around us.

Becoming aware of your assumptions is a very powerful accomplishment. Most people think the world they perceive is reality. If you start to understand that much of it is in fact your own model—the map, not the territory—then you can start to ask the question: is this or that assumption useful to me?

GENERALISATIONS

"Generalisations are seldom if ever true and are usually utterly inaccurate."

Agatha Christie, Murder at the Vicarage

We've already encountered some of the most commonly used generalisations: the maximisers always, never, everyone and nobody. However, these are far from the only examples, and if you are in the habit of generalising it may well be transformative to become conscious of this and to temper it—especially when it comes to arguments with loved ones. Big and negative generalisations (BANGs) are very dangerous, whether we say them to and about ourselves ("I can't dance") or to and about others ("You just don't care"). If we repeat them enough we can start to believe them, and they can even become real.

Exercise: Be specific

Review your use of generalisations. Ask your friends and loved ones to help you. If they are a problem for you, set yourself the goal of being specific—of saying exactly what's so, without absolutes and maximisers, keeping the conversation limited to this specific situation or a well-defined set of experiences. Using phrases like "I feel as though..." can help to moderate those BANGs and reduce their impact dramatically.

Discuss with your significant other (with careful framing and a commitment not to get upset) any BANGs each of you tend to deploy. Make an agreement to be conscious and avoid them, and have a code word one can use when the other deploys a banned BANG.

EMOTIONS

There is an inverse relationship between listening and upset emotions. The more upset you become, the harder it gets to listen to someone: strong negative emotions like anger, self-pity or sadness turn our focus inward, removing it from the process of listening, which requires full attention to be effective. And if someone is upset, really listening to them will almost always calm them down. If you want to defuse an argument, the best way is to stop speaking and start listening.

This is worth knowing because we all experience strong emotions sometimes. Negative emotions such as sadness, anger, or personal dislike filter what you hear so that it matches your mood. They can even distract you from listening at all. Other people may read or sense your state and censor themselves, or struggle to communicate. At the same time, good feelings can generate carelessness: being optimistic, excited or liking a speaker can make you go along with whatever you hear. You may lose focus, neglect details, or stop thinking analytically. In short, you may stop listening effectively. Even staying neutral can descend into apathy and partial listening. When you stop putting energy into listening, you no longer do it attentively.

The key is to be aware of your state. If you know that you can't listen so well because of your current emotional state, you can take action, for example to move important conversations to a better time or to compensate by making greater effort than you naturally would. In the case of arguments at home, it can be very helpful to agree on a system of calling time-outs that allow all parties to take a break and calm down so that, when conversation resumes, listening can take the place of shouting. All parties must agree in advance that, when a time-out is called, there is no negotiation or carrying on; also, calling a time-out must include agreeing a time to resume the conversation within a pre-agreed maximum limit.

NOISE

Now that you're conscious about sound and its effects—and about noise and the damage it can cause—you will be taking control of the context for your conversations much more than ever before. Noise makes communication more difficult, obscuring the signal we want to pay attention to. In hospitals, research shows that high noise levels increase dispensing errors, probably because people mishear instructions. Noise is all around us, so it pays to have a simple system to deal with it when you want to have an important conversation or get some work done. Here's my suggestion: if noise is an issue, take an MBA.

The M is MOVE. Whenever I see people in the street shouting at each other next to a building site or a jack hammer, I think: "Why don't you just move?" It's not helpful to go unconscious, ignoring noise and carrying on regardless, in a bellow. If we remember the communication model that underpins this whole book (the circular relationship between speaking and listening, inside of the context of background noise) then it makes sense to plan the context for significant conversations, avoiding unhelpful noise. It might not be the best idea to try and make a complex sales presentation in a coffee bar, or to propose marriage in a nightclub—although I'm sure both these things happen! When you know what you want to say, how and to whom, the next question is: where?

The B is BLOCK. If you can't move, try to block the noise. Close doors or windows. If you're trying to work or make phone calls, headphones can be your friends here, blocking the background noise. For concentration in noisy spaces, non-distracting masking sound like the Study app or some birdsong can help too.

The A is ACCEPT. If you can't move and you can't block, then it pays to have an internal conversation and choose to be there. If we fight the inevitable, getting upset about the noise, the upset itself becomes the problem and adversely affects our conversation or our work. If, instead, you decide to accept the noise and the suboptimal context, and adjust your expectations accordingly, then the upset doesn't occur and you make the best of a bad job. As my father used to say: "The best is the enemy of the good." Sometimes good is the best we can do.

TIME

"You cannot truly listen to anyone and do anything else at the same time."

– M. Scott Peck

It takes time to listen properly, which is an issue in our increasingly time-poor world. For decades, marketers have been selling time-saving: faster, easier, quicker. The pace of life seems to accelerate year by year as we try to cram more and more into every day, multi-tasking in order to get things done and stay on top of life with all its complexities and calls on our time. We are always on, doing email in bed, texting as we walk in the street, and having phone or even face-to-face conversations as we do two or three other things simultaneously.

I believe that there are billions of people on this planet who have never had the experience of being properly listened to—that is, when the other person stops their world for a while and devotes 100 percent of their time and attention to the act of listening.

There is a cost to this of course... but there is such a benefit too. True listening like this is one of the most generous gifts you can give to anyone. You may not have done it for years. Try it today and see what happens! (See the exercise below.)

By the same token, we can gain enormously by being conscious of time when speaking. Face to face, it's often (though not always) possible to see if someone is open for a conversation. Remotely, especially in voice-only communication, we don't have that data. We are not likely to achieve a good outcome if we speak to someone while they are focusing elsewhere, especially if that focus involves emotions. By making a polite request ("Is now a good time for you to talk for five minutes?") we can ensure that they do give us their full attention for the agreed period.

Exercise: timing

1. Listening

Make a list of the most important people to whom you listen. Choose one at a time and decide that, next time they speak, you will stop everything else and give them your full, undivided attention. Do this for a week for that one person and make a note on your list against their name of any changes you detect in your relationship or how they are with you. After a week, add the next person, and so on. When your list is complete, sit and read through the notes to see the transformations you have effected simply by giving people your time.

2. Speaking

Unless nonverbal information makes it clear there is an opening, always ask: "Do you have a few minutes?" (or however long you know you need). Or you might say: "I want to discuss x; is now a good time?" You are making a contract to buy their attention. Not doing this and butting in without permission often lands as arrogant or selfish, and yields far less returns than this explicit agreement.

3. Meetings

In meetings, always confirm a start time AND a finish time. I have lost count of the number of meetings I have attended where only the start time was agreed and very different expectations existed (unspoken) about the finish time. At the start of the meeting, confirm that everyone agrees on the finish time and is clear to be present for the whole meeting.

SEMANTICS

The S of AGENTS is about meanings. Semantics is another word that comes to us from ancient Greece, where *sēmantikós* meant 'significant'; it is the study of meaning. It focuses on the relation between 'signifiers' like words, phrases, signs, and symbols and what they stand for—their 'denotation' and 'connotation'.

Denotation of a word is its essential, central meaning: for example, dog, a domesticated carnivorous mammal that typically has a long snout, an acute sense of smell, non-retractile claws, and a barking, howling, or whining voice.

Connotation describes the word's implications and emotional associations—the additional layers of meaning that we ascribe to it.

There was an advertising campaign in the UK recently that used the slogan "Be more dog," meaning be more enthusiastic, playful and excited about life. This is a perfect example of connotation.

As we will discover in the next chapter, context and listening are critical when it comes to connotations. We are meaning-making machines, and we often collapse what happened with what we made it mean. It can be very liberating to become conscious of the meanings you make, of your ability to change them at will, and of the fact that others may construe things very differently!

Semantics impair communication clarity more obviously when languages get involved. Even English versions vary widely, as I found recently when I was talking about the problem of noise from trolleys to a group from a US hospital. Faces were blank until I showed a picture and the lightbulb came on: "Oh, you mean *carts!*"

If we can retain humility and realise that others may not make the same meanings we do, communication is less likely to be derailed by potentially destructive misunderstandings.

BUTTONS, TRIGGERS, BARBS AND BOMBS

As we saw in the discussion of the AGENTS that affect our speaking and listening, each of us develops a model of the world based on assumptions that in turn derive from our experiences; we mature with an emotional landscape and our own habits and systems for meaning-making. We also develop our own sensitivities, and in relationship we become aware of the sensitivities of our loved ones, families, friends and colleagues.

As a result, most people have buttons and triggers. I differentiate these two by their results. A button produces an emotional response—for example say that thing to me, and I immediately become incandescent with rage. A trigger produces a behaviour—for example, remind me of this memory or put me in that situation and I will behave in a certain way.

When we deliberately, or perhaps instinctively, aim for other people's buttons or try to trigger them, we may use barbs or bombs. A barb is a niggling, pointed remark that tends to hook the recipient because it's unkindly meant. A bomb is that phrase we deploy *in extremis*—the one that's going to cause a nuclear explosion in the other person.

Involuntary emotions or behaviours can be very destructive, so it's generally wise to avoid pressing buttons, pulling triggers, casting barbs or dropping bombs.

Exercise: Map the minefield

As usual, consciousness is key. Take some time to reflect on your own buttons and triggers. What sets you off? When did you last lose it, or behave in a way you later regretted? Start a notebook on this and collect examples. In time, you will have a very clear idea of your own sensitivities, and you can do the same for the important people in your life. Life is not always a walk in a minefield, but it definitely helps to know where the danger areas are so that you can avoid them.

CHAPTER TWO: THE DARK SIDE

Chapter Three

Exploring listening and speaking

We don't teach the skills of listening and speaking much, if at all, in formal education. That leads many people to take them for granted, assuming that it's natural to have these abilities—but in fact they are both skills that can be learned, practiced and improved. In this chapter, we unpack them to explore exactly what listening and speaking really involve.

THE MIRACLE OF HEARING

Hearing is a form of touch. You feel it through your body, and sometimes it almost hits your face.

Evelyn Glennie

Hearing is a miracle, and far too complex and extraordinary to be taken for granted the way we do. As you read this, you are hearing the sound around you with your whole body. You were doing this from as early as 12 weeks after conception in your mother's womb, until your ears developed enough to start working properly at around 20 weeks. What you were listening to back then was mainly your mother's heartbeat, which was in three-time, like a waltz (lub-dub-pause, lub-dub-pause). Perhaps this is why music in three-time tends to be happy, while four-time (which is more associated with walking or marching feet) can be much more aggressive.

In the womb, you could also hear muffled sounds from the outside world: remember, sound travels even more effectively through fluids than it does through air. These sounds shaped you as you listened. Research shows that pre-birth babies learn to recognise their parents' voices and become familiar with the cadences and sounds of what will be their native language; they even get to appreciate their parents' favourite music. Although there is absolutely no evidence to support the popular idea that playing classical music makes a baby more intelligent, nevertheless it's probably a very pleasant experience!

The moment of birth transformed your hearing experience. Suddenly, the high frequencies that had been blocked by your mother's body assailed you all at once. I often think this must be one of the most startling aspects of coming into the world, equal with seeing bright light and starting to breathe air instead of fluid. It must take some time to get use to sharp, high-pitched sounds.

Although your eyes don't learn how to focus for some time after birth, your ears are already working perfectly when you enter the world. Unfortunately, many babies' first experience is very noisy. Hospitals are chronically loud: as already mentioned earlier in this book, a study of US hospitals found that noise levels were up to 12 times the World Health Organisation's recommended maximum by day, and eight times as loud by night.

Neonatal units are no exception, as I remember very well from the birth of my son Ben, who came six weeks early by emergency C-section. Long before I was working in sound and understood its effects on human beings, I intuitively felt very distressed by his surroundings as he lay in an incubator, surrounded by hissing sounds, beeps and intermittent alarms.

I'm glad to report that Ben has grown up a fine young man, but recent research shows that this kind of environment can affect development. This is because the senses affect one another in a process scientists call cross-modal effects. The power of these effects is becoming clearer with research by scientists like Professor Charles Spence at Oxford University; for example, one paper found that we taste food less well in noisy restaurants, probably because overloading any one sense displaces our sensitivity in others.

Restaurateurs need to take note of this because restaurant noise is becoming a ubiquitous hazard. I'm sure you've had the experience of going home with a sore throat and a sore head after bellowing across the table at your dinner companion for hours. A few years ago, I took my fiancée Jane to the world-famous Manhattan restaurant P.J. Clarke's, the bar where Johnny Mercer wrote *One for My Baby (and One More for the Road)*. I'd first been there with my father at the age of 15, and was looking forward to a romantic and atmospheric evening. We got atmosphere all right, but the romance all went out of the window the moment we walked in. The din inside was unbelievable (I measured it at a consistent 90 dB) and the only way to communicate was to shout at the top of your voice. Sadly, many people now confuse buzz with noise. I wish restaurateurs would realise that you can have a quiet buzz!

Tip: If you want to speak to someone in a noisy bar, restaurant, club or gig, teach them first to press firmly with a finger on their tragus (the solid flap of skin and cartilage in front of their ear canal) then speak normally very close to their ear. It works like magic and you can speak rather than shout whilst being heard perfectly; you also don't damage their hearing by shouting straight into their ear. I wish I'd known that in P.J.Clarke's!

We tend to take our hearing for granted, but it is a complex and, to me, rather a wondrous process. Sound waves travel through the air and enter your ear canal, collected by the brilliantly designed pinna, the complex folds of skin on the side of your head that we generally think of as the ear. They enter your head and vibrate your tympanic membrane, an eight by 10 millimetre (roughly quarter-inch) oval better known as the ear drum. This is an amazing process: we manufacture loudspeakers with three or more vibrating cones in order to reproduce all the frequencies of sound, and yet in your ear this one little membrane manages the whole thing perfectly.

Three tiny, linked bones (the smallest ones in your body) transfer this vibration to an even smaller membrane called the oval window. The engineering is rather remarkable when you consider it: those three tiny bones vibrate thousands of times a second for many decades, and they very rarely fail.

The oval window in turn vibrates fluid in your inner ear, a shell-shaped structure called the cochlea, containing tiny hair cells, each of which responds to specific frequencies; when triggered, these cause the release of neurotransmitter.

The auditory nerve takes all the information from the ear's hair cells to your brainstem, where its first task is to trigger subconscious reflexes in the midbrain, starting with fight/flight because your life may depend on it. A little after the subconscious responses, the auditory information reaches many other parts of your brain, where it becomes consciously perceived and may further affect your physiology, as well as impacting on your emotions, cognition and behaviour.

Hearing goes very deep, very fast, as we discussed in the section on the four effects of sound. Vision is a cone in front of you, while hearing is a sphere all around you; you can hear, but not see, danger coming from behind, which is why hearing is your primary warning sense.

The human hearing range is 10 octaves, from 20 to 20,000 Hertz; by comparison, we see less than one octave, from roughly 430 to 770 teraHertz. Also, your ears are always on: you may have noticed that you have no earlids! A strange noise in your house at night will probably wake you, because your ears are working even while you sleep.

Hearing is vulnerable to damage, as we've seen with the troubling phenomenon of youngsters abusing headphones. Industrial and construction noise, loud music and even working for extended periods in noisy restaurants or clubs, can create permanent hearing damage. Many famous musicians are now suffering from years of exposure, among them Sting, Bono, Neil Young and Pete Townshend, who is an active campaigner for raising awareness of the dangers of loud music among young musicians and fans alike. Townshend wrote: "I have terrible hearing trouble. I have unwittingly helped to invent and refine a type of music that makes its principle proponents deaf." He blames his hearing loss not only on high-volume gigs, but also decades of headphone use during recording. These days he has to take 36-hour breaks between sessions to let his ears recover. He reflects: "Hearing loss is a terrible thing because it can't be repaired. Music is a calling for life. You can write it when you're deaf, but you can't hear it or perform it."

Dr. Seth Horowitz wrote a terrific book called *The Universal Sense: How Hearing Shapes the Mind*. A former neuroscience professor at Brown University, he currently works on ways of improving wellbeing through applied sound: for example, he created some effective sleep-inducing sonic products that I can vouch for, as they worked very well when my daughter Alice was suffering from insomnia. I spoke to Seth about hearing, and the full interview is on this book's website in both audio and transcript forms. Check the panel for an excerpt and for instructions for accessing the full interview online.

Hearing is a powerful and rather miraculous sense. It places us in the world as we become aware of the sounds all around us, warns us of danger and permits us all the joys of music and spoken communication. We need to look after it.

Hearing—the universal sense:
Seth Horowitz

This is an excerpt from the transcript of a conversation with Seth Horowitz. For the full transcript, and the audio recording, visit www.howtobeheardbook.com and use the password **conscious**.

Dr. Seth Horowitz is a former professor in the Department of Neuroscience at Brown University. His work covers comparative and human hearing, balance and sleep research, brain development, the biology of hearing, the musical mind and neuroethology (the evolutionary and comparative approach to the study of animal behaviour and its underlying mechanistic control by the nervous system). He has applied his research skills to real world applications of designed sound, ranging from sleep enhancement to combating motion sickness. His work has been covered in popular media including NPR's *Hear and Now* and *All Things Considered*, the *Boston Globe*, Wired.com and numerous other online and print publications. His book *The Universal Sense: How Hearing Shapes the Mind* has received critical acclaim by *Publisher's Weekly* and *Nature*. His New York Times article *The Science and Art of Listening* was one of the most emailed articles in 2012.

Julian Treasure: Seth, your book was called "The Universal Sense" and I'm fascinated by how you came to that title—why you feel that hearing is the universal sense. Perhaps you could say a word about that.

Seth Horowitz: Well, it was really my first quest given to me as a graduate student where my advisor was doing a series of lectures on animal senses and said, "Go find some animal that doesn't hear." There are plenty of animals that don't see very well or don't see at all, like blind cave fish. There are plenty of animals with limited sense of touch, taste, smell, but it turns out that there are no vertebrates, creatures with backbones, that do not have a functional sense of hearing and vibration. Once I realised that, it made complete sense because vibration is one of those forms of energy that you're going to find anywhere. Chemical senses need to be close to the body, light will be dependent on time of day and environment, but no matter where you go, there are always vibrations. A truism about lifeforms is that if there is a source of information, somebody will evolve to use it.

Julian Treasure: And of course, vibration ultimately is life. It's everything. Everything is vibrating at subatomic level right up to cellular level. Vibration is all around and, I imagine, just self-preservation for most species would dictate that they need to be very sensitive to vibration.

Seth Horowitz: Of course, because even if you're a visual species, like humans, there's going to be a time when you're going to want to hear something even if it's behind you or it's dark out. So, vibration and sound act as our alarm system. What that has grown out of is the fact that hearing and vibration detection are very fast sensory systems. We think about something being as fast as sight or the speed of light being very quick, but in biological terms hearing can be 20 to 100 times faster than vision. This is because vision has to be processed through multiple stages. It has to be synthesised to create an image; whereas, hearing is a very mechanical sense. Our ear actually carries out many of the really critical analyses even before it gets to our brain. Within the first .0051 of a second you can tell where something is, what it is to some degree, whether you should be afraid of it or whether you should be possibly running towards it. Long before you can get any kind of conscious response, your ears have already set up the very basic survival parameters...

It hits the preconscious regions of the brain very early. That's why sound colours all other sensory and perceptual and emotional phenomena, because it's gotten in there long before anything else has driven. By the time someone has said, "I want you to listen to me" you have heard that person's voice, identified their gender, where they're talking from, might have some idea about their culture, their age, how important what they're saying is and their emotional status. That colours long before you actually hear and understand the words that they're saying.

Julian Treasure: Can you say a word about the difference between hearing and listening?

Seth Horowitz: Hearing is a sensation. It goes on all the time, whether you're paying attention or not. Listening is hearing plus attention. Paying attention is something that we do to increase our resolution on a task, but what attention really is, is a way of filtering out everything but one particular thing. All your friends who say they're multitasking because they're so busy—no, they're not. You can only really focus on one thing at a time. People who claim they're multitasking just have a decent mental transmission and are shifting between things very quickly and often just not spending any depth on any one thing. Listening requires taking all that auditory information, finding elements that are similar and aligning them in your brain.

Attention is about signals that synchronise in time. If a whole orchestra is just doing that tune up thing where everyone is making it up, there's no melody, there's nothing you're tracking, you just hear this wall of sound—but if during the tune up, a cello and a flute start playing a similar line, the same scale, you'll pay attention to that scale. It's like they're both playing the C major scale or they're both playing the opening from some song you know: your ear has locked on the same frequency content over time.

THREE KINDS OF LISTENING

Nature hath given men one tongue but two ears, that we may hear from others twice as much as we speak.

– Epictetus

Dame Evelyn Glennie is the world's only full time solo orchestral percussionist—and she is profoundly deaf. When Evelyn lost her hearing aged 12, her enlightened music teacher had her feel the different vibrations in timpani skins as he struck them. Gradually she became so sensitised that she could discern different notes through touch, and as time passed she learned to hear with her entire body. Today, she plays with symphony orchestras, listening with every cell. Naturally, Evelyn has some strong views on hearing and listening, as expressed in her excellent 2007 TED talk, and also in my interview with her, an excerpt from which is in the panel, along with instructions for accessing the complete interview online in both audio and transcript forms.

If they think about listening at all, most people think that hearing and listening are one and the same, a natural process we don't have to think about. That may be why we do not teach listening in schools.

In fact, hearing and listening are not the same thing at all. Listening is a skill, one that can be learned and improved. It's also a lot more complex than it may initially appear.

I distinguish three kinds of listening, each of which we will explore in this chapter.

First is **outer listening**. This is the listening you immediately think of when you consider the topic—listening to sounds from around you. I define this kind of listening as 'making meaning from sound'.

Second is **inner listening**. We all have an inner voice that speaks to us inside our heads. You know the one: it may have just said to you: "What inner voice is he talking about?" The way we listen to that voice can shape our whole life experience.

Third is **created listening**. Our actions and words fashion a listening for us in other people, and this joins with the unique listenings they bring from their life experiences to create *a listening into which we always speak*. This may be individual if we're speaking to one person or it may be a compound listening from a group or an audience.

Dame Evelyn Glennie

This is an excerpt from the transcript of a conversation with Evelyn Glennie. For the full transcript, and the audio recording, visit www.howtobeheardbook.com and use the password conscious.

Evelyn Glennie is the first person in history to successfully create and sustain a full-time career as a solo percussionist, performing worldwide with the greatest conductors, orchestras, and artists. She fondly recalls having played the first percussion concerto in the history of The Proms at the Albert Hall in 1992, which paved the way for orchestras around the world to feature percussion concerti. She had the honour of a leading role in the Opening Ceremony of the London 2012 Olympic Games.

Evelyn regularly provides masterclasses and consultations designed to guide the next generation. With over 80 international awards to date, including the Polar Music Prize and the Companion of Honour, Evelyn is also a leading commissioner of new works for solo percussion, with more than 200 pieces to her name from many of the world's most eminent composers. The film 'Touch the Sound' and her enlightening TED speech remain key testimonies to her approach to sound-creation.

To this day, Evelyn continues to invest in realising her vision—to Teach the World to Listen—while looking to open a centre that embodies her mission: "to improve communication and social cohesion by encouraging everyone to discover new ways of listening. We want to inspire, to create, to engage and to empower".

Evelyn Glennie: I knew I wanted to play in percussion and participate in music making, but I thought that sound came through the ears. There was this huge build-up of sound. It wasn't that I wasn't hearing sound. It was actually that I was hearing too much of it and I couldn't then separate the sounds and decipher where they were coming from. So that actually then affected my balance. And the sense of touch was just completely out of the door, even though I knew what needed to happen, I couldn't make that happen because I was being directed by what was happening here.

Until one day, one lesson … He happened to be striking a timpani. There were two timpani in the room, or kettledrums. He struck the drum and he just sort of paused for a moment. He said, "Evelyn, can you feel that drum?" He said, "That drum is really resonating. Can you feel it?" And he struck it and I said, "Well actually I think I can. I think I do. I think I do feel this." And he said, "Okay, right. Where are you feeling it?" And I listened and listened and I said, "Well I think I'm feeling it in part of my hand," or wherever I was feeling it. He then said, "Evelyn, put your hands on the wall of the room." These were thin, just thin music rooms. Sure enough, the amount of vibration that came through the wall and through my hand was enormous. Then, he changed the pitch and then said, "Right. Where are you feeling that?" And I said, "Ooh, from there to there." Then he changed the pitch again. "Ooh, that's now less." It was getting higher and higher.

That completely changed the way I saw sound. I knew that I needed the patience to listen to the sound after the drum had been struck. I knew that, heavens above, this body was perceiving sound in many different parts. What I don't do and can't do is decipher the pitch. So I can't say, "Oh yes, if I feel it from there to there, that's a B-flat." That's not going to happen, because what you're playing is just simply too fast. It's too much. It's too many notes. If you're playing with an orchestra, there's just simply too much going on to just kind of pick these things out. And even with tuning, you need to be completely alone, completely that's the only thing happening, as it were, in your environment.

So that was a hugely important turning point for me, because from then I had the confidence to take the aids out, actually hear less through the ears, but more through the body. It also meant that, suddenly, I knew that the sense of touch was the most important sense for me. Also the sense of sight, just being aware of how other people were playing, really using the eyes to see if something was aggressive, if something was loving, if something was gentle, if something was cheeky, whatever it was.

Suddenly, all of the senses became developed and each one couldn't do without the other, actually. So in a way, all of these senses sort of form this, what I think is the sixth sense, frankly. But that's always fluid in the kind of situation that you're in. It's not a case of "This is how I always do it". It's your launch pad, and it depends on the room you're in. It depends on the piece you're playing, the instrument you're playing. It depends on all sorts of things.

What we do as musicians, is that nine times out of ten we rehearse in an empty hall, and that has a certain feel to it. But then suddenly the audience comes in and it's a completely different feel. So in my mind, when I'm in my own home I make a difference between practice, rehearsing, and performance. So practice is, for me, the mechanics of playing. How can I get this more however I want it to be? But rehearsing, which is what I do most of the time, is really imagining the audience there and thinking to yourself, "Today I'm going to imagine myself in a cathedral, so what is that sound palette going to be? How am I going to interpret what I want to play?" Could be an exercise, but how am I going to play that exercise in a cathedral, or in a really dry acoustic, or in a small room, or in a drawing-type room, or wherever it may be, in an outdoor venue? How am I going to project that sound? It makes me decide which mallets I may want to use because they'll be different according to those situations.

That's helped me broaden the sound palette that I use as a player so that I'm not hostage to, "Well, this is how I always play it, and this is how it worked in my practice room, so why doesn't it work now when I'm in this particular room?"

Julian Treasure: Are there any sounds that you particularly love listening to, Evelyn?

Evelyn Glennie: Well, it's whatever sound is around, that's my favourite sound. It's a little bit like an instrument, whatever is in front of me, if it's a triangle or a marimba or snare drum, that's my favourite instrument. Whichever piece of music is in front of me, that's my favourite instrument. But it is interesting what you said, because you can play any kind of music to youngsters, to infants really and if you play those in certain concerts people might say, "Goodness, what on earth was that? That was just nonsense," or, "That was just awful," or whatever. But for kids it may be, "Well that sounds like my dad's lawnmower," or, "Ooh, that sounds like the fridge door," or something. They're relating it to things, and I find that really quite interesting because there is that imagination not to be a hostage to sound really; they're really thinking about their environment.

I enjoy the exploration of sound, so it is hard for me to pick out what my favourite sound is. Because really, if I'm participating in sound, then I have to pay attention to that 100%, so that's my favourite one. It has to be, yes.

OUTER LISTENING

You hear every sound around you, but you don't listen to them all. During the complex process of distributing the mass of sonic information to various parts of your brain, you select what to pay attention to. This is the first stage of listening: filtering. As we'll see shortly, this filtering shapes your whole experience of life.

The second stage of listening gives rise to my definition of outer listening: '*making meaning from sound*'. As you filter, you also interpret and create meaning. Language is the most obvious example: we learn how to decode a stream of sounds as words with meanings. If you listen to a language you don't understand at all, you will hear a wall of incomprehensible vocal stylings, and you may get a fresh sense of how amazing this process is. We tend to take for granted that our own language means something, but there is nothing inherent in this: decoding language is a learned process with enormous complexity.

We ascribe meaning to all sound, not just language. Instinctively, we recognise potential danger in sudden or unexplained sounds. Consciously and subconsciously, we create and access a huge mental library of sounds and what they mean, to help us understand the world around us: the sound of a car, train or plane; the alert sounds of our phones and computers; our doorbell; all the richness of music; feedback sounds from household devices and public street furniture; nature sounds; the nuances of our baby's vocalisations or the subtle inflexions in our loved one's voice.

The problem is that most people do not listen consciously at all. They are not aware that they are *doing* something, deploying a skill that can be worked on, improved, refined and mastered. When you start to listen consciously, you move to a whole new level of life experience and you gain unprecedented levels of control over your happiness, wellbeing and effectiveness. We will be learning how to listen consciously in the next chapter.

THE LISTENING FILTERS

Here's a potentially transformative concept: your listening is unique! It's as individual as your fingerprints, your irises, your voice print or your face.

A common, persistent and very damaging assumption is that everyone listens the same way. We do not. This is because we all listen through a set of filters, and these filters are not the same for any two people because they are shaped by our life experience and by our character. Taken together, our filters create a default listening that can become a little like a bunker with a small slit open to the world outside: only certain things get in, and much simply bounces off. If we are unconscious of this process, we can firmly believe that what we perceive through that small opening is reality, whereas it is in fact a small, selected part of reality that we interpret in our little bunker. Of course, what we think of as reality actually happens between our ears: it is just our perception and thus never complete. The trick is to become aware that we are viewing the map and not the territory, in which case we can start to manage, and even change, the limitations.

Let's explore the listening filters.

Culture

You were born into a complex of cultures, each influencing the way you listen. These may have included your nuclear and extended family; your ethnicity; your neighbourhood; and your city, state and country. Any or all of these environments may fashion your listening as you grow up.

Language

The language or languages that you learn to speak will further forge your listening. Languages differ widely, not only in how they work but in the words they have, or don't have.

Tonal languages like those used in China, Vietnam and Thailand distinguish identical words by using different pitches or inflexions, giving them completely different meanings. Some of these languages create seven different meanings for the same syllable, depending on whether it is said high, low, with or without a croak and so on. Speakers of some African tonal languages can communicate across long distances playing the tones on drums, and there are hundreds of whistled languages where people in places as diverse as France, West Africa, Madeira and Mexico can have entire conversations with nothing but whistling, delivering the tones of the language without the words.

Some languages treat time very differently to the way Indo-European languages conceptualise it with the future in front of us and the past behind, and tenses of verbs to indicate temporality. There are tenseless languages, such as Hopi, and the Amazonian Amondawa language has no words for time periods such as month or year. The Amondawa people do not refer to their ages, but rather assume different names in different stages of their lives or as they achieve different status within the community.

Languages also emphasise the importance of things in the words they use, or don't use. The urban legend about Eskimos and words for snow and ice is true. Central Siberian Yupik has 40 such terms, while the Inuit dialect spoken in Canada's Nunavik region has at least 53, including *matsaaruti* for wet snow that can be used to ice a sleigh's runners, and *pukak* for the crystalline powder snow that looks like salt. In the Inupiaq dialect of Alaska, there are about 70 quite poetic terms for ice, including *utuqaq* (ice that lasts year after year), *siguliaksraq* (the patchwork layer of crystals that forms as the sea begins to freeze) and *auniq* (ice that is filled with holes, like Swiss cheese).

Equally, languages can miss words, either because they are not relevant to the experience of the people speaking that tongue, or simply because nobody ever bothered to make one. In Czech, *vybafnout* is a single word meaning to jump out and shout boo, a word lacking in English. The reason is unclear: Czech children are probably no more playful than English-speakers. In Brazilian, *cafune* is the act of tenderly running your fingers through your loved one's hair. Perhaps Brazilians are more romantic than most!

One of my favourite books is *The Meaning of Liff* by Douglas Adams and John Lloyd, where the brilliantly witty authors suggest hundreds of things that really ought to have words but don't (in English, anyway) and give them words taken from obscure place names. So, a 'berriwillock' is an unknown workmate who writes 'All the best' on your leaving card, while a 'grimbister' is a body of cars on a motorway all moving at exactly the speed limit because one of them is a police car.

Our language shapes our perception, something that may be behind many differences and conflicts.

Values

As you grew, you accreted values from parents, friends, teachers, role models and authority figures. You selected some and discarded others, probably largely in your teenage years where most people try on a range of identities before settling on the one they choose to make their own.

As we saw in our discussion of the People Pleasing leech, most people never make their values explicit and many don't know what they are at all. The values exercise in that section can be very valuable to identify and be conscious of the values that drive you and underpin your behaviour, and your listening.

Attitudes

Less formal and grand than values, attitudes also shape listening. You will have accumulated attitudes about many things from your individual path through life. Some will be based on fact or first-hand experience, while others may be arbitrary and even simply prejudice or bias. Most people find it hard to listen to someone who has highly opposed attitudes to their own, especially if they appear capricious or unjustified. Attitudes such as religious bigotry, racism and sexism absolutely affect the way people listen and respond to others, with serious and sometimes fatal consequences that appear all too frequently in the news media worldwide.

Beliefs/Assumptions

We saw earlier in the section on AGENTS how assumptions can colour our listening to other people. Beliefs can do the same, whether they are religious, philosophical or scientific. So much of human conflict and cruelty has come from people refusing to tolerate those with opposing beliefs, to the point where violence becomes justified in their minds. We have seen this in the 21st century in vicious, uncompromising groups like ISIS, who continue a long and tragic history of pogroms and 'ethnic cleansing'. Peace depends on the ability to tolerate those with opposing beliefs. That requires trying to understand them, which is only possible if we work hard at listening despite our filters.

Expectations

I try very hard not to form too many expectations, because expectation is often the mother of resentment. Of course, we need to plan, and it's great to look forward to things, but if we set expectations too firmly—especially of other people, and especially if we keep them secret—then we set ourselves up for a fall, probably into pain and anger. Expectations can affect our listening profoundly if things don't turn out as we wanted them to. As usual, the key is consciousness: if we are aware of having an expectation, we can challenge it or be willing to let it go if life turns out differently (and sometimes for the best!).

Intentions

We enter most conversations with some sort of intention. This will inevitably shape our listening as we listen out for things that will help us achieve our goal or that will get in our way, and ignore or discard things we deem entirely irrelevant to the intention. Intentions can cause confusion, embarrassment or conflict if we're not clear and explicit about them, for example if a speaker and a listener have different intentions for a conversation. I remember at the TED conference in Monterey in 1988 the sound system failed. My intention to listen and learn from what was on the stage was unwavering, so when someone a few seats to my left started shouting I felt annoyed and disapproving—until I realised that it was the late and much missed Robin Williams, who then proceeded to amuse and entertain the audience with brilliant improv comedy until the technology was fixed and the show could go on.

Emotions

As we saw in the AGENTS section, emotions often colour and affect our listening. When we're upset, we don't listen so well, while we can defuse another's upset by really making them feel listened to. Another example is romance: when we're in the first flush of love, our listening for the object of our affection is both overwhelming and unconditionally positive: the very sound of their voice can make our heart skip a beat, and nothing they say is wrong. That usually changes as romantic passion matures into a more sustainable, long-term loving relationship, where we accept that nobody, not even the love of our life, is perfect. We'll be examining loving listening later in this book.

These, then, are the filters. Yours are different from mine, because we've walked a different road. This observation chimes with recent neurological research, which indicates that individual experiences shape our brains through a process called hippocampal neurogenesis. In a 2013 German lab experiment, 40 genetically identical mice were raised in a closed environment. What transpired was fascinating: the mice diverged in their behaviour, with some becoming more adventurous and others being very conservative. The differences grew over time, despite identical environment, diet and genes. The reason was that every individual experience led to the growth of new neurons, creating individuality through a sort of neurological butterfly effect. The same process operates in human beings, which may be why twins with near-identical genes and upbringings often lead very different lives and develop different personalities, strengths and weaknesses. If individual experiences can have such a strong effect, it is no surprise that one twin might be a great listener and the other very poor.

I suspect this brain plasticity is part of the process of developing unique listening filters. No two people have identical experiences, so the setting of each individual's filters is unique to that person—in other words, every person's listening is unique, which is a transformative realisation that we will work through in detail in the section on created listenings later in this chapter.

Taken together, the listening filters create our reality—the things we pay attention to, and what we make them mean. It also means that, by becoming aware of your own filters, you create the possibility of changing them—of using them like the control surfaces on a plane to change your reality for the better. Now that's an exciting prospect! We'll learn how to do it in Chapter Four.

INNER LISTENING

It's generally accepted by neuroscientists that most of the activity in our brains is unconscious. We are rarely aware of the management of our bodily functions, even though they all are clearly regulated. It's a little like being the CEO of a huge organisation: you have a good general sense of what's going on, but as far as the details are concerned, all you get to know about is the odd piece of important information relayed to you by those who choose what's significant and what it means.

However, we do also think consciously, in imagined words, pictures and sounds. The weight of each varies from person to person, but note that two of them are sound-based. Even if you would describe your thinking as primarily visual, your mind's ear is probably quite active, whether it's listening to the voice in your head, enjoying remembered music or imagining the voice of a loved one saying something to you.

It's the little internal voice that we need to focus on here. Our inner listening to that voice plays a major role in our relationship with ourselves, which is to say our opinion of ourselves and our emotional response to ourselves, whether that's expressed in self-love and high self-worth, or in self-loathing and/or self-pity.

Most of us have an inner critic, and for some it's a very strong voice, possibly carrying on the destructive work of an over-critical parent or teacher. If you've ever heard the words "You idiot!", or worse, in your head, you know what I mean. Many people suffer greatly from negative self-talk.

Even if your inner critic doesn't run the internal show, you will almost certainly receive negative messages from time to time. Messages like these…

"Don't you dare get up to dance, people will laugh at you!"

"If you go and speak to him/her you will only make a fool of yourself!"

"Don't put your hand up, people might notice you!"

"Don't try that, you'll fail!"

It's easy to think that the inner voice is you, the boss, telling you the truth all the time. If that's so, then the negative comments hit home hard and cramp your style, stopping you from doing things and from expressing yourself, causing low self-esteem and even self-hatred.

Let me offer you a potentially transformative perspective: *you are not your inner voice.*

But if that's true, then who are you?

You are the one who's listening.

The voice you hear is not all of you; it's probably a part of you that got hurt once, or has learned to fear or be cautious about something. It may be doing its best to protect you, or it may be carrying on negative feedback you became familiar with in your childhood. (Sadly, very often we prefer familiar pain to the scary unknown, even if that route might lead to happiness.)

The father of behavioural economics, Daniel Kahneman, distinguishes two selves in his great book *Thinking, Fast and Slow*. The experiencing self does our living, experiencing everything in the moment. The remembering self summarises all this experience, interprets it and assigns meaning; it also overstates peaks and valleys and endings in its version of our life experience. The remembering self is what dominates our view of the world. This is why we tend to assume that the future will mirror the past, and form biased judgements about the likely outcomes of our current choices.

Whether your internal voice is a damaged fragment or your remembering self, and whatever its motives, if you accept that it isn't the whole of you, you put yourself in a completely different mindset when hearing it. Think of yourself as the king or queen on a throne with the little voice coming to offer you counsel based on a very incomplete set of data. If you don't like what it says, dismiss it! Alternatively, think of the little voice as an unruly youngster who doesn't understand the world yet and can't stop blurting things out as they enter his/her head; you can listen, tousle its head and send it packing!

Exercise: retrain your inner voice

1 That's interesting!
Practice using this phrase. It helps to distance you from the negative self-talk if you immediately think: "That's interesting! Why did my inner voice just say that?" I learned this one on the golf course! It's far more productive than diving into anger, frustration or despair to coolly ask: "That's interesting! Why did I hit that shank/slice/hook?"

2 True, kind, helpful
Ask yourself: was that comment true? Was it kind? Was it helpful? If the answer to any of these is no, say thanks for sharing and send the little voice on its way.

3 Transforming your self-talk
Take some time to write down the things you hear most from your inner voice. Some are probably negative. Many of them might be in the first person, like "I'm so useless!"

First, if your voice uses the first person (I this, I that), translate everything into the second person. Research shows that positive self-talk using the word 'you' or even the third person, using your name, is more effective, possibly because it makes us feel that someone else is talking.

For each of the negative comments, write a positive counter. So, for example, if you often hear "I'm so stupid", you might write "You are intelligent and perceptive." Or to counter "I have nothing interesting to say", you might write "John is a complex and fascinating human being." Or for "My stomach is so fat" try "Your stomach is round and you are going to take steps to slim."

You can write the positive statements on post-it notes and put them on the mirror you see in the morning. If there are a lot of them, take them one at a time. Repeat them to yourself enough times and they will gradually replace your negative tapes.

CREATED LISTENING

Just as you are a listening for others due to your filters, so others are a listening for you. This 'created' listening is a combination of their own unique, individual listenings and any experience they have of you. In other words, it is co-created.

Your part

Your contribution is your behaviour and way of being. How you are, and what you do and say, create a listening for you, especially in those who know you well. If you are always late for appointments, people may start telling you the meeting is earlier than it really is, because their listening for you is that you are a late person. This is where the seven deadly sins really play out: any of those behaviours that becomes habitual will impair the way people listen to you and make it harder for you to be heard and get your point across.

However, it doesn't take repeated behaviours to change people's listening for you. Sometimes that can happen instantly, either for better or for worse. In a world where reputation is becoming more and more important in business and in personal relationships, it is now vital to be aware of this process, as a salutary example shows.

In the 1980s, the UK's leading jeweller was a nationwide chain called Ratners, which was the default destination for any young couple planning to get married. It looked unassailable until, in April 1991, its Managing Director, Gerald Ratner, gave a speech to the Institute of Directors conference at the Royal Albert Hall. He decided to be humorous and self-deprecatory, but he badly misjudged the potential consequences. In his speech, he joked that some of his company's products were so cheap because they were 'crap' and that their earrings were cheaper than a prawn sandwich, but probably wouldn't last as long.

He did not anticipate the backlash. The popular national daily newspapers ran headlines that screamed 'Rotners'. Customers (who generally resent being depicted as mugs) boycotted Ratners stores. The value of the group plummeted by £500 million and the company almost collapsed completely. Gerald Ratner resigned and the company relaunched with a new name, though it never regained its former market position.

Instant changes in listening can also occur due to spoken or printed gossip, which is why we have laws against libel and slander. However, the law doesn't protect individuals from having their reputation destroyed in their own social circles, and damaged listenings can generate very destructive behaviour, as Desdemona finds with tragic consequences in *Othello*. On the other hand, a single action can transform the listening for a person from derisory to respectful, as T. E. Lawrence finds after the taking of Aqaba in David Lean's wonderful epic film *Lawrence of Arabia*.

The lesson from this is: **take responsibility for the listening you create through your actions and your words**. The listening you generate—public, professional, within your organisation, among your community, or among your friends and family—determines how you are received when you speak, and to a large degree what you can accomplish in your life. Take care of it.

Their part

Other people's contribution to the co-created listening for you is that they bring their own filters. As we've already noted, it is a grave mistake, and one that many people make, to assume that everyone listens like you do. Each human being brings his or her unique listening to every conversation. Becoming sensitive to this is a key skill in speaking effectively. We will look at this in more detail in Chapter Five.

EXPLORING SPEAKING

As already noted, humans have been communicating with complex language for up to 100,000 years. I often wonder what it sounded like when Palaeolithic people were speaking to each other tens of thousands of years ago. Living in Orkney as I do, the abundance of Neolithic antiquities such as the famous village of Skara Brae serves as a constant reminder that 95 per cent of human history is undocumented, including the words and ways of speaking our ancestors used and the music they made.

The anthropologist Steven Mithen postulates in his book *The Singing Neanderthals* that music came before language. Backed by an impressive, sweeping survey of the available data and scientific thinking, he suggests that early humans communicated using 'proto-hum', a non-verbal and quite musical form of vocal expression not unlike the wordless tonal languages of today that we discussed in the section on listening filters.

I do an exercise in my seminars that shows the power and universality of non-verbal vocal communication. I have the group pair off and then ask them to express to one another joy, anger, sadness, saying sorry, and asking for something—all in sound but without using any words. It is remarkable how everyone uses almost identical sounds for each of these tasks: anger is a low growl; sadness is a high, gentle tone that descends by about a minor third (could this be the reason minor keys sound sad to most people?); saying sorry is a gentle sound that goes quickly from high to low and back up again; and asking for something is pure questioning intonation where the tone rises as the object is indicated.

Mithen argues that infant-directed speech (IDS)—the sounds mothers make to their babies—may go back 500,000 years, and certainly this is the first form of verbal communication most of us receive, with its exaggerated prosody and simple, repeating vocabulary. However, from this simple and age-old starting point, modern babies then set out on the journey to learn an entire, complex language with up to 50,000 words they may use, along with all the complexities of intonation, gesture, facial expression and timbre that combine to form complete vocal communication.

Speaking is very simple: you force air through your vocal cords, which are folds of tissue stretched horizontally across the larynx from the front of the throat to the back, forming a slit, the edge of which vibrate to produce the sounds of your voice. The process is controlled by the Vagus nerve, the largest nerve in your body that also carries information to and from your ears, and reaches all the way down into your digestive system, passing by most of your vital organs on the way.

At the same time, speaking is very complicated: you have to create a wide range of tones, timbres, dynamics, sounds, vowels, consonants, words, phrases and sentences, instantaneously selecting from your working vocabulary in order to communicate.

The issue is that very little of this is actively taught or formalised. Yes, good parents know to read to their infants and converse as often possible in order to transfer these skills. Yes, kindergartens and schools know how to teach and develop vocabulary. But the ubiquity of low-value children's TV (especially cartoons) and screen-based games is a real challenge—and in any case mastering basic vocabulary is only a small part of the skillset required for really effective self-expression. People know that they don't know how to play this extraordinary instrument we have all been born with like a virtuoso, and they realise how powerful that skill can be.

Let's explore some of the secrets of powerful speaking.

BREATH

Your voice is simply breath.

Breathing in and out is the most fundamental way in which we are all connected to the world around us. Respiration is an autonomic process which fortunately doesn't require any conscious thought at all; controlled by the brain stem, your diaphragm and intercostal muscles tense and release to expand and contract your lungs, each breath pulling in the volume of a grapefruit containing trillions of air molecules, and within them trillions of trillions of oxygen atoms. About half of that oxygen comes from plants, the rest from algae and cyanobacteria in lakes and oceans. All your cells need that oxygen to drive the cellular respiration process, which creates energy for biosynthesis, movement and more.

The mechanics are straightforward, but breath has more dimensions than simple anatomy. Controlled breathing is the foundation of meditation in every one of the world's spiritual disciplines. Possibly the most focused practice is to be found in pranayama yoga, which comprises a wide range of breathing techniques. The Sanskrit word prāṇa means life force but can also be translated as breath, and this connection between breath and life itself is found in many other traditions: the Chinese word qì or ch'i has the same two meanings; pneuma in Ancient Greece meant breath, and also soul; indeed, the English word spirit derives from the Latin word spiritus, which meant breath.

More practically in the context of our needs in this discussion, the better you breathe, the better you will speak. Most people breathe very lightly, which feels like using just the top of one's lungs. For many, whole days can pass without taking a really deep breath, or indeed being conscious of breathing at all.

Most of us hardly scratch the surface of our potential breathing capacity, which can be greatly extended through diligent practice: international Ashtanga yoga teacher Kisen can inhale for one full minute and exhale for the next. Try emulating that! Free divers manage even more amazing feats. I knew they could hold their breath for over 10 minutes whilst diving, but I was staggered to find that the world record for static apnea—holding breath underwater without moving—is (at the time of writing) a mind-blowing 24 minutes and three seconds, set by free diver, Alex Segura Vendrell in February 2016. People like this train for years and alter their biology to achieve these potentially dangerous records. They also probably start off with larger-than-average lung capacity, as do many Olympic athletes, particularly in rowing (crew) and swimming. But it doesn't take years to achieve remarkable improvements in lung capacity: Tom Cruise and his *Mission Impossible - Rogue Nation* co-star Rebecca Ferguson trained to be able to shoot long underwater sequences with no breaks—up to six minutes long in Cruise's case.

We don't need to go that far of course, but learning how to breathe well is a great contributor to wellbeing as well as to the power of your voice. We'll be exploring some exercises to improve your breathing when we rummage through the Vocal Toolbox in Chapter Five.

THE INSTRUMENT WE ALL PLAY

This is a phrase I often use to describe the human voice, because it reminds me of the incredible capacity that we all possess and yet so often take for granted. Think of what can be done with this extraordinary instrument, from the throat singing of Tibetan Buddhist monks to the soaring soprano of Maria Callas in her prime; from the visceral, distorted wails of Robert Plant on Led Zeppelin's *Immigrant Song* to the sublime scat signing of Ella Fitzgerald; from the sumptuous sound of the superb choristers at King's College, Cambridge to the mind-blowing Qawwali vocal gymnastics of Nusrat Fateh Ali Khan... and that's just singing. In speaking, imagine the lithe and dangerous baritone of Sean Connery saying "Bond, James Bond", or another famous baritone, the passionate and inspiring Dr. Martin Luther King intoning "I have a dream...", the bass of James Earl Jones as Darth Vader, or the husky tones of Lauren Bacall telling Humphrey Bogart: "You know how to whistle, don't you, Steve? You just put your lips together and blow."

The human voice is the most expressive sound maker on Earth, and probably the most powerful sound too—it's the only sound that can start a war, or say "I love you." It seems tragic to me that we do not teach our children how to master this complex and supple gift. I've had people in my workshops whose version of a shout is almost inaudible, or who are deafening in one-to-one conversation; others whose voice is locked in a tight, restricted throat, who speak in a lifeless monotone, or who seem never to breathe at all... I hope they went home greatly changed, but what a waste of this almost limitless capacity for the years before.

Your voice is probably capable of far more than you ever ask of it, in range (from high to low), in power (from a whisper to a shout or a roar), in resonance and depth, in projection and in expressiveness. We will be exploring ways to unleash all that potential in Chapter Five.

THE ELEMENTS OF SPEAKING

Powerful speaking combines two elements: content and delivery.

Both are crucial: a great speech that's delivered in a shambling, dull monotone will fall flat, while the most passionate delivery can't make nonsense memorable. However, for most people, the greatest value lies in working on delivery because a person with excellent delivery is immediately impactful; most people fall far short of their potential simply through having never worked on the basics.

We'll be covering both content (what you say) and delivery (how you say it), in reverse order for the above reason, in Chapters Five and Six. But first check the panel to see what Chris Anderson, TED's curator, sees as the essential elements of effective public speaking. The panel also contains instructions for accessing the complete interview in audio and transcript forms online.

What makes a great talk: Chris Anderson

This is an excerpt from the transcript of a conversation with Chris Anderson. For the full transcript, and the audio recording, visit www.howtobeheardbook.com and use the password **conscious**.

After a long career in journalism and publishing, Chris Anderson became the curator of the TED Conference in 2002 and has developed it as a platform for identifying and disseminating 'ideas worth spreading', and as the gold standard for public speaking. In June 2015, TED posted its 2,000th talk online. The talks on www.ted.com are free to view, and they have been translated into more than 100 languages with the help of volunteers from around the world. Viewership has grown to approximately one billion per year.

Julian Treasure: What are the essential elements of a great talk Chris? And I know you're going to say, at the heart of it is that powerful idea... is that enough or is there anything else?

Chris Anderson: There are many different types of great talk. I think one important piece of advice is not to take any single set of guidelines as definitive, because that can be the recipe for something formulaic, and what matters is that you say what you want to say in your authentic way: that really matters more than anything. But, I think mostly talks work best when the speaker comes with an attitude of generosity, not selfishness. If a speaker comes on stage and is basically pitching in some way, whether it's a business, a cause, a book, whatever...

Julian Treasure: ...or just to be liked...

Chris Anderson: ...yeah, or just to be liked, it's frustrating and fundamentally ineffective. The stance to come with is a belief that you have something you're really excited about that is going to be valuable to people in the audience and your job is to offer them that gift and to try and do something, which is kind of a miraculous thing to do, which is to recreate in their minds the same idea that is in yours. And, usually the way to do that effectively, is to just be very clear about what is the core that you want to communicate, and anchor everything in your talk to that—to have a crystal clear through-line to the talk, which every element connects to in some way.

Julian Treasure: Achieving that lovely holy grail—I know there's been research showing that the brain waves of audiences actually attune to the brain waves of the speaker if they're doing it really well. Okay, next question, the three most irritating things that people do on the stage. When would you say, just don't do that?

Chris Anderson: The single most irritating to me is visible manipulation of an audience, and that can take several forms. It may be emotional manipulation—that's telling an emotional personal story in a way that just doesn't feel authentic, it feels formulaic in some way, or feels contrived. Or, an attempt to grandstand. There are a lot of people who are just seduced by the idea of "I want to be a charismatic presence on stage" and they come over as full of themselves. Those are really the things that irritate me. It's when people are in it for their own ego.

Julian Treasure: Okay, so, how about some tips if somebody's about to speak in public for the first time, what things would you suggest they focus on?

Chris Anderson: I think one of the key things is to basically delete most of what you want to say. You just don't have time to say most of what you want to say and it's the hardest thing to do, to get rid of the excess and instead pick the one thing that is most important but then develop it with enough depth. It's far, far better to be narrow but deep than broad and shallow, by and large. And so, for a talk to be meaningful, people need to know why it matters; they need to have their curiosity about it stimulated; they need to engage with you; probably stories need to be told that connect to this thing; and the explanation needs to go deep enough to be interesting. Often that means exploring to some extent dead ends, and showing why they're dead ends, which helps reinforce why the idea you're trying to communicate is the right one. That's the single biggest tip: focus the scope of the talk so that you can go deep enough to really let it land.

Chapter Four

How to listen consciously

*"I like to listen. I have learned a great deal
from listening carefully. Most people never listen."*

– Ernest Hemingway

SEVEN LISTENING PRACTICES

*"We are what we repeatedly do.
Excellence then, is not an act, but a habit."*

– Aristotle

As we've found, listening is a skill, not a natural capability like hearing. Any skill can be improved—and the first step in that process is to become conscious that you're doing it. If you know what you don't know, you have a chance to learn it. If you don't know what you don't know, there is nothing you can do

So, the first step here is to admit this to yourself, using the adverb that's most appropriate for you:

"I am sometimes/often/generally unconscious in my listening."

In my TED talk on conscious listening I suggested five practices to improve your conscious listening skills. In this Chapter, we not only explore each of those in detail; we add two more, bringing the total to seven.

Conscious listening is really a subset of conscious living—the practice of being aware and mindful as we move through life. The main secret to conscious listening (and indeed to conscious living) lies in *intention*. Simply by recognising that you have been unconscious in your listening and setting the intention to become fully conscious, you open the door to a wonderful new dimension of experience, adding to the richness of your reality and enhancing your wellbeing, effectiveness and happiness.

These practices will help you on that journey.

1. SILENCE

If you live in a city, as more than half of humanity does now, it's rare to experience silence, and perfectly possible to forget that it even exists. Let's take a moment to consider silence.

Dame Evelyn Glennie made a superb DVD called *Touch the Sound*, in which she reflects on silence, listening and music and performs her art, including a stunning solo snare drum performance in Grand Central Station's magnificent hall. (I highly recommend watching this film if you have any interest in sound.) At one point, she says: "Silence is a sound." I totally agree with this, and have experienced different qualities of silence in my life. Four of them spring to mind.

First, the glorious, expansive silence of a windless day far above the tree-line in mountains. If you can find a spot isolated from human-generated noise, there are very few birds at that altitude, and with little or no air movement you can experience lengthy periods of complete silence—a silence that seems to go on forever, like the view.

Second, the reverential silence in an empty place of worship. I remember sitting in Worth Abbey Church in Surrey, England whilst on a retreat there. The vast upturned dome of the church caps a modern, circular building that's partly submerged in the South Downs landscape. Designed by France Pollen and built in 1974, it's a huge space that seats 1,400 people; at night, there is a single spotlight on the altar in the centre. It was evening, in between monastic offices, and I was the only person in there. I enjoyed half an hour of silence, punctuated (and paradoxically emphasised) by one intrusion as a monk entered and left and the door opening and closing echoed through the huge room. This was a cloaking, velvety silence that felt peaceful and intimate.

Third, the intimidating silence in a deep cave. I am slightly claustrophobic, so caving is not high on my list of hobbies. Many years ago, I visited Kents Cavern in Devon, England, which was inhabited by Upper Palaeolithic period humans, possibly up to 40,000 years ago. At one point in the tour, the guide had us sit quietly, and then switched off the lights. The darkness was absolute, and the silence seemed to press in and become almost suffocating, the auditory consort to the absolute darkness that enveloped us. As I sat, I reflected on those early humans and how their hearing must have been so important: they probably shared that extensive cavern system with cave bears, lions and hyenas. In the dark, intense listening would have been an essential, and often life-saving, skill for those ancient people. It was a relief when the lights went back on and we started to make sound ourselves, happy to be back in the 20th century after that brief, primal experience.

Finally, the sterile silence of the desert. With no fauna at all, the silence of a windless day in the desert speaks of the stillness of death, emphasising the hostile and inhospitable environment and reminding one of the inevitable outcome of being in that place for too long without the specialist skills and equipment needed to survive. I have experienced this in Dubai, far from the slick intensity of the city. Intractable and uncompromising, it felt as though the desert's silence signalled nothing less than a haughty indifference to my existence.

Silence is not only a sound: it is the context for all sound. Without the gaps, words and musical notes would be a meaningless jumble. Losing contact with this context can result in ever-increasing desensitisation, evincing itself as a tendency to add inputs or edge the volume up. I see this more and more in younger people, and I worry for the future as virtual reality and endless innovations in delivering entertainment create an addictive relationship to intensity.

Silence is your baseline. Try to stay in conscious contact with it by emulating recording engineers. These are listening professionals; their ears are their livelihood. They know they need to take regular breaks, moving away from the loudspeakers and recalibrating their ears with some silence, or at the very least some quietness.

In 2015, I was honoured to take part in a brilliant feature film entitled *In Pursuit Of Silence,* since described by *Huffington Post* as "a luminous and vitally important movie". Directed by Patrick Shen, the film explores our relationship with silence and noise, travelling the world from a traditional tea ceremony in Kyoto, to the streets of the loudest city on the planet, Mumbai. After the film's release, I spoke with Patrick about many aspects of silence; check the panel for an excerpt from the interview and instructions on accessing the full interview in audio and written form online.

Our key objective in this first practice is to recalibrate. By reminding yourself of the baseline in the exercises below, you can right-size your listening and become able once again to appreciate quiet sounds—and to be more sensitive to loud, possibly unhealthy sounds. It's a little like eating a sorbet in the middle of a rich meal: your palate is cleansed and refreshed and your sensitivity is renewed. Silence is your aural sorbet. It pays to develop a taste for it.

In pursuit of silence: Patrick Shen

This is an excerpt from the transcript of a conversation with Patrick Shen. For the full transcript, and the audio recording, visit www.howtobeheardbook.com and use the password **conscious**.

Patrick Shen is a writer and award-winning film maker and founder of Transcendental Media, an independent motion picture production company dedicated to making films "to agitate the sleep of mankind". His work includes *Flight from Death*, a seven-time Best Documentary award-winning documentary about death anxiety, inspired by the works and writings of cultural anthropologist and social theorist Ernest Becker; *The Philosopher Kings*, a documentary about the wisdom gained by janitorial workers in prestigious universities, and in 2015 *In Pursuit of Silence*, a meditative film about our relationship with silence and the impact of noise on our lives. (You can find out more at www. pursuitofsilence.com).

Patrick Shen: Silence is scary, it opens us up to a lot of our inadequacies, I think. Things that we just happen to be avoiding to think about. So I think there's a huge deficit of this type of experience in our modern world. But, I also think that people are sensing that something is amiss in the busyness of our lives and this very superficial existence and encounter that we have with the world around us. I think that silence can bring us back to that and I think people are starting to realise that.

Julian Treasure: I think one of the meditations from the Island of San Giuliano: "In the silence you meet yourself." Perhaps that's what's scaring people.

Patrick Shen: I think so. I think absolutely, it is. You know, we had the privilege of interviewing Susan Cain not too long ago and she talks a lot about how we value those who fill that silence. The loud speakers, the dominant speakers. Science has even showed that we find these people even more attractive and smarter. We tend to follow their ideas over those who aren't as eager to fill that silence. I think that speaks a lot into what that silence does for people and the fear that people associate with that silence. A lot of our experience with silence has been negative, in this culture. I think that's one thing that we wanted to tackle in this film, and kind of reshape our understanding of silence.

Julian Treasure: When you say negative, in what way negative? Is this silence equated with death, for example?

Patrick Shen: Absolutely. I think if you sit with silence long enough, it ultimately opens you up to, well, our impermanence, right? Our mortality. I think that's very scary for a lot of people. It ultimately opens us up to our frailties and the things that we simply aren't good at dealing with. Death being one of them. So, yeah, I agree with that, absolutely.

Julian Treasure: Now, I've had the honour of contributing something to your film and I'm fascinated to know, in the world of silence, what have you learned, what have been the highlights and the most impressing things that you've come across?

Patrick Shen: When I began the journey, I expected to be making a film more about sound and how we relate to sound itself. Or the lack of, I should say. But, I quickly learned that silence is much more than the absence of sound. It's been chased after throughout the ages by cultures all over the globe. All these cultures have very different, unique, multidimensional ways of looking at silence and interacting in silence in ways that I think can really speak into our humanity. It's led me to circle back to this ancient silence that we've been after since the beginning of time, it seems. This has led me to read the works of a lot of theologians and Zen Buddhists and a lot of the monastics that began these traditions of living in solitude and living a life of silence. Henri Nouwen, the theologian, I think summed it up perfectly. This is probably the most potent thing that I've come across so far in my research. He says, "Silence makes us pilgrims, silence guards the fires within and silence teaches us to speak." I think that sums up exactly what silence can be and what it is for anybody who wants to interact with it.

Julian Treasure: Well, that is fascinating. So, it's the spiritual dimension of silence that's actually become most engaging to you. As you rightly say, I think there's not a spiritual path on this planet that doesn't involve, on some level, quiet contemplation. Which in a sense, is listening, isn't it?

Patrick Shen: Yeah, very much so. I think it's not just listening externally, but it's listening to what's happening internally, isn't it? Which makes up the core of a lot of spiritual seeking that people have done throughout the ages. I think what happens when you listen internally, sure, there's a spiritual component, but I think it also benefits us on multiple levels. Where we are now becoming in touch, when we're in touch with silence, that is, interacting with silence, we're now in touch with an authentic part of who we are. Because there isn't that noise to block out the inner thoughts and the inner chatter and all the inadequacies and the things that we're avoiding having to think about. But, it's making us ponder who it is that we bring to the conversation. Who it is that we bring to the collaborative process. Who we bring into the community that we're a part of. I think that's lacking in the world, I think that we aren't even asking the question of who it is that we are, in community. Who is the authentic self that we bring?

Exercise: Silence

I offer you two exercises here.

The first is the simple practice that I recommended in my TED talk, which is to experience a few minutes of silence every day. This takes discipline at first, but like all beneficial practice it becomes a habit with daily repetition. If you can't get absolute silence, the nearest, quietest equivalent will be just fine. When you do this is entirely up to you. You might find it easiest and more beneficial first thing on awakening, or in the middle of a busy day, or as a reflective exercise before retiring. Aim for at least three minutes a day, and ideally two such sessions.

The second is to enjoy a wonderful set of meditations on silence. Not far from Milan is the beautiful alpine lake district of Italy. One of the smaller and less well-known lakes is Lake Orta, in the middle of which is an island called San Giulio, which houses a convent and a basilica. Around these buildings is a flagged path, which the sonically enlightened Sisters of the Monastero Mater Ecclesiae built in the 19th century. They dubbed it 'The Way of Silence' and decorated it with signs containing meditations on silence. You are requested to do the circular walk around the small island in silence; every so often you encounter a meditation sign and you stop to absorb and reflect on its message. The meditations are surprisingly eclectic, even secular.

We can't all get to Lake Orta and physically do the walk (though I do recommend it), but I reproduce the meditations here so that you can enjoy them at home. I suggest you make a card for each one, sit quietly and reflect on one card at a time, taking as long as you feel you can for each one. If you're technically inclined, you could alternatively create yourself a slide show with a timer on each slide (and a nice gentle transition between them!).
In the silence you accept and understand

Silence is the language of love
Silence is the peace of oneself
Silence is music and harmony
Silence is truth and prayer
In the silence you meet the Master
In the silence you breathe God
Walls are in the mind
The moment is present, here and now
Leave yourself and what is yours
In the silence you receive all

2. THE MIXER

In a recording studio, the central device is the mixing desk. This contains multiple channels or tracks, so that you can record one instrument on each track and then blend them all together (a process called mixing) to create the final stereo master.

In life, we are often surrounded by complex soundscapes comprising many individual sounds. I experience this often when carrying out Sound Audits of large commercial spaces like shopping centres. The myriad of individual sound sources may include many people; a range of mechanical and electrical machinery such as escalators or catering equipment like coffee machines and dishwashers; and music (all too often mindlessly deployed and played through low quality sound systems). The combination of all these sounds, in what are usually large, reverberant spaces, becomes something we call 'mall mush'. It takes conscious effort to disentangle the individual sound sources from the mix.

If you listen unconsciously, most of the world will be mush. Paying attention to the individual components of the soundscapes around you is a wonderful way of engaging more with the world, and the result is that you live more fully in the present moment. I recommend it.

Exercise: The Mixer

Whenever you are in a complex soundscape, be it a noisy café or restaurant, a room in your home or a natural location like a garden or forest, try to identify the individual sound sources that make up the 'mush'.

If you like visualisations, imagine the mixing desk in front of you and bring up the faders one at a time to focus on each individual sound. If you are primarily auditory, then simply listen and ask yourself the question: how many sounds can I identify?

The main secret to conscious listening is simply intention.

As you get into the habit of analysing the sounds around you, you will naturally start to recognise the constituent tracks that make up any soundscape. This practice enhances the quality of your listening, as well as enabling you to deal with counterproductive sounds that might otherwise have remained hidden from you— for example small hums and buzzes that are largely masked by other, more dense sounds.

3. SAVOURING

There are great benefits to treating your hearing like your sense of taste and smell, becoming discerning about what you experience and seeking out enjoyable sensory encounters.

You instinctively reject bad tastes and smells, while you seek out and buy food, drink and scents that you take pleasure from; however, if your listening has gone unconscious like most people's, it is likely that you are assailed by sounds that adversely affect you without realising it, and equally likely that you miss out on really pleasing sounds.

The exercise to combat this numbness and potentially dramatically enhance your wellbeing, effectiveness and happiness, is called savouring.

Exercise: Savouring

Consciously 'tasting' sound allows you to be more discerning about how it's affecting you, and, over time, to change the typical soundscape around you, taking more control over its components and replacing negative sounds with positive ones.

Start by exploring the sounds in your home. Sit quietly in each room and listen carefully and consciously. You will discover many small sounds you may never have noticed before. The more constant ones all combine to create a 'noise floor' in each room, and any intermittent sound that happens in that room occurs on top of that noise floor. Buzzes and hums may come from electrical or electronic equipment such as fridges, heating, ventilating and air conditioning (HVAC), computer fans, coffee machines, dishwashers, cookers, washing machines and tumble dryers. Hisses and gurgles may come from boilers, water pipes or HVAC.

You may be surprised how many sounds there are that you never noticed before. Some of them may be pleasant or reassuring for you; others are just noise and may be able to be silenced or tamed. If you're buying new equipment, be sure to check the noise output; for white goods, this is often on the information label these days. At The Sound Agency we recommend a maximum of 40 dB at one metre for any piece of equipment. I recommend the same for your home.

Don't forget to notice interesting or pleasing sounds in your home too. In my TED talk on conscious listening, I played the sound of a slightly faulty tumble dryer I used to own; its rotating drum had a characteristic sound in waltz time. I used to find that pleasing, and indeed, once when I appeared on a US radio show a small orchestra played a piece of Mozart to accompany a recording of my tumble dryer, which made it even more pleasing for me as a sound from then on. Sadly, that machine is no more. In the TED talk I also played a beautiful recording of a kettle boiling, which is actually a rich and fascinating sound.

There is great complexity to many sounds you experience, including the harmonics I described in Chapter One, when I recounted the extraordinary experience of becoming conscious of them even in a car engine. The point of this exercise is to change your relationship with sound from passive and unconscious to active and conscious.

After working through your home, tackle all the other environments in which you spend a lot of time: your work place, your car or transport, your hobby locations... in some cases, you will have control and can improve them; in others, like public transport, you have little control and have to adopt the MBA strategy we learned in the AGENTS discussion of noise in Chapter Two. In all cases, be in an active enquiry by asking: "How can I improve my experience here?"

4. LISTENING WITH

I had the pleasure of working with a Florida-based teacher named Cathryn Lokey on a curriculum for teaching listening skills to children. (The curriculum we developed is available as a download from my website at juliantreasure.com.) She had created an excellent way of sensitising young children to the facts that listening takes work, that you can focus on it and that focus helps you do it better. This was a little mantra the kids would repeat, which went: *"We listen with our ears, with our eyes, and with our heart!"*

Becoming conscious of what you are listening *with* is an excellent practice and this mantra provides a simple, memorable way to improve your listening skills by doing exactly that.

It's tempting to assume that we simply listen with our ears although, as we discussed at the start of Chapter Three, the whole body is in fact involved. Nevertheless, the ears are the primary channel for sound and the first part of the mantra reminds us to *focus our hearing on the subject at hand.*

The second reminds us to *look at the person we are listening to.* This is also covered in my RASA practice (the last one in this list). If your eyes are busy with other tasks, your listening is degraded because the visual information is incongruent; it displaces attention you would otherwise be giving to the speaker. Being seen to pay attention is just as important as paying attention itself. We all know the feeling of frustration and even despair when we are trying to communicate and the other person is looking at a screen, their watch, or indeed anywhere but at us. The dance of eye contact in dyadic conversation varies from culture to culture and even more from person to person and situation to situation: if we like someone, we look more than if we don't, while the context of the conversation is key—for example, it's no surprise that confessionals preclude eye contact because when we are admitting something with shame or guilt, eye contact is the last thing we want. It is important to be culturally sensitive: people from some Hispanic, Asian, Middle Eastern, and Native American cultures may consider eye contact to be insulting. On average, we look more at the other person when listening than when speaking: in his book *Bodily Communication*, eminent social psychologist Michael Argyle estimated that, on average, listeners gaze at the speaker 70 percent of the time, while speakers gaze at the listener only 40 percent of the time, often in small bursts at the end of statements, and mainly to check that the other person is listening. Listening with our eyes is important.

The third part of the mantra reminds us to *empathise*. As you'll discover in the pages immediately following, there are many places you can listen from, and not all of them involve listening with your heart. Compassion is the basis of understanding, which is why it's a vital component of conscious listening. If your heart is hard and you stand in judgement and condemnation whilst listening (one of the seven deadly sins of course), then the conversation is likely to be 'nasty, brutish and short', to quote Hobbes.

Exercise: Listening with

This exercise trains you in listening with your ears, eyes and heart.

This is best done with a friend who's up for a little communication training. Sit facing one another and then whoever chooses to go first starts to speak about something s/he cares deeply about—maybe their favourite holiday destination in the entire world.

The listener starts by looking down, very neutral, consciously disengaged but listening carefully with the ears. After a little while (you could set a timer for 30 seconds), the listener looks up and establishes eye contact, taking in all the nonverbal communication that's being sent—but still emotionally cool. After a further 30 seconds or so, the listener engages the heart, feels the feelings and takes the shackles off any nonverbal responses that might come naturally, such as facial expressions, nods, posture adjustments and so on.

Stop and both share how that was. Swap and repeat.

If you can't find someone to try this with you, simply focus on listening with ears, eyes and heart for a day and see what you experience. If you like it, keep it up until it becomes second nature to you.

5. LISTENING FROM

Consider this: there are many listening positions—places to listen *from*. This is entirely metaphorical: I am not speaking of physical positions or places. Perhaps an analogy will help to explain. Imagine you are standing at the foot of a hill, on top of which there is a house. If you don't like the way the house looks from here, you can walk around the hill and see if the other side looks better. That's changing your viewing position.

Now, remember that we all listen through a set of filters, which we listed and explored in Chapter Three. These are:

- Culture
- Language
- Values
- Attitudes
- Beliefs / assumptions
- Intentions
- Expectations
- Emotions

Every human being has their own individual listening, shaped by their personal set of filters. Over time that listening tends to ossify into a default listening position that's like a concrete bunker with a slit in the front. Much of reality bounces off, and only a small amount gets through the filters and is listened to. We sit in that bunker year after year, believing that the world is what we perceive through our little window, never realising that there is a door in the back—and it's open! We can leave our bunker and move to a completely different listening position simply by becoming aware and making an act of will.

In reality, most people have more than one window in the bunker, using different ones depending on the situation: for example, you probably listen rather differently to your children than to your friends or work colleagues. But the essence of the listening is very similar, and for most people the fundamental position does not change.

The good news is that there are as many listening positions as you choose to create. You can move to them by using your filters as control surfaces—being aware of them and choosing to alter them consciously for this conversation. The following exercise will help you to start that process; afterwards, I'll get you started by listing a few listening positions that are so common they may resonate with you. Remember, you can create your own personal set of listening positions. The main point is to be aware that you can move!

Exercise: Know your filters

Using a notebook or a computer, write each filter at the top of a page:

Culture
Language
Values
Attitudes
Beliefs / assumptions
Intentions

Expectations
Emotions

Now write as much as you need to about how each of these filters affects your listening. Aim to describe each filter, how it occurred or developed for you, and how it helps or hinders you.

When you're done, you have effectively identified your autopilot settings. Now you can take control!

LISTENING POSITIONS

Now let's look at a few common listening positions. I will offer them as three scales: active to passive, critical to empathic, and reductive to expansive. None of them are intended to be presented as good, bad or for you; the intention here is simply to get you thinking about positions you might want to create for yourself. Of course, if you see something in these positions—either something you like, or something you want to move away from—then take whatever is helpful from them.

ACTIVE TO PASSIVE

Active listening

Active listening is used widely in therapeutic professions such as counselling or psychotherapy as well as in education and journalism, and forms an important element in parenting courses like Parent Effectiveness Training and in relationship programmes like Imago Therapy (both programmes I heartily recommend). Active listening can also be very powerful in selling.

This position involves intention, focus, reflection and summarising. The listener must fully set the intention of listening with total attention and no interventions—those interventions we so often make, where we interject, interrupt, correct or attempt to clarify. Then they focus on what is said, and reflect it back exactly as it was said, or as near as possible to that. This might sound something like: "What I heard you say is…" and then "Is that right?" to check the reflection was accurate. At the end of the conversation, or every so often if it's a very long talk, the listener summarises what has been said to ensure that everything has been safely and accurately received. The intention is to leave the speaker feeling fully heard.

It takes practice to do this without sounding robotic, but it can be immensely powerful in defusing upset, whether dealing with customer complaints or an angry teenager. We've all done this when being given driving directions—the alternative being another brilliant definition from Adams and Lloyd's *The Meaning of LIFF*:

Dinner *vb*: To nod thoughtfully while someone gives you a long and complex set of directions which you know you're never going to remember.

Passive listening

This position tends to be applied to things rather than people, as it involves no interaction and minimal interpretation: it is simply being aware of the sound and savouring it. We might use this listening position when enjoying music, or the sound of a beautiful place—or in our daily practice of three minutes of silence, perhaps. I always think of this as a serene Zen master sitting by a stream, simply listening to the sound of the moving water. There is room for a little passive listening in even the busiest life.

CRITICAL TO EMPATHIC

Critical listening

You may recognise this one, because so many people have variations of it as their primary listening position. In business, in education and in any debate or argument it is the natural place to go, and it's very powerful. It involves critical assessment of the other person's message, often involving the little noise in your head giving a running commentary. If you have a particularly strong voice for you (and if it habitually criticises you, I hope you got a lot from the section on inner listening earlier in this book).

Of course, it's valuable to assess and to be discerning in what you take on board so, in many conversations, this listening position is indispensable. In business, we quickly get used to listening for what we deem useful and discarding the rest; it's not unlike panning for gold. We become quick to give our opinion, and we have a rating system constantly at work in our heads. However, even at work there are times when this is not desirable. I have seen many efforts at brainstorming founder because people could not switch off their critical heads and accept rule one of a brainstorm: "Every idea is acceptable." It becomes very hard to switch off the critical filters.

If critical listening becomes your default position and you get stuck there, it will cause problems for you, especially at home, because it does not facilitate intimacy. When someone shares their pain or their fears with you, it can be very destructive to respond with a critique or a set of instructions, even if your intentions are of the best. That kind of managerial interaction, which works so well for practical matters, can be very problematic when applied to emotional communication.

I suspect this is one major way in which the always-on nature of modern business is so threatening to our emotional wellbeing. Not only does it blur the lines and rob us of family time and focus, but it also forces us into critical listening at home. If you are reading work emails in bed, you are much less likely to be able to flip positions and respond tenderly to your partner's fear about a challenge he or she is facing tomorrow: it's far easier to stay in critical listening and give some practical advice or even dismiss the fear as irrational with a "Don't be silly…" comment. I do urge you to avoid this practice. If you must do it, be prepared to consciously jump out of critical listening at any moment or your relationship is likely to suffer.

People who get stuck in critical listening tend to find it hard to give unconditional affirmation. This is particularly sad for parents, because it robs them of heart connection with their children, not to mention creating young people with major self-worth issues. If nothing short of perfection is good enough or warrants any praise, the result will almost certainly be a child who is bent out of shape in some way, either suffering low self-confidence or grimly obsessed with perfection, and in either case probably emotionally repressed after being knocked back so many times.

The worst kind of critical listening moves into the other definition of the word—a tendency to find fault. That's a doorway straight into condemning, the second of the seven deadly sins, as discussed earlier.

Empathic listening

The opposite end of this scale is empathic listening. This means feeling the other person's feelings. It's like going onto their island and experiencing their reality, rather than staying on your home turf and filtering what they say through your own reality.

It's said that we seek three things in a relationship: to be heard, to be understood and to be valued. Empathic listening achieves two of these and indicates the third. If you listen empathically, to hear, you understand and, by taking the time and making the effort, you indicate how much you value the other person. It's a very powerful listening position, and one that's usually appropriate when listening to strong emotions like pain or grief, or indeed joy or love.

Professor Marisue Pickering of the University of Maine, a leading researcher on interpersonal communication, listed four characteristics of empathic listeners, and 10 skills that help achieve this listening position.

The four characteristics are all conscious intentions, because we need to be conscious of our listening filters in order to change them and move our listening position.

1. Desire to be other-directed, rather than to project one's own feelings and ideas onto the other.

2. Desire to be non-defensive, rather than to protect the self. When the self is being protected, it is difficult to focus on another person.

3. Desire to imagine the roles, perspectives, or experiences of the other, rather than assuming they are the same as one's own.

4. Desire to listen as a receiver, not as a critic, and desire to understand the other person rather than to achieve either agreement from or change in that person.

One or more of these may immediately occur to you as challenges, which could reveal something about your own filters and default listening!

The ten skills she identifies will sound quite familiar, as they are all covered in one way or another is our own work here, but this checklist for empathic listening is so useful I want to pass it on to you, with great thanks to Professor Pickering.

1. *Attending, acknowledging*: providing verbal or non-verbal awareness of the other, i.e. eye contact.

2. *Restating, paraphrasing*: responding to person's basic verbal message.

3. *Reflecting*: reflecting feelings, experiences, or content that has been heard or perceived through cues.

4. *Interpreting*: offering a tentative interpretation about the other's feelings, desires, or meanings.

5. *Summarising, synthesising*: bringing together in some way feelings and experiences; providing a focus.

6. *Probing*: questioning in a supportive way that requests more information or that attempts to clear up confusions.

7. *Giving feedback*: sharing perceptions of the other's ideas or feelings; disclosing relevant personal information.

8. *Supporting*: showing warmth and caring in one's own individual way.

9. *Checking perceptions*: finding out if interpretations and perceptions are valid and accurate.

10. *Being quiet*: giving the other time to think as well as to talk.

Empathic listening builds intimacy, trust and loyalty, but it also does involve some risk and vulnerability on both sides. It's very powerful, but as with all the listening positions, the trick is to judge when to use it and not to get stuck in it.

REDUCTIVE TO EXPANSIVE

Here we get into the sensitive area of gender. I offer you this scale of listening positions with the caveat that it is something of a gender stereotype. The following is certainly not true of all males and all females—remember, everyone has a unique listening—but, after interacting with thousands of people on this distinction, I believe there is some value in it, and for many people it has been powerfully revealing. One gentleman came up to me after a workshop in Philadelphia and proclaimed: "That was the best marital advice I've ever encountered!", while at another a doctor, with tears in his eyes, shared that he had just realised that on arriving home each evening after a hard day at the hospital, his wife tried to share her day and he was simply unable to listen to her – and now he knew how to do that. So, with a health warning about gender stereotyping, let's consider 2 gender-based listening positions.

Reductive listening

Men (not all men, not all the time) *tend* to listen from a position I call reductive. Reductive listening seeks a point, a solution, a destination for the conversation. It can appear as impatient, or even rude: if a reductive listener sees (or believes he sees) the point, he may interrupt in order to short-circuit the conversation and arrive at the destination with less time wasted. I have seen male friends and acquaintances of mine have rather dysfunctional conversations when each participant has decided the conversation has a different destination! Reductive listening loves solving problems, gathering facts and generating opinions, and this is what a lot of male conversation comprises—stating problems, swapping information and offering solutions or opinions. The archetypical male conversations about driving routes, sport and cars are great examples of reductive communication. It's very effective when there is a problem to solve or a practical challenge to face, or when time is tight.

Expansive listening

Women (not all women, not all the time) tend to listen in a way I call expansive. As I always joke onstage: "In expansive listening there is no point!"... by which I mean, of course, that expansive listening is not seeking a resolution or a destination. It focuses on the journey itself, being with the other person, sharing and validating feelings, smelling the roses, with little or no concern for where the road eventually leads. Expansive listening is inquisitive, curious, prepared to be surprised and delighted. It notices the small details, and it changes direction on a dime when it spots something worth paying attention to. It dallies and it flits. Most of all, it is interested, not because it has an agenda, but because it cares. Expansive listening is useful in business too: brainstorming founders without it, and I believe it's the wellspring for flow and creativity. Without it, there is only fixing things.

In relationship, these positions can create disconnection and conflict. She comes home after a tough day, collapses into a chair and shares: "Darling I had such a bad day... this happened, then this, then this...". He looks up from the football game and says: "Have a bath baby; you'll feel much better. You always do." In the male world, it's problem solved and back to the game. In the female world, that was not at all what she was looking for! The expansive response would have been more like: "Oh, I'm so sorry darling, that must have been awful! Let me fix you a drink and you can tell me all about it." It works the other way too: posing any issue as a problem to be solved is a great way of engaging a reductive listener and getting them to help. "How *are* we going to get the trash out on time every week?"

Learning to move from your natural listening position to the other side can be very fruitful: it can even reconnect relationships that have suffered from communication that's been constantly missing, like two ships in the night. Try consciously taking the helm and you just might meet!

Exercise: Listening from

Take some time to think and then write about your own default or favoured listening positions. Think about all the situations or contexts in which you listen to people, and how your filters affect you. You may find one default position that recurs or underlies all these situations; or there may be a small set of them. The listening positions may include some of the examples I have given here, or they may be unique to you: there are as many potential listening positions as you care to imagine.

Now you have the situations and positions identified, ask in each case: is this the most effective listening position for this situation? If not, describe a better one and then practice consciously moving to that position each time you are in that situation.

This is best done one context at a time or it can become overwhelming and demotivating: it's not easy to change the habits of a lifetime, so it will take perseverance.

6. LISTENING FOR

This practice is very close to the critical listening position, but much more active and variable. Instead of simply allowing your inner critic to run the show, this is conscious. It's like mining: you have a goal in mind and you are actively seeking it. You might listen for affirmation or encouragement; information that's vital for the task at hand; similarities rather than differences; inspiration; connection; ways to help; solutions; confirmation of your worst fears; the ending in a story; the truth in an interrogation—or anything you choose. The list is probably endless, and the choice is up to you.

You probably often do this unconsciously, focusing your listening on a specific goal and discarding anything that doesn't move you closer to it. Bringing this to the realm of consciousness makes you more alive and builds your skill as a listener.

Exercise: Listening for

Tale a week to do this one. Ask yourself in every conversation: "What am I listening for?" After a while, the consciousness becomes natural and you qualify as a professional miner, choosing the most appropriate and effective thing to be listening for in each conversation.

7. RASA

Rasa is the Sanskrit word for juice, but in this context it's another acronym, this time one that works when you're in conversation.

R is for **receive**. Remember the quote from Scott Peck in Chapter Three... true listening involves your full attention and cannot take place if you are doing something else. Effective listening means being in full receive mode: looking at the speaker (alias listening with your eyes); using attentive body language (usually, leaning forward rather than back, facing the speaker squarely, and not making any irrelevant or distracted-looking gestures or movements).

A is for **appreciate**. This means giving little visual and auditory cues that you are fully engaged. These may include small affirmatory facial expressions like eyes widening, eyebrows lifting, smiling, nodding and so on—you know how to do all this naturally!), as well as those little noises that oil conversation: aah, ohh, mmm or whatever fits your personal style. I tend to forget these on the phone and people say: "Are you still there?" I am, and listening intently, but of course without the visual cues they have no feedback at all. Positive feedback creates a friendly, receptive listening for the other person to speak into, and conversations thrive on that.

S is for **summarise**. This usually involves a powerful and important little word: 'so'. I sometimes feel like forming a society for the protection of this vital little conjunction. It implies a logical sequence from what has just been said, often involving cause and effect. For some reason, it has been press-ganged into starting almost every sentence among the hipster and entrepreneurial classes, as in:

"What does your company do?"

"So, we have an app that..."

This unfortunate habit has even found its way into many TED talks, where the speaker walks on stage and starts with the word "So...".

I would love for this word's vital work, when used as intended, to be recognised. When you respond to a few minutes of someone speaking with "So, what you're saying is...", you affirm and they can check you've received what they were trying to send. This is particularly vital in meetings—those places where we can take minutes and waste hours! Without a 'so' person, a meeting can go round and round for a very long time. It's invaluable to have someone in the group who will say: "So, we can all agree on *this*, and now let's move on to *that*."

A is for **ask**. If you ask relevant and appropriate questions throughout, and especially at the end, you again assure the speaker that you are there with them on the journey, alive, interested, engaged and, most of all, listening!

Exercise: RASA

Memorise the four steps of RASA and then use it in conversations for a week. Note down any changes you notice in the way people talk or relate to you in your RASA week. You may choose to continue indefinitely!

HARAH

Here's another useful acronym that offers a different window onto effective, conscious listening. I offer all these perspectives so that you can try them on and choose the one that works best for you.

H is for **humility**. Listening comes best from humility, not self-importance. With a modest or at least right-sized self-image, we are able to admit much more easily to the possibility of learning, of receiving gifts, of being surprised and delighted by what someone is saying, rather than having to know everything or be right.

A is for **awareness**. Conscious listening is active, which means you need to be aware that you are doing something if you are to do it effectively. In my experience, the vast majority of people listen unconsciously, in their default listening position, unaware that they are filtering and making meanings. If you can stay conscious, actively part of the process, aware that you are deploying a skill, then you can dramatically change your outcomes in life.

R is for **respect**. We'll see in Chapter Six that wishing people well is a crucial element of powerful speaking. Respect is the corollary for listening. I have learned over the years that judging books by their covers is a very ineffective way to go through life. Many times I have been astonished at the wisdom, the searing honesty, the imagination, the creativity, the compassion or the profundity that has come out of people I arrogantly thought would not be worth listening to.

A is for **attention**. It's no accident that this one arises time after time. Listening with full attention is one of the most wonderful gifts you can give to anyone.

H is for **humour**. In my experience, it's a grave mistake to take oneself too seriously. Retaining a sense of humour when listening, especially to things we disagree with, is a great antidote to pursed-lipped disapproval and superciliousness.

THE FOUR CS

Conscious listening takes effort. It's also helped by choosing some compatible states. Here are four Cs that will move you a long way in the right direction.

Commitment. You've listened in a certain way all your life. Habits that established will not change overnight, so commitment is essential on two levels. First, the exercises and practices in this book require it: they won't change you instantly, and most of them will take some time and repetition to work their magic. Second, in every listening situation you can commit yourself to listen consciously.

Consciousness. As we've discovered, for most people natural listening is unconscious, which means they are not aware of how they are shaping their reality. Go conscious and you take the controls, disengage the autopilot and choose your own destination!

Compassion. You can substitute 'care' if compassion is too weighty, but I do urge you to try it on. This may be a feeling of loving-kindness, well-wishing, empathy or simply identification. If you listen from any of these positions you will extract more juice from almost every conversation. If you don't care, you are probably not going to listen at all.

Curiosity. Generating a state of curiosity is a marvellous way of spicing up your listening. You could do this by listening for "what might I learn here?", or practicing being what one trainer I worked with used to call 'ferociously curious'.

SPECIAL LISTENINGS

Some listening contexts deserve special mention because they are so important. Let's touch on a few of them now.

LOVING LISTENING

Not listening *in* love, because that's probably one of the few times when we do afford someone our complete, undivided attention. Loving listening can be universal, as with *agape* love in Christianity or loving-kindness in Buddhism: in our language, this could be listening for the gold in other people, in the complete confidence that it is there, even if sometimes deeply buried!

Loving listening can also be very specific, and in a long-term loving relationship it becomes fundamental and crucial. You may well have come across Gary Chapman's book *The 5 Love Languages,* where he categorises five ways that love can be expressed and suggests that each of us has our own preferences for the one(s) that really get through to us—so if you are sending the wrong one, it's like speaking a different language to your partner: they just don't get it. The 'languages' that he lists are: words of affirmation; acts of service; receiving gifts; quality time; and physical touch. These may resonate with you, or you may even have something of your own that means the world to you—and the same for your partner. If you've never done this, listen to your partner to understand their preferred love language and you may break through to new levels of connection. If confused, just ask!

Another wonderful practice in relationship, particularly long-term relationship, is to set yourself a listening position for an hour, a day, or even for good, of listening as if for the first time. This means consciously casting aside all the "Oh, there you go again..." thoughts, stopping all the mental (or even verbal) sentence-completing, and absolutely being determined that you do *not* know what is coming next out of your partner's mouth. Your aim is to get to a place of innocence, naivety, not-knowing and allow yourself to rediscover what delighted you about your partner when you first met.

LISTENING TO CHILDREN

There was a Victorian parenting adage in England that 'children should be seen but not heard'. What a tragic way to teach the opposite of confident self-expression! Banning children from speaking is definitely not a good way to encourage speaking and listening skills. Every time we shush a small child, we chip away at their natural, exuberant self-confidence.

But does that mean we tolerate unconstrained vocal expression at all times? Certainly not. The answer lies in careful, appropriate listening.

Children often get short shrift when it comes to our attention. We have important things to do, people to communicate with, tasks or chores to carry out... especially in this time-poor, always-on world where I see many parents paying more attention to their phones than to their children.

What a different world it might be if every child regularly had the gift of proper listening, with their parent giving them eye contact, setting aside for a moment any other activity or distraction, taking them seriously, possibly being in empathic or active listening position. Children who are really listened to develop confidence, and learn that they don't have to shout, scream or throw tantrums: they can talk.

I am not saying that listening is a sinecure for all bad behaviour, or that it will work every time. But I do believe that children deserve to be listened to as much as everyone else, and that listening consciously and fully to children is one of the most loving things a parent can do.

LISTENING TO MUSIC

I have loved music since my mother made a practice of buying me records like *Carnival of the Animals* by Saint-Saëns, Prokofiev's *Peter and the Wolf*, and Britten's *The Young Person's Guide to the Orchestra* to play on the family's precious Rogers stereogram, which still had an option for 78 rpm (yes, I am that old!). I remember my father bringing home a copy of *Sgt. Pepper's Lonely Hearts Club Band* in 1967 and saying it was supposed to be the greatest pop LP ever (true even today, in many people's opinions). The first 45 I bought was *Ride a White Swan* by T Rex in 1970; the first LP *Bridge Over Troubled Water* by Simon and Garfunkel in the same year. I used to save up my pocket money for my weekly pilgrimage to the tiny local record store, where I would browse through the latest releases and choose the one I could afford to buy. I well remember the excitement of walking home, impatient to play the precious 45. I changed my school piano lessons to drum lessons (without telling my parents!) and invested every penny in getting my own stereo and later, at age 15, a drum kit. I have played music ever since, and have been lucky enough to have had some wonderful experiences recording, playing live and being broadcast on radio and TV through the years in numerous bands.

If you're getting the impression that music matters a lot to me, you're right! Playing in a band, group or orchestra develops a person's listening, much like the Mixer exercise we explored earlier in this chapter, because you cannot be a good musician without listening to multiple streams of sound simultaneously and being conscious of each of them to spot cues, pick up tempo and rhythm, and feel the way the ensemble is changing the feel and volume. That responsiveness, brought to its peak in jazz music, brings music alive; it is there in any group performance, even a highly rehearsed one where all the players have the 'dots' in front of them and every note is fixed. Perhaps this is why research shows that musicians have slightly larger brains than non-musicians!

It was my musician-listening that got me into my career in audio branding. I often listened to the world like a live performance, and when I sold my publishing business in 2003 I really focused on my long-standing observation that the world sounds pretty unpleasant, at least in cities. I wondered: does this matter? Months of research later, I was convinced that I had discovered a hidden opportunity to transform soundscapes that were impacting with major negative consequences on millions of people in shops, offices, hospitals, schools, airports and the like, and so The Sound Agency was born.

Music has been here as long as humans have, and it's everywhere humans are. There is no culture on earth without it. It combines all the aspects of sound—melody, harmony, rhythm and tempo, often enhanced by the human voice and words. As a result, after the human voice, I rate music as the most powerful sound of all.

You know what they say... with great power comes great responsibility. Particularly since music has one major aspect that makes it a fickle servant: association. We could play Robbie Williams's *Angels* in a store to two people with identical demographic and psychographic profiles. One could feel a million dollars because they fell in love to it and it was their song at the wedding. The other could leave the store in tears because they just got dumped by the person who sang it to them.

If you are going to listen to music, I encourage you to listen with care and attention and at high quality whenever possible. Yes, we can all enjoy portable music or background music when we're doing something boring like commuting or ironing. But there is a joy to fully decoding the skill, passion and imagination of the people who make good recorded or live music: taking these things for granted is a rather sad and, to me, impolite way of consuming something that can express some of the best aspects of humanity.

I encourage you to watch the world-famous conductor Benjamin Zander's terrific TED talk about actively listening to classical music. I was in the room for that one, and when he had us all stand up and bellow the chorus from the fourth movement of Beethoven's Ninth, the communal joy was palpable.

I spoke with Ben Zander about many aspects of listening to music, and you can hear and read the full interview on this book's website at www. howtobeheard.com, using password conscious to access your special book-owners' area. An excerpt follows this section.

Music can also heal, and I suspect we are just scratching the surface of its capabilities in the modern world. I have no doubt that, for many thousands of years of prehistory, music was used in many more social and therapeutic ways than today, where it has become commercialised and rather stuck as a form of entertainment. There is a growing body of research about music's positive effects of many illnesses and conditions. Just some of them are: addiction, Alzheimer's, asthma, autism, behavioural difficulties, communication disorders, depression, disability, dyslexia, eating disorders, epilepsy, HIV/AIDS, learning disabilities, mental health, pain relief, stress management, stroke recovery, and vision loss.

Music deserves our respect and offers much we are not currently receiving. I recommend that you take up an instrument if you don't already play. Even if that's not for you, I urge you to explore the powerful benefits available from music, and do it actively and consciously.

Listening to music: Benjamin Zander

This is an excerpt from the transcript of a conversation with Ben Zander. For the full transcript and the audio recording, visit www.howtobeheardbook.com and use the password **conscious**.

Benjamin Zander is the conductor of The Boston Philharmonic Orchestra and the Boston Philharmonic Youth Orchestra and a guest conductor around the world. His recordings with London's famed Philharmonia Orchestra of Mahler symphonies have been received with extraordinary critical acclaim (including Grammy nominations) both for the performance and Ben's famous full-length disc explaining the music for the lay listener.

Ben is one of the most sought-after speakers in the world. He has given both the opening and the closing keynote address at the World Economic Forum in Davos, where on another occasion he received the Crystal Award for "outstanding contributions in the Arts and international relations". In 2002 he was awarded the Caring Citizen of the Humanities Award by the International Council for Caring Communities at the United Nations. In honour of his 70th birthday, and of his 45 years of teaching, he was awarded an Honorary Doctorate by the New England Conservatory. With Rosamund Zander he wrote a best-selling book, *The Art of Possibility*, which has been translated into fifteen languages. His TED talk on listening to music is legendary and highly recommended.

Ben Zander: I think my life is about enrolment. It's about giving the people the opportunity to see something that they otherwise wouldn't see. I spent a great deal of my life with a woman whose father was a professional gardener. She became a wonderful gardener, and I didn't pay any attention at all to what was going on. Now, I have the most exquisite garden, and I love every single flower. But it took being around it. It took people caring about it, enrolling me in it, and that's what I feel teachers do. They enrol people in their passion, and listening is one of the great human arts, the great human capacities. Part of the job of a teacher is to enrol people, train people, lead people towards greater, and greater listening...

It's an unbelievable capacity. My father was blind, and I remember saying to him "Which of the senses would you prefer to lose?" And he said, "Oh, there's no question about it. The eyes are unimportant. The ears are essential." So, it's one of the great human capacities, maybe the greatest. Our job as leaders of any kind is to train people to listen. When they don't listen well, and we're in the midst of a morass of bad listening in the political world, it's terrifying.

Julian Treasure: We can improve our listening, and music must be a great way of doing that, surely.

Ben Zander: It's a fantastic way of doing it... For 50 years almost, I've run these youth orchestras, taking them on tour and playing these extraordinary performances. There's no doubt in my mind, although I can't prove it, that their lives are immeasurably enhanced and improved by the fact that they're listening to each other, they're listening to themselves, they're listening to the music as a whole: they're listening to clarinets immersed in trumpets, and violas, and it's just a world, which is kind of a model for life.

If you just bash through a piece from beginning to end, and it's as loud and raucous as you can make it, you learn nothing, neither about music, nor about life. But if you pull it apart and tell them what to listen for, and give them the meaning, and share with them what you think the composer is trying to say, and then they play over a long period of time, and then they take it on tour, and they play it in concert... You can't tell me that this is not going to profoundly affect the way they lead the rest of their lives, and I have countless letters from people in their 40's and 50's who say that this experience is what shaped them as leaders in other fields—as doctors, and lawyers, and political people.

So, to me, it's one of the essential life forces. I'm just working on my discussion for the Beethoven Ninth, and I'm very clear that Beethoven was one of the great teachers that humanity has ever had. I love *Eleanor Rigby*, but to suggest that *Eleanor Rigby* is an equal to the Beethoven Ninth is grotesque to me. It's on a level of such subtlety, and sophistication, and depth, and profundity, and open heartedness in meaning and philosophy—and on a scale that is beyond comprehension.

Julian Treasure: Well not to mention joy, Ben. I remember very well being in the room when you gave that TED Talk, and you had the entire TED audience belting out the fourth movement of Beethoven's Ninth.

Ben Zander: I know! Isn't that amazing?

Julian Treasure: It was very joyful, which is what it's supposed to be, isn't it?

Ben Zander: And you know what's interesting about that, Julian, is that it's irresistible joy. It doesn't matter how depressed, or self-absorbed, or frightened you are. You listen to that music, and whatever state you're in, it takes you away. It takes you with it, and that's a very powerful aspect of music. Mendelssohn said that music is much more powerful than words—he actually said something more important: it's much more precise than words, which is extraordinary. It seems like a complete paradox... Our job, all of us, every single one of us is to make sure that the people around us, whoever they are, know what's going on in the things that we love the most. We love music, and we know the power that music has, to transform people's whole lives. So, it's our job to keep training people.

LISTENING TO NATURE

Another therapeutic and richly beautiful sound is what my friend, leading sound recordist and TED speaker Bernie Krause, calls *biophony*: the sound of nature. I interviewed Bernie about listening to nature and more, and you can hear and read the full interview on this book's website at www.howtobeheardbook.com, using the password conscious to access the special area for book-owners.

Many people walk into a room and feel they need to switch on some sound, which I think may often be a form of pining for the nature sounds that surrounded human beings until we invented cities. I class them as WWB: wind, water and birds. All three have been on this planet far longer than we have, and the gentler, more beautiful versions of them are, I believe, universally health-giving and also great for promoting energy and concentration or rest and sleep, depending on how they are deployed.

Wind has a huge range, like all the WWB sounds. Howling gales in the Antarctic are not generally the kinds of sounds I want to surround myself with! However, gentle breeze in leaves or grass is one of my favourites, and can work very well as a background sound on a hot, airless day or on headphones as a masking sound when I'm trying to work and people are speaking nearby.

Water can work its magic too. If you ever have problems sleeping, the sound of gentle surf may well be the answer. Its typical frequency is very similar to the breathing pattern of a sleeping person, so there's a strong physiological association. Emotionally, we tend to associate it with being relaxed, stress-free, on a beach somewhere—all excellent overtones to have resonating within you as you settle down to sleep. Gentle rainfall is another soothing sound, though not so soporific, as is the lovely tinkling of a bubbling brook or stream. Pick your favourite sounds consciously: I do not suggest trying to work or rest to pounding storm waves or a large waterfall. As well as being very intense and eventually fatiguing, the latter makes communication very difficult, because it effectively masks the important sibilant consonants (s and t). We understand language largely by hearing consonants, which is why it's hard to understand someone on the other side of a good wall: you may be able to hear the vowel sounds, which tend to be lower frequencies and thus transmit through anything but highly effective attenuating materials, but those aahs and oohs are almost impossible to decode without the consonants.

Finally, I've mentioned birdsong before in this book, and make no apology for again extolling its virtues as a sound that promotes mental alertness (it's time to be awake when the birds are singing) and emotional security (when birds are happily singing, we feel safe). There are apps and recordings available that allow you to play birdsong from your mobile device or computer. Choose the type that you like best, because there is great richness and variety in birdsong; I wouldn't recommend the sound of crows or parakeets, for example! For ideas and to explore this topic more, I recommend the lovely book *Why Birds Sing: A Journey into the Mystery of Bird Song* by David Rothenberg.

To have fun with nature sound, and to engage your kids in the same pursuit, I highly recommend getting a copy of Bernie Krause's book *The Great Animal Orchestra*, plus the extraordinary symphony that evolved out of it—a collaboration between Bernie and the composer Richard Blackford, featuring imaginative and entrancing match-ups between the instruments of a full orchestra and many of the astounding recordings from Bernie's archive. Bernie's contention that nature sound is like an orchestra, where every animal knows both the right place (high or low frequency and its own specific timbre) and the right time for its sound, is borne out by the amazing duets and conversations between sampled animal sounds and instruments. Highly recommended.

Listening to nature: Bernie Krause

This is an excerpt from the transcript of a conversation with Bernie Krause. For the full transcript and the audio recording, visit www.howtobeheardbook.com and use the password **conscious**.

Dr. Bernie Krause is a musician, a naturalist and the world's leading nature sound recordist. During the 1950s and '60s, he devoted himself to music, replacing Pete Seeger as the guitarist for the Weavers and then, in Beaver and Krause, playing a key role in developing the tools and methods of electronic music, working with The Byrds, The Doors, Peter Gabriel, Stevie Wonder, George Harrison and Van Morrison, among others. For more than 40 years since then, Bernie has traveled the world, recording and archiving the sounds of creatures and natural environments. He has recorded more than 5,000 hours of wild soundscapes, over half of which no longer exist in nature due to encroaching noise and human activity; these include the sounds of over 15,000 species. He gave a TED talk in 2013 on the voice of the natural world. He has made countless albums, written numerous papers and books, and recently collaborated with UK composer Richard Blackford to create *The Great Animal Orchestra Symphony for Orchestra and Wild Soundscapes*. Bernie and his wife, Kat, live in Sonoma, CA.

Julian Treasure: Bernie, you've talked to me in the past about biophony. Could you tell us what you mean by that word?

Bernie Krause: Well, biophony is one component of what we consider the soundscape, what Murray Schafer referred to as the soundscape. I've reduced it to three basic sources. The first source is the geophony, or the non-biological sound that occurs in a wild environment, wind in the trees, water in a stream, waves at the ocean shore, that sort of thing. It's non-biological, natural sound. The second is the biophony, and this is the most important, because it's the collective voice made up of all vocal organisms in a given habitat. The operative term here is collective, because each habitat expresses itself very much like we distinguish one human voice from another. It has its own signature. The signature is made up of all of the organisms that vocalise at a given time, in a given habitat. It actually defines the habitat, by the way.

Julian Treasure: What's the third element of the entire soundscape?

Bernie Krause: Well, the third element is the sounds that we humans make. I call it anthropophony. Anthropophony is made of two classes of sound. The first class is controlled sound, like speech, music, theatre. The second is sound that's more chaotic, incoherent. That's what we call noise, because it's not conveying any particular kind of information. It's just sort of random sound in a given moment and in a given place, wherever we are, like automobiles going by, or leaf blowers, or lawn mowers, that kind of thing, jet planes flying overhead.

Julian Treasure: Just raises the question in my mind, do animals make noise as well, or is everything, all the sound that they create, useful? Is noise, to some extent, the garbage of sound?

Bernie Krause: I believe so, but animals, of course, do make noise as they shuffle through leaves, or walk through a forest, and step on twigs, they crack, and so on. Yes, they make noise, but their noise is relatively little compared to what we humans produce.

Julian Treasure: The planet has changed a huge amount in the last few hundred years, with anthropophony starting to dominate more, and more, and more. I remember reading something from you, and in fact, I quoted it in my book, some time ago, about the time it now takes to record a few minutes of nature sound unpolluted by anthropophony. What is your experience with that now, Bernie?

Bernie Krause: I actually make the point in my recent book, *The Great Animal Orchestra*, that when I first began to record, I could record for 10 hours and capture one hour of usable material. That was in 1968. Now, it takes me almost 2000 hours to capture the same thing in many habitats.

Julian Treasure: My goodness.

Bernie Krause: Yeah, yeah.

Julian Treasure: That is shocking. Presumably, the kind of intrusive noises, even if you were out in the wild somewhere, would be a distant leaf blower, or an aeroplane overflying the area.

Bernie Krause: Yes. That's another problem. There's almost no place on Earth now that doesn't have some human signature that intrudes on the silence and solitude of a place.

Julian Treasure: Can you think of anywhere that still is truly natural, and there's no anthropophony going on?

Bernie Krause: I've found a couple of places, actually. You have to think about this in terms of times of quiet intervals. One of them is not very far from where I live, about 20 minutes from our home in Glen Ellen, California. We can drive to this spot, and very often, in the mornings, just before and until just after sunrise, we can record in that spot and maybe hear one plane flying over in an hour. There are places in the panhandle of New Mexico, in the United States, a state that borders on the Mexican border, where we recorded for two weeks and heard one aeroplane in a two week period. In Alaska, where there are only 500,000 people in a state that's a third the size of the lower 48 in the

United States, and I've recorded there in the Arctic National Wildlife Refuge, and we've recorded for 10 days without hearing another intrusion of human noise, just ourselves.

Julian Treasure: I remember you talking about Alaska. I think you've said that's your favourite place in the world. Is it still?

Bernie Krause: Yes, because there are so few people. You can get to places where there are no trails. You can walk for a week in any direction and not come upon a fence, or a road, or another human habitation. What's nice, also, about Alaska, is there's signage. There are no eager rangers describing to you the life cycle of an elk or a wolf. Best of all, of course, there's nothing to buy.

Julian Treasure: Although, I imagine, your life is on the line. If you're that far from civilisation, you slip and break an ankle, and you're in big trouble, aren't you?

Bernie Krause: Well, I'll take my chances in Alaska anytime over Hollywood!

LISTENING IN SALES

Ask any top-performing salesperson what the most important part of the sales conversation is, and they will probably say: "Listening." Empathic selling builds long-term relationships because it creates connection and empathy by listening to the customer's needs, unlike high-pressure selling where the customer hardly gets a word in and feels bullied rather than understood.

The active listening position, when deployed by a master, can be an incredible business generator. In my magazine publishing business in the early 1990s, our first advertising sales executive was the opposite of the stereotypical sales executive. John was so quiet that you could hardly hear his side of the phone conversation. He never got excited, or pumped himself up, or did a countdown at the start of the day, or slapped himself in the face before a call: his was a gentle, quiet and polite nature. When he listened, customers really felt heard—so despite the lack of energy and buzz going down the phone line, people just seemed to love buying from him. His figures were amazing. He went on to launch a division, buy it out from us, and sell it for a large sum—all, I am sure, at imperceptible volume levels.

Sales listening can also employ the 'listening for' techniques we reviewed a few pages ago. In any sales conversation, it's important to listen for two things: context and cues. The context may include the other person's listening for you and your business (including any opinions, past experiences and so on—here, a great question to ask is: "What do you know about us?"). It may also include their high-level goals and current situation, which are again great things to ask about, because people generally love speaking about themselves. If you understand someone's hopes, fears, dreams, aspirations and problems then you can map that onto your own product or service and accurately fit your solution to their problem. Also, if you can spot their listening style, you can respond appropriately. Some people want the big picture, and fast; others like data and proof or technical details; still others relate emotionally and love a chat. It's only possible to build rapport by matching styles if you are actively listening for their style from the very beginning.

Cues are little conversational hooks to hang your benefits on—opportunities to match your solution to their problem in some way. They include what sales trainers call 'buying signs', where the other person expresses latent intention by asking for more information or details.

We'll come back to selling when we discuss powerful speaking.

LISTENING LEADERS

In effect this means listening while you are talking, which may sound impossible, like breathing in while you are breathing out, but in fact it is a hugely powerful business technique. Sadly, it is rarely taught in management training courses.

It seems obvious to observe that good leaders are situationally very aware. Like a squirrel, a good leader combines strength, speed and agility with awareness. And like a squirrel, a good leader needs to be listening all the time—for danger, and for opportunity.

Sadly, many of those who achieve leadership positions do so because of their dynamic, powerful, extrovert personalities, which are much more expressed in speaking than in listening. I remember very early in my career, with my first promotion to manage a small team, being taught four modes of leadership: tell, sell, consult, join. Three of these four require good listening. From time to time, tell-mode is the most effective place to be, but managers who deploy the Nike slogan 'just do it' as a matter of course can only be successful in the long term if they have extraordinary genius and an intuitive feel for their market. Those people do exist—Steve Jobs is the most obvious example—but they are very rare, and for every one blessed with the talent to be right most of the time when ordering people to 'just do it', there are many habitual tell-managers who manage a resentful, repressed and ineffective team.

A great manager will be able to move mode to suit the situation, and will always be aware of all the factors that may affect success. That means knowing the people in the team: their skills, knowledge, attitudes, motivators, current state and any issues they are dealing with. The only way of knowing people like that is to listen to them.

I have worked for managers who inspire their whole team to give of their best; people for whom the team would walk across hot coals if need be. I have also worked under managers who have inspired only fear or contempt. The most significant difference has always been listening skill. Listening is a way of showing respect, of valuing another human being. Even the most charismatic leaders will have trouble binding a team with passion, care and commitment in the long term if they fail to listen to their people.

The best leaders I have encountered use both informal and formal methods: an open-door policy for people to ask for help or advice; a no-blame atmosphere where it's okay to make mistakes as long as the intention was right and they don't get repeated; a culture of respecting and valuing differences; a sense of humour at all times; a structure that ensures two-way communication and appraisal, from informal check-ins at the coffee machine to formal 360-degree appraisals. They move to the most appropriate listening position, avoiding getting stuck in critical listening, which is one of the most common business mistakes—and of course a massive issue in many relationships when that stuck listening position comes home! They avoid the seven sins, especially dogmatism (which produces interrupting), gossip and negativity. They are not concerned with personally looking good, but instead are focused on bringing the best out of every member of their team. They have humility, knowing their limitations and trusting the people to whom they delegate tasks without interfering or obsessive checking.

All of this is made so much easier when a leader listens—to the point where I believe that if you look at any successful team, its leader will probably be a good listener. Despots, tyrants and dictators may have their days, but if they don't listen they will eventually fail, probably through the burden of their own ego and hubris, or the resentment of those they rule. I believe listening is a fundamental skill for a good leader.

I was lucky enough to interview Franklin Covey co-founder and best-selling author Hyrum Smith about leadership listening and speaking.

Check the panel for an excerpt from the interview and instructions on accessing the full interview in audio and written form online.

Hyrum Smith

This is an excerpt from the transcript of a conversation with Hyrum Smith. For the full transcript and the audio recording, visit www.howtobeheardbook.com and use the password **conscious**.

Hyrum W. Smith is a distinguished author, speaker, and businessman. In 1983 he co-founded the Franklin Quest Company to produce the Franklin Day Planner and train individuals and organisations in the time management principles on which the planner was based. In 1997 it became the Franklin Covey Company. As the co-founder of these companies, he was directly responsible for training over 6 million people over the course of his career in time management skills and increased personal productivity; he was the time management guru, or more accurately put, the life management specialist. He "retired" from Franklin in 2004 to pursue other interests. For four decades, he has been empowering people to effectively govern their personal and professional lives, combining wit and enthusiasm with a gift for communicating compelling principles that incite lasting personal change. Hyrum is the author of several nationally-acclaimed books, including *The 10 Natural Laws of Successful Time and Life Management*, *What Matters Most*, and *The Power of Perception: 6 Steps To Behavior Change*.

Julian Treasure: Do you think listening is really important as a skill for a leader?

Hyrum Smith: You know, I'm not sure there's a more important skill for a leader than listening. In fact, if I had to list the skills and rank the skills that a leader ought to have, I would put listening at the very top of my list. It's a skill that not many leaders have, and it costs them a great deal of money, it costs them a great deal of productivity. In my opinion, listening is at the very top of the line.

Julian Treasure: Why is that, why is it so important to listen if you're a leader, Hyrum?

Hyrum Smith: Well, if you don't know what your people are thinking and what their ideas are, then you're going to have to come up with all the ideas to run your company. I mean, I started the Franklin Planner Company back in 1983, and I discovered very quickly that I did not have all the skills necessary to take it from my garage to what it became, which is a billion dollar company on the New York Stock Exchange. I discovered very quickly that I had some really bright people around me, and we attracted bright people, and I don't say this in a bragging way, but I think one of the reasons we were able to attract bright people is that we not only listened to people, but we actually implemented their ideas.

There's so much going on that a leader can never see, and if he or she is not willing to listen to the people that are working with and for them, then it is very costly. Just the economic cost of not listening. You've got a guy down on the line who created our binders who came up with an idea for a new binder. Had we not been willing to listen to him, we'd miss about a 30 million dollar opportunity, which it turned out to be.

Julian Treasure: And what are the speaking skills that you think would be helpful for a leader?

Hyrum Smith: The ability to reach into someone so that they feel what you're saying is a very special skill. There's a difference, for example, between telling and teaching.

Julian Treasure: Mm-hmm.

Hyrum Smith: The great speakers are *teaching*. They're not telling, they're teaching. In my opinion, the greatest sales people in the world are teachers. They're selling their students on an idea and experimenting with the idea. A leader has to be the quintessential teacher in my opinion. What the leader needs to do is to make the presentation in such a way that it goes in through their chest first and then up to the brain. Most people go in through the intellect. They have 47 slides that they're going to show, and all this stuff, and it's all very intellectual, but they don't grab the people's hearts. If people walk away from a presentation by their leader, their manager, that hasn't grabbed them in their heart, their chest, I don't care how much data they had, how on line the speech was, they've got to learn to get into their heart.

Great teachers instinctively teach with parables. The modern day word for parable is an apperception. That means that you teach an idea and then you share a story that solidifies the idea. That's like Christ—I hope you don't mind me using that example.

Julian Treasure: No, it's fine.

Hyrum Smith: Christ taught with parables. The reason he was such a fabulous teacher is because he used stories that the people related to. The people there understood sheep, and they understood that whole thing. Great speakers, in my opinion, are great storytellers.

Julian Treasure: Well, I think you've raised a fascinating point there, Hyrum, which is to feel it, then think it, then say it, not just think it.

Hyrum Smith: Right. Absolutely.

Julian Treasure: It kind of wells up from the heart to the head, and then out of the mouth, which is a tremendous physiological metaphor really for giving a great speech, and certainly, I know many people have intellectualised speaking, and it becomes a kind of robotic, mechanical process. If you can touch, move, and inspire people, and they feel it, then that connection is invaluable, I think, isn't it?

Hyrum Smith: Absolutely. The fact is, people may forget what they've heard, forget what they've seen, but they never forget what they feel.

THE LISTENING ORGANISATION

The danger of not listening

I have first-hand experience of the problems that can arise in an organisation that has the opposite of a listening culture. I sold my magazine publishing company to a US-owned marketing services group whose premier London advertising agency was large, long-established and well-regarded. Unfortunately, its CEO was a man with a ferocious reputation for not taking bad news at all well. People were terrified of him, so the habit had developed of editing out the bad news, and of embroidering average news to make it good, and good news to make it great. (Remember, exaggeration is one of the seven deadly sins). The result was that the agency had been over-reporting its success, claiming that it had won business that was only promised, and that client billings were larger than they really were. Its accounts were effectively fabrication. This was obviously unsupportable in the long term, but nobody had the courage to tell the emperor that he was without clothes. Eventually, an audit revealed the extent of the problem. The London agency had to reissue years of financial accounts, which resulted in the whole global group having to do the same. Falsifying accounts is not taken well by financial markets, and the group's share price on the New York Stock Exchange tumbled to less than a quarter of its previous value. I felt the effect of this anti-listening culture keenly, because we had accepted shares in our purchase price and had to watch, unable by law to sell the shares, as they tumbled to a fraction of their value at the time of the deal. Just one reason that I passionately believe in the importance of a listening culture!

The benefits of a listening organisation

All the innovation gurus I have ever encountered stress the importance of accepting mistakes if your organisation is to be truly innovative. Many companies give an award for the year's biggest mistake! If we don't try new things or new ways of doing things, we get stuck in historical attitudes and behaviours, and the result can be devastating, as Kodak and many others have discovered to their cost.

Openness to mistakes and a 'let's try it' environment absolutely require a listening culture. When someone is reporting a major failure, an innovative manager will be listening for the positives: the courage to try something new; the imagination in isolating the problem to be solves; the ingenuity involved in engineering a new solution... this is very much listening for the gold, in order to encourage the positive aspects, coach on what went wrong and even assess whether the failure is a failure after all; sometimes just the criteria for success need to be changed. Always remember: Post-It notes were a failed effort to invent a strong paper glue.

Other listening benefits include being able to spot problems earlier and thus deal with them before they become major; improving skills and performance everywhere with 360 degree reviews that contain honest, fearless and accurate feedback from all directions; producing better managers who really understand their teams' challenges and can be asked for help without fear of loss of face; and of course the massive benefits that come from listening to customers and understanding their needs and experiences.

Creating a listening culture

It's never easy to change an organisation's culture. Making a management decision and emailing everyone that 'our culture is now...' certainly doesn't work! To create a genuine listening culture takes planning, communication, involvement, commitment, persistence, continual training and accountability. Recruitment has to consider people's relationship with listening (it's always better to recruit the right type of people and train the required skills than to recruit the right skills and try to change the people). The regular performance review process equally needs to include listening explicitly. Most of all, listening has too come from the top and be consistently practiced and encouraged.

Chapter Five

How to achieve perfect content

I n 1939, Jimmy Lunceford and Ella Fitzgerald recorded the song *T'aint What You Do (It's The Way That You Do It)*, which became a global hit many years later for Fun Boy Three and Bananarama. Well, in powerful speaking, it *is* what you say *and* the way that you say it. Both are vital: a brilliantly-delivered speech with trivial or meaningless content will be quickly forgotten, while even the most brilliant content will fail to land if the speaker is tedious, flat and uninteresting. We'll deal with both these aspects of speaking, starting in this chapter with the foundations of powerful speaking and then answering the question I am most often asked: how can I make my ideas concise, effective and powerful?

HAIL: THE FOUNDATIONS OF POWERFUL SPEAKING

Throughout my career at The Sound Agency, my professional concern has been the sound of organisations, brands and their spaces, such as malls, airports, shops, offices, hospitals and places of education. I created a scientific model that describes how sound affects people, and we helped to move many organisations towards conscious design of sound instead of unconscious creation of noise.

As time passed, I started to realise that it's not just organisations that make important sound. Human beings do too: your body can't make light, but it can, and does, make sounds, of which the most important is speech. As I explored this aspect of sound, my TED talks started to focus more on personal sound, and on interpersonal communication, culminating in the fifth talk entitled 'How to speak so that people want to listen', which as I've already mentioned has over 20 million views compared to the five million of my talk on conscious listening. Epictetus's adage about two ears and one mouth (quoted in Chapter Three) seems to have been tossed aside... it appears that, in the modern world, most people are much more concerned about the effectiveness of their speaking than that of their listening. I do hope you have received the central message of this book—that in fact a balance between the two skills is essential, because they are so interrelated. In order to be good speaker, I believe you must also be a good listener.

Nevertheless, we now come to focus on powerful speaking. When I came to assemble my thoughts and experiences into the content for that fifth speech, I asked myself what were the foundations for speaking with authority, power and effect. I reviewed my own experiences, both in hundreds of talks on stage around the world and in personal communication; I also reviewed some of the great speakers I'd had the pleasure to watch live, and some of the most powerful speakers in history.

The result was HAIL: an acronym of the four cornerstones of powerful speaking. The H stands for honesty; the A is authenticity; the I is integrity and the L is love. Let's explore them in more detail.

HONESTY

Honesty is the first chapter in the book of wisdom.

– Thomas Jefferson

Honesty is the absence of falsehood. This sounds simple enough, but is in fact extraordinarily challenging, because lying is part of human nature. In her excellent book *Liespotting: Proven Techniques to Detect Deception* and the fine TED talk that arose from it, Pamela Meyer recounts research showing that on any given day we are lied to between 10 and 200 times, and that strangers lie three times within 10 minutes of meeting each other. We are all liars, even if most of them are relatively harmless white lies, the kind that reduce friction and keep home and work from needless upset and conflict: "I was just about to call you!", "Of course you don't look fat in that!" or "So sorry, my spam filters got that email for some reason."

The scale of lying, and public tolerance for it, have definitely increased in the past few decades. I remember a time when we held our politicians (and indeed all professionals such as doctors, lawyers, teachers and accountants) to the highest standard; when being caught in a lie was sufficient cause for resignation or dismissal. Now we live in the post-truth world, where inconvenient stories are dismissed as 'fake news' and we have the interesting euphemism "I misspoke" to replace, and dilute to an apparently acceptable level, the admission of lying.

Lying is so prevalent that it will help in our pursuit of honesty to understand it—and to have compassion for some expressions of it. Pamela Meyer distinguishes nine motives for lying, four of which are 'offensive' (designed to advance our position) and five 'defensive' (designed to avoid some sort of damage).

Offensive reasons for lying

- To obtain a reward that's not otherwise easily attainable.

- To gain advantage over another person or situation.

- To create a positive impression and win the admiration of others.

- To exercise powers over others by controlling information.

Defensive reasons for lying

- To avoid being punished or to avoid embarrassment.

- To protect another person from being punished.

- To protect yourself from the threat of physical or emotional harm.

- To get out of an awkward social situation.

•To maintain privacy.

You probably recognise many of these, as I do, and you may be able to think of examples from your life where, with the best of intentions (or sometimes not!) you have intentionally 'misspoken'. I wonder if there has ever been a completely honest human being. The truth can hurt, and I am certainly not advocating brutal honesty at all times: "You look terrible today!" is neither kind, nor necessary.

Despite the prevalence of lying, we value honesty highly, and many people say it's the most important value they seek in their key relationships. I want to emphasise two facets of honesty that I believe are critical if your speaking is to land with power.

Be clear

Many a book has been written on plain speaking, and for good reason. In business, government, the legal professions and academia, a combination of pomposity and hubris (in particular, the desire to appear clever, expressed by using long, complicated and obscure words) have given rise to millions of documents, speeches and conversations that have left the recipients more confused at the end than they were at the beginning. I remember being turned off the entire subject of sociology during my economics degree at Cambridge when the first lecture included words such as 'systemativity' and 'performative conception'.

In their entertaining book *Made to Stick*, which investigates why some ideas stick and others evaporate, Chip and Dan Heath reflect that, had he been a CEO, President John F Kennedy might well have said in 1961: "Our mission is to become the international leader in the space industry through maximum team-centred innovation and strategically targeted aerospace initiatives." Instead he said: "I believe that this nation should commit itself to achieving the goal, before this decade is out, of landing a man on the moon and returning him safely to the Earth."

That level of clarity was inspiring enough (and precise enough) that the almost impossible goal was achieved eight years later. Governments seem to be learning this lesson: on October 13, 2010 President Obama signed a Plain Writing Act requiring that federal agencies use "clear government communication that the public can understand and use." In the UK, the Plain English Campaign has its international Crystal Mark, which rewards well-written documents, as well as an annual Foot in Mouth Award for baffling spoken language, such as the 1994 winner by then Shadow Chancellor Gordon Brown, who gave a speech about "the growth of post neo-classical endogenous growth theory." My own bugbears are the classic corporate words provide, utilise and facilitate (what's wrong with give, use and help?).

Of course, written language is even worse than spoken in most instances, and, although it's not the subject of this book, the Plain English Campaign's Golden Bull awards offer a salutary pool of examples of how not to write. One insurance survey asked the recipient:

"When you changed your retirement date, did you intend to align your lifestyle switching strategy to your revised retirement date?"

They didn't explain what on earth a 'lifestyle switching strategy' is. Lawyers, of course, rule the roost when it comes to incomprehensible written language. Most people who have had to deal with legal agreements have struggled with passages like this single sentence from the winner of the 2016 Golden Bull award:

I do hereby for myself, my heirs, executors, administrators and assigns guarantee to you and your heirs, executors, administrators and assigns and the owner of the premises for the time being the punctual payment of said rent now payable by the Tenant or as same may be varied or permitted to be varied by law and for mesne rates that may accrue due until full clear and legal possession shall be delivered up to you and I agree for myself, my heirs, executors, administrators and assigns to indemnify you and your heirs,

*executors administrators and assigns and the owner of the premises
for the time being from all loss or damage done to the said premises by
the Tenant or through his negligence or by reason of non-fulfillment
of any of the stipulations and conditions on the part of the Tenant
contained in above agreement and for all costs of any proceedings
for the recovery of the rent or possession of said premises and should
Notice to Quit be served by the Landlord or Tenant, or ejectment
summons issued or eviction decree obtained in respect of said
premises and afterwards withdrawn or waived by either party with
or without my knowledge.*

Are you still with me? Unnecessary complexity, vagueness and indirectness tend to be confusing. Keep sentences short wherever possible, avoiding too many subordinate clauses. Try to avoid the passive tense unless it adds strength or clarity; it usually does neither—for example, "We will achieve this by the end of the year" is much more powerful than "This will be achieved by the end of the year." Always check for that little self-aggrandising imp that lurks in us all: ask yourself if there's a simpler word you can use, a plainer way of putting this. If you set goals for anyone (or for yourself), make them SMART, as President Kennedy did: specific, measurable, achievable, realistic and timed. Remember, the objective is to be understood, not to be impressive: this is about getting the ball over the net and keeping the rally going, not hitting a crowd-pleasing winner.

In sum, make your speech simple, easy to understand, logical, plain, direct, complete and specific, and you will generally find it effectively received.

Be straight

Politicians have always been the masters of deflection and obfuscation (a lovely old word meaning the practice of making things unclear). Often this is because they can't, or don't want to, answer a question in an interview. In their defence, they are now facing journalists who have become more and more aggressive, due partly to politicians' deviousness, and partly the public obsession with blaming and shaming—see the discussion of being right in Chapter Two. As a result, the two groups are locked in a grim dance that doesn't really serve anyone. We hear interruptions, soundbites, unfounded accusations, straw man fallacies, and often complete avoidances, often preceded by "I'm glad you asked me that question..." (because I'm now going to answer a completely different one).

Being straight in your speaking means being frank—in other words, saying what you mean. Many relationships at home and at work are blighted by twin-track communication, where the frank conversation is unspoken and what's said is at best allusive (using suggestion rather than explicit mention), at worst completely different from what is meant. The famous scene from Woody Allen's 1977 movie *Annie Hall* where the two lead characters have an entire discussion without saying what they're thinking, with subtitles so that the audience can see the real conversation, is so painfully funny because we all recognise that process.

Of course, sometimes it's kinder or safer not to say what we're thinking, and I am not advocating removing the editor that works between your mind and your mouth: not all our thoughts are worthy of being spoken and we've all had the experience of saying something we later regretted. However, I am suggesting that falling into the habit of indirect, allusive speaking is something to be avoided. It requires mind-reading on the part of the other person, which is hard work for them and will often be inaccurate. Also, it tends to go hand in hand with a habit of meaning-making because we assume that other people are the same and don't say what they mean either, so their speech requires decoding just like ours does. These things give rise to misunderstanding and conflict because they involve so much unconscious filtering and guesswork, often resting on the assumption that others are just like us (which is not true) and arising from a fear of being known or a need to be right that translates into making others wrong. Remember, being judgmental or even condemnatory in your meaning-making is deadly sin number two!

Many people's feelings of not being understood arises here. The fear of being poorly received can itself produce indirect speaking that's harder to understand, producing a self-fulfilling prophecy. Equally, the need to be right and justified can create speaking that demands mind-reading, producing the desired feeling of righteous indignation when the other person's mind-reading is off the mark, as it often will be. If you recognise any of this obliqueness in your own speaking, or you have relationships where mind-reading is regularly necessary on either part, try the exercises below.

If you want to be powerful in your speaking and fully understood, be straight: say what you mean and mean what you say. Be steady, reliable and unambiguous in your speech and people will learn that when you speak, it's worth paying attention.

Exercise: Be clear and straight

Be clear

Your writing will have many similarities to your speaking, so the easiest way to check your clarity is to examine your written communication. Take a look at your recent emails, letters and even texts, and check for the following.

Unnecessary complexity, for example ~~utilising~~ using ~~lengthy~~ long ~~verbalisations~~ words where ~~more concise~~ shorter ~~conceptualisations~~ ones will ~~serve more than adequately~~ do just fine.

Habitual use of the passive tense where active is clearer or more direct; ~~this is to be avoided~~ try to avoid this.

Redundant words, e.g. ~~absolutely~~ unique or ~~carefully~~ scrutinise.

Multiple or nested subordinate clauses, which, while tempting, as things often are, can, if overused, become, to the casual listener, who may not give you more than partial attention, very confusing!

Long sentences—no need to give an example here, you know what I mean.

Jargon—any words or expressions whose meaning is understood by a restricted group when used outside that group or when used unnecessarily, including acronyms and Initialisms. There Is now an acronym EUUA, meaning excessive use of unnecessary acronyms! A good example of jargon-laden incomprehensibility is this sentence from a UK National Health Service Trust letter to a patient: "The criteria are embedded within an indication of needs matrix, encompassing the continuum of care needs." Eh?

Clichés, which in business might include "Going forward", "To your point", "Touch base", "Take this offline", "On the same page". You can probably think of many you encounter; do you use them yourself?

Euphemisms, which abound in society and bear deep thought as they can disguise unpleasantness and are often woolly and imprecise or even downright misleading (for example "Ministry of Defence", "correctional facility" or "collateral damage"). We all tend to use them where the right word seems too blunt, for example 'passed on' instead of died or 'restroom' instead of toilet, and I'm not suggesting losing that polite habit; however they can be disingenuous and it's worth reviewing your relationship with them. I remember a software giant where people weren't sacked, they were 'uninstalled'.

Some of these habits may translate into your speaking. If you have people in your life whom you trust to give you honest feedback, ask them if you are ever unclear, and even use the above as a checklist. Another approach is to record yourself on phone calls and listen back to your end of the conversation.

Be straight

In your notebook, list all your important relationships and speaking situations and mark yourself out of ten in each case for how straight you are. Do you say what you mean and mean what you say, or do you soften, disguise or even withhold your real message? Is mind-reading involved, in either direction?

Where you have a score less than seven, think carefully about the reasons. I am not advising you to abandon practices that may be keeping you safe in difficult relationships; if you have genuine cause to fear the consequences of straightness, please seek professional help. However, where the habit is all yours or you judge that the fear is disproportionate or inappropriate, take one relationship or situation at a time and set yourself a goal of straight talking. In some cases, you may even be able to share that this is what you're doing and inspire the other person or people to help you in your project.

A great starting point for increasing your clarity is to practice making clean requests. Instead of hinting, intimating, suggesting or simple wishing the other person would guess what you want, ask. The request might go something like this: "When you [do or don't do something], the effect on me is [I feel something or I have to do something]. My request is that you [do something different] in future. What do you say?"

AUTHENTICITY

It is possible to treat all speaking as a performance, either consciously or unconsciously. The desire to fit in, to be liked, or to be respected is a strong one in many people, and it can drive a chameleon-like approach to speaking where different personas come to the fore depending on the audience. I remember that my mother's accent and pronunciation varied significantly from the family version of her to the public version: we got the genuine, natural delivery, while strangers got a more refined, impressive version.

However, people can often feel the artifice of an assumed persona, and it can take a lot of effort to switch, particularly if there are several to move between. In my younger days I separated my contacts, presenting different versions of me to work colleagues, band members, friends, my family and so on. My new workmates secretly went through my address book and organised a surprise 30th birthday, inviting everyone. When the lights went up on what I thought was an empty office, the feeling of overwhelm was so intense I fell to my knees as I looked around and saw intermingled all these people I had conscientiously been keeping separate. Of course, I was touched and astonished, but there was also a sense of fear because my secret walls had all come down. Who was I to be?

The party was wonderful, and I learned a big lesson that night, later encapsulated by a phrase spoken to me by a wise friend: *stand in your own truth.*

To be authentic is to be yourself. That sounds simple, but it may not be. You may, like the young me, have several selves to choose from. Which is the real one? Even if that's not the case for you, the task does raise an important question, and one that not many people ponder: who am I?

The exercise below will help you to answer this question, making it easier for you to speak with authenticity. In my experience, authenticity rings true with listeners; fakery tends to be detectable unless a speaker is highly skilled at pretence (like great actors), or the adoption of a persona is deliberate and comes from a desire to serve others or to make a point, and not from self-regard.

I am not suggesting that you wash your dirty linen in public. If you have an argument with your spouse just before making a business presentation, it will not serve the listeners to hear about or see the results of your upset. With their best interests at heart, you will have to generate a different, more positive you if you are to make your speech effective. Your privacy is your decision: Steve Jobs gave many speeches in public without mentioning his fatal disease. This was not inauthentic; he was a very private person. Intimacy is being fully known, and few people decide to open themselves up for all the world. You can decide your own personal boundaries whilst retaining authenticity; there is a big difference between levels of an authentic self and assumed personas.

One great benefit of clarifying who you are is being able to introduce yourself clearly and succinctly. The exercise below also helps you to develop a powerful personal introduction, so that next time someone asks: "What do you do?" you can answer powerfully and confidently without the common fumbling ("Oh goodness, where do I start?" Or "Well, at the moment I'm...").

Exercise 1: Who are you?

We tend to take for granted that we are who we are, but without definition that concept can be rather woolly, and it changes over time as our experiences shape our personality. Here are some questions for you to ask yourself. When you settle on clear answers, you will have a much firmer concept of who you really are.

What are your values?
Use single, simple nouns here, and try not to go past four or five or it gets too hard to remember.

What are your skills/knowledge?
You may surprise yourself here. List everything you're good at, even if it's not anything to do with work.

What are you known for? What are you seen as?
Think what your friends or colleagues would say. I wonder if the public perception of you matches your own.

What is your visual image?
Do you have a style? Do you change it for different situations?

What is your commitment?
In other words, what, if anything, do you stand for in life?

What difference will you make? To whom?
Do you have a mission in life, and if so whom will it affect and how?

Exercise 2: Your elevator introduction

The aim is to write a 30-second personal introduction that you learn and can recite instantly when the need arises. You may create more than one if you really do have a hybrid life. In most cases, this will be about what you do for work, so let's focus on that.

By way of example, mine is:
I'm a sound consultant, international speaker and author. I have helped hundreds of brands and organisations to make effective, healthy sound, and millions of people to speak and listen better.

My passion is to make the world sound beautiful.

You can sculpt your own powerful personal introduction by answering three questions.

What? What are you? Your title, or a short description. Make it as simple and pared down as possible. If your job title is long and involved, summarise it. If you have two or three significant roles, that's fine. Check TED.com to see how speakers are described for some inspiration.

Who? Who gains (or have gained) from your work and what do they gain (or have they gained)? Be as specific as possible about this, whilst keeping it as simple and short as possible.

Why? What's your driving force? Your motivation? Your passion? The difference you want to make in the world?

Write the answers, then speak them. Edit, refine and rework until they are like diamonds, brilliant, clear and compressed. Try the whole thing out to the mirror, then to friends who know you well and will give you honest feedback. (They may gain from this too by deciding to do their own!) When you are happy, learn it by rote and practice so that it rolls out naturally whenever needed. It must never sound forced, laboured or scripted, which becomes easy when you really inhabit it and remember that this is you, and your genuine passion.

INTEGRITY

My definition of integrity is this: be your word. If you say it and it happens, your words have weight. I remember once visiting the abandoned city of Fatehpur Sikri, the one-time capital of the Mogul emperors. At one point in the tour, you get the chance to sit in the seat once occupied by the all-powerful ruler. It's a strange sensation to reflect that, a few hundred years ago, the person in that seat had absolute authority: what he said is what always transpired, whether that was a boon or a horrible death.

A relatively small number of people have had such authority in the world's history, and I am not in any way advocating autocratic leadership for you or me! Nevertheless, within our own lives we do have domain over one important thing: our own actions. If your actions back up your words, people will listen to you with respect and seriousness. If, on the other hand, your words, once spoken, evaporate like puddles in the sunshine and the action fails to happen, then people will learn to discount your speaking and pay your promises scant attention.

If you break your integrity, remember the tip from the seven deadly sins about excuses: simply apologise and explain what you are putting in place to make sure that never happens again. Your integrity will be repaired and maintained if you adopt this practice in all your affairs.

Exercise: Conscious agreements

I have come to believe that integrity is closely bound with a practice of making conscious agreements in relationships.

You can make agreements at work, for example defining etiquette for meetings (being on time, not using mobile devices while someone is speaking and so on) or for the open plan office (for example, not shouting across people's desks or not having loud conversations behind people when they are working). You can make agreements at home, for example dividing up chores (I'll do the clothes washing and drying if you put them all away) or the give and take of social life (I'll go to your work dinners if you come to my club socials). Agreements can be proactive, defining boundaries and responsibilities in advance, or they can be reactive, solving problems as they arise, whether short-term or long-term.

It's a powerful, effective and healing thing to align with someone and agree on a solution to something that has become a problem for one or both of you. If the debate has become heated, it may take a time-out to get to the negotiating table at all... so the first agreement might be to have a code for time-outs that both people agree to respect, whatever happens.

Unless both people have exceptional memories, I also suggest that you record agreements in a book or an app of some kind, and review them weekly to keep them fresh and ensure that one or both parties don't simply forget them. Try to keep the list of agreements short so that it doesn't turn into a piece of legislation, pedantically defining every small piece of behaviour. With luck, the next section on the L of HAIL will help you to avoid having to write agreements for things that are best left to happen naturally, like being kind or thoughtful. Try also to avoid becoming litigious and punctilious: it's not a recipe for success for one party to become a frequent judge, jury and executioner, which is of course being right and making the other party wrong.

This practice will take time to work, as people will tend to forget at first. With time and diligent review, and with goodwill on both sides, conscious agreements can make even the most fractious relationship work by injecting integrity.

LOVE

People are often surprised by the L of HAIL. What, they ask me, has love to do with effective communication?

First let's clarify the kind of love we are discussing here. It's not romantic love ("I love you"), the love of friends or family, or self-identifying love ("I love golf"). Rather I am suggesting you focus on what Buddhists call loving-kindness, and Christians call *agape*: a non-specific, non-possessive feeling that I think is best summed up thus: **wish them well**.

If your speaking comes from well-wishing love, then honesty, authenticity and integrity flow much more naturally. At the same time, love can shape the other three cornerstones, for example tempering the tendency to be brutally honest when that is not in the other person's best interest. If you are genuinely wishing someone well, your speaking (and your listening) will tend to be in tune, building rapport and creating connection—very different from speaking out of self-interest or desire to manipulate, dominate or even harm, in which circumstance honesty will be compromised, authenticity absent and integrity challenged or destroyed.

Whenever you are on a stage or platform, or speaking to a group, remember: **it's not about you**. I can generally spot a speaker who is self-absorbed and in the business of seeking approval or affirmation, and I think most other people can too: the speaking feels somehow contrived, artificial, thin, performed. You are there to give something to your listeners or your audience: it might be the growth you can provoke or promote; the joy, inspiration or delight you can inspire; or the new information or perspective you can transmit. If you focus on the gift you are giving to people you genuinely feel kindly toward, they will listen with much more natural attention and warmth.

Exercise: Bless you

I was taught this exercise many years ago by a wise old friend named Charlie. I was bemoaning someone being in my way and Charlie put his hand on my arm. "You know, resentment is like drinking poison and expecting the other person to die," he said. "If you go through life silently blaming, judging and condemning other people, your insides will be a mess. Why don't you try this instead: think 'Bless you' towards everyone you meet."

I tried it, and the results were remarkable. Consciously wishing people well in my head changed my posture, my demeanour and my experience of life. Instead of skulking around full of negative emotion, I felt taller, lighter and happier: it was like walking on air. Instead of avoiding eye contact because I'd been thinking something bad about them and feared they would see it, I was happy to meet people's gaze—and mutual smiles sometimes even broke out!

I commend the exercise to you. You can choose whatever phrase works for you and your convictions: 'Bless you' is very simple; 'I wish you well' is equally clear and genuine. The important things are to do this in your head, not out loud; to do it to everyone you meet; and to mean it from your heart—this is not to be confused with a polite but rather empty social nicety such as 'Have a nice day'.

With practice this can become a habit and I believe you will find it one of the best you've ever developed. In my experience, loving and judging are mutually exclusive. Practicing this exercise can exorcise the habit of being judgmental, which can lift a great weight.

SPEAKING INTO

In Chapter Three, we distinguished the concept of a created listening, and noted that each one is partly fashioned by our own actions, and partly by the filters of the listener(s).

It is possible to spot the listening and thus adapt your speaking to make sure that you hit the target every time.

I realised this many years ago, when I was regularly pitching for new business for my magazine publishing company. I gradually became aware that I could very quickly spot who was positively disposed, and who was not, in a group of strangers around a meeting room table, even before they had spoken.

I puzzled over how this was possible, and read books on body language and nonverbal communication. There are countless small 'tells' in how people sit, where they look, fleeting facial expressions, gestures and head movements, vocal timbre, physical tics, pupil dilation and even breathing patterns. Today, I believe that you do not have to read up on all this in order to read the signs: I think most human beings can understand the compound message of all these small, subtle signs simply by *having the intention to do so*—in other words, by consciously paying attention.

The lesson from this is: **you always speak into a listening**. It may be an individual listening in a one-to-one conversation, or it may be a more complex group listening as you chat in a small social group, present to a team or a prospective client group, or even give a TED talk to 1,500 titans from leading edge businesses. If you reflect, you will find that you knew this intuitively before reading it here: you probably wouldn't speak the same way to your grandfather as to your best friend, because you instinctively know that the listening for you is different. Nevertheless, the power of consciously seeking the listening, and then consciously speaking into it is enormous.

I remember giving a talk once in the wonderful *Musiikkitalo* concert hall in Helsinki—a beautiful building with superb acoustics, thanks to the brilliant acoustician, Yasuhisa Toyota. Now, Finns are somewhat restrained, to put it mildly. At the end of my talk, there was a quiet ripple of polite applause. "They didn't much like that," I thought—until several people came up to me afterwards and (very quietly) said that it was the best talk they'd heard for a long time. I now understand the understated listening in Finland and adapt when I'm speaking there.

You also have the power to affect the listening you are speaking into. Your actions and words in the past may have created a listening for you in the people you are about to speak to. If this has developed and solidified over years, it will be hard to change. If they have never met you, your reputation may affect their expectations and intentions. If you are giving a talk, there may have been promotion or publicity beforehand. The way you appear from the very beginning, the way you speak, what you say, how you stand and move... all these will dynamically be affecting people's listening for you as you talk. We'll explore the secrets of the vocal toolbox and stagecraft in the next two chapters.

Exercise: Spotting the listening

If you have ever had the experience of feeling mortified after making an inappropriate comment, or increasingly desperate as you seem unable to get through, it was probably because you were speaking into the wrong listening.

This is a simple but immensely powerful exercise. In every conversation, presentation or speech, simply ask yourself: what's the listening? This works as well at home and in your family as it does on a platform or at work. People's listenings are not fixed, as we saw when we discussed the filters. Things like intentions, expectations and emotions vary from moment to moment, so even with someone you know very well this is a valuable exercise. As you practice asking yourself this question, it will become an unconscious habit and you will become more and more sensitive and able to listen to the listenings for you and around you.

By all means, read up on nonverbal communication, but I believe that most people are automatically equipped to decode the complex signals very well without knowing the theory and the intricacies; in some cases, all that knowledge can make things more difficult and get in the way of the natural skills we are born with. The trick is to make the effort consciously. In our tech-crazy world where sending into the ether (personal broadcasting) is so common, I think many people are losing this sensitivity. Nourish yours by starting this practice today.

SPEAKING FROM

You may be starting to feel that speaking is rather more complex than you used to think! There are many dynamics involved in that circular relationship with listening that we laid out right at the start of this book, and there are many ways to direct and shape your speaking. Here's another one: speaking *from*. Rather than simply being your natural self, you may decide that you want to stand in or for something specific, and speak from that place, concept or feeling.

This is particularly powerful if you are aiming to transform people's attitudes or perspectives, or move them to action, by engaging their emotions. In my professional life, I often encourage brands to be clear about their emotional message and deliver it congruently through all the senses, because research shows that we buy brands, products and services mainly emotionally, then we post-rationalise our purchases.

So, for example, speaking from a passion for justice can make a talk compelling and unforgettable. I was lucky enough to be in the room for Bryan Stevenson's extraordinary TED talk about the imbalances in the American justice system, which received the longest standing ovation I've ever seen at TED. His passion was infectious; he changed our listening and charged the room with fervour by speaking so resolutely and passionately from this one place.

In the same way, speaking from compassion or pity can make a charitable appeal much more powerful; speaking from affection can make a wedding speech charming, touching and delightful; and speaking from kindness and compassion is what makes the Dalai Lama so quotable.

Sadly, this works for the negative emotions too: speaking from hate, righteous anger or fear can be very powerful and infectious, as so many tragic victims of mob violence have found throughout history, and as we are still finding today in the radicalisation of young people by extremists.

Speaking from is powerful. Use it wisely and well.

PERFECT CONTENT

Standing in HAIL or speaking from a strong place are powerful constructs, but I can hear you wondering: "OK, but how do I decide what to say specifically?" Let's move on now to the practical side of deciding on your content.

Impact stems from delivering great content well, in the right place at the right time. Here's the equation:

Content + Delivery + Context = Impact

It's easy to forget context, but as we learned right at the beginning of this book, context can make or break verbal communication. We'll be unlocking the secrets of delivery in the next chapter; here we unpack the way to plan and structure great content.

I like the model of learning that moves through four levels. It starts at unconscious incompetence: we don't know what we don't know, like a two-year-old who has no idea she doesn't know how to drive. Later, the lack becomes known and the intention grows to learn; this is the level of conscious incompetence, where we do know what we don't know. The lessons are taken and the test is passed, so the new driver ventures out, gripping the wheel tightly with heart pounding, grimly determined to remember all those instructions. This is level three: conscious competence, where we can do it but only with real effort. Years go by and driving becomes instinctive, with complex vectors and multiple scenarios being processed in the brain at lightning speed while the driver is chatting, listening to the radio or planning lunch. This is the fourth level: unconscious competence.

When it comes to speaking and listening, I believe that most people are stuck at level one. If that's where you started, I hope you are now at level two and moving to level three as you practice the exercises in this book. Most people speak intuitively and informally, for which you can substitute in most instances unconsciously incompetently. If your experience is that people don't listen to you as you would like them to, I urge you to apply consciousness to your content planning, at least for a time. Start by becoming consciously competent and the ease will follow in time.

So, here are the tools for preparing excellent content, whether your challenge is asking someone to marry you, closing a big sale, requesting a pay rise, presenting to 500 people, or becoming socially charismatic.

INTENTIONS

It's impossible to plan a route if you don't know the destination. If you want to create effective content, the first step is to be clear on three sets of intentions.

Your intentions for you

What do you want to achieve? What will success look like, sound like, feel like? Be clear, specific and descriptive as you visualise it. If possible, write it down, in the present tense, including as much detail and sensory information as possible, like this: "It's 4:15 pm and we've just finished the big meeting. I presented really well and the clients agreed to all the proposals. They've signed the contract and left, happy and excited. My boss is still shaking my hand, the team have all congratulated me and I feel proud of myself and exhilarated as I enjoy a glass of cold champagne, with the bubbles tickling my nose."

Your intentions for them

Equally important, and often forgotten, what do you want to give? How will your audience feel, think, and be after you have spoken? You may want to touch, move and inspire them, or to educate, enlighten, or entertain them. Be clear and you will be much more effective.

Their intentions

Finally, try to put yourself in the shoes of the listeners and ask yourself: what are their intentions coming in? This will help you to be sensitive to the listening and to predict any concerns, doubts, fears or other obstacles that you may have to deal with.

THE BIG IDEA

The slogan of TED, the Holy Grail of speaking, is 'Ideas worth spreading', and for good reason. Ideas have been central to all human progress, whether giving rise to actions (making fire, farming, going to the Moon), to discoveries (gravity, electricity, relativity) or to concepts that work because we all agree to believe in them (paper money, democracy, laws).

Most effective movements, political parties and organisations work because they are clear about their central premise, otherwise known as the Big Idea (used in a strictly non-ironic way). BMW's is in their advertising tagline: "The ultimate driving machine." Apple's centres on simplicity, stated in an inspiring way: "We make technology so simple that everyone can be part of the future." Disney's is equally aspirational: "Where families share the magic."

Sadly, the information overload that's swamping you and me in the Internet age is potentially threatening the existence and propagation of new, rich ideas, because people, media and organisations are starting to value knowing things more than thinking about things. In the past, information was useful because it allowed us to create wisdom, knowledge and ideas. Now it seems to have become an end in itself, to be shared in endless merry-go-rounds of gossip and opinion on social media. Few profound ideas can be fully expressed in 140 characters.

Before you plan a speech, talk or conversation, I encourage you to ask yourself:

What's the Big Idea?

What, in a nutshell, am I trying get across? Aim to sum it up it in around 10 words, or even less if you can: crystallise the essence of what you are trying to say to ensure that your content has a clear, simple focus. When you have answered that question, ask the second:

So what?

This is the question old newspaper editors used to ask trainee journalists over and over again. Why should the audience care? I have cringed at speeches where the entire subject matter was effectively "I am a wonderful human being", featuring constant use of the word 'I', frequent exhortations to the audience to applaud yet another great achievement by the speaker, and absolutely zero value or relevance to the audience. You must give a gift! This second question is the key that will unlock that gift and ensure that your speaking has value to the listeners. Use it often.

4MAT

We now look at two content design systems that I think have value. Some people like one, some the other, and some neither. Please make up your own mind and take from these pages anything you feel is useful to you.

In 1979, Dr Bernice McCarthy synthesised 25 years of classroom teaching experience into a model of the way kids learn. She called it 4MAT and its modern, expanded version offers a powerful way to think about structuring content for all audiences.

4MAT suggests that there are four types of learner. Each has a favourite question.

1 (WHY)

Imaginative learners. They like feeling and watching and making connections; they seek personal associations, meaning and involvement.

2 (WHAT)

Analytic learners. They like listening to and thinking about information and formulating ideas; they seek facts, think through ideas, like to know what the experts say,

3 (HOW)

Common-sense learners, they like thinking and doing and applying ideas; they experiment, tinker, build and test.

4 (WHAT IF)

Dynamic learners, they like doing and feeling and creating original adaptations; they seek hidden possibilities, explore, and use trial and error.

Of course, most people are hybrids, but the research indicates that one type will tend to dominate. By making sure that you answer all four questions in your content, either explicitly or implicitly, you can increase your chances of engaging everyone in your talk.

THINK-FEEL-KNOW

In his 2013 book *Connect: Through Think Feel Know*, Clive Hyland argues that human beings process information in three levels, associated with the three main areas of the brain. A very simplified summary is below, again giving some sense of the different language and emphasis you might like to build into your speaking to make sure that you engage all sorts of people equally well.

Think

The cerebral cortex is the centre of thinking. People who operate primarily at this level are rational, and like to have details and numbers. Your weather forecast for a 'think' person might go along these lines:

the chance of rain tomorrow is 55% and the predicted maximum temperature is 14 degrees Centigrade, with gusts of 25 mph.

Feel

The limbic system in the centre of the brain is the engine of emotions and sensory information processing. People who operate primarily at this level are creative, emotive, and focus on relationships and sensations. Your weather forecast for a 'feel' person might be: it'll feel a bit chilly tomorrow in the wind, and you may get wet.

Know

The basal region of the brain is the oldest part, sometimes called the reptilian brain, and it deals with instinct and gut reactions. People who operate primarily at this level are intuitive, no-nonsense and action-oriented. Your weather forecast for a 'know' person would be: take an umbrella, sweater and jacket tomorrow.

BRAINSTORMING

I doubt this is a new concept to you, but you may never have applied it to what you say. It works particularly well when you are going to deliver a long or complex speech, or you have multiple concepts to communicate.

You may be a mind mapping aficionado, in which case that tool will be your preferred option. Start with the Big Idea and mind map all the nodes until you are happy you have a structure that works and covers everything.

The other option is to buy several pads of Post-It notes and find a large wall and start writing on the notes. Just write. Any concept, idea, word, issue, objection... absolutely anything that might be part of your talk.

Stick them all on the wall as you write them. When the writing stops, get a cup of coffee, stand back and take in the wall. Little by little, start to cluster the notes: you will spot key concepts or groups of notes that relate to each other. The process will gradually gather steam until you end up with a group of clusters. These are your core ideas. Photograph them for safety, then move them into the order that seems right to you, going from left to right across the wall. I usually favour going from the general to the specific, but there are no rules about this. You now have the horizontal (timeline) flow of your talk.

CHUNKING

*I always wanted to be somebody, but now
I realise that I should have been more specific.*

– Lily Tomlin

The body of work known as neuro-linguistic programming (NLP) has many passionate advocates and probably an equal number of detractors. As someone who loves language and communication, I studied it, and I found it contained some useful concepts. One of the best is chunking.

Chunking describes shifting focus upwards, downwards or sideways as you speak. Chunking up puts something in context, moving toward the bigger picture: landing gear is part of a plane; a plane is a method of transport and so on. Chunking down is getting more specific: the plane is a midrange type, specifically a Boeing 737. Chunking across is adding examples of the same type: flowers include daisies, roses and irises.

In planning your content, this concept may help you to consider the vertical dimension as well as the horizontal (timeline). Whilst moving through your talk from start to finish, try to make sure that you chunk up and down enough to engage the people who like the big picture (chunk up) and the little details (chunk down). There may also be times when you want to chunk across to add depth, for example in listing the benefits of your proposition or the examples that prove your point.

Conscious chunking on the fly can be a lifesaver if, for example, you spot that your audience's listening is largely 'know' or 'feel' and your presentation is full of facts. I have had conversations where I was interrupted 30 second into an elegant sales spiel that started with empathising and defining the client's problem with an impatient: "Just tell me what you're offering and how much!"

SAY, SAY, SAY

There's an old essayist's trick that is worth remembering when you're planning your content: say what you're going to say, say it, then say what you said. I used exactly that structure in my fourth TED talk which was called 'Why architects need to use their ears'. If you watch that talk, you'll see that I start by saying "It's time to start designing for the ears". I then explain why this is true, and finally close the talk by repeating the phrase I started with. Say, say, say. This can also help you to ensure that you end with a powerful summary of your whole talk, which is often a very potent and memorable close.

CLEAN LANGUAGE

I am a fan of clean language. This is not the practice of avoiding expletives (though I try to do that too) but another piece of NLP-related thinking that I think has serious value. It's a system of questioning developed by New Zealand-born psychologist David Grove in the 1980s. Intended for counselling sessions but potentially applicable just about anywhere with great benefits, clean language aims to eliminate as far as possible the questioner's metaphors, assumptions, paradigms and sensations (MAPS) to leave neutral questions that don't steer or influence the questionee.

Most of us unconsciously pad our language with our own stuff, imposing our world view, attempting to steer or control the other person's answers, or attempting mind-reading, for example: "Did you have the eggs and bacon for breakfast, or the fruit?"

The clean version of that question would be simply: "What did you have for breakfast?"

I think there is great mileage in being attentive to our language, stripping out the unconscious or conscious manipulations we so often deploy by rephrasing what someone said, asking leading questions, embedding assumptions or generalisations or invalidating the other's point of view. To me, clean language involves saying exactly what I mean, and asking without leading.

Exercise: speak cleanly

Here is a fascinating game to play with yourself: set your sights on 100 percent clean language: say exactly what you mean without injecting assumptions, generalisations, invalidations of the other or any form of manipulation or attempt at controlling the answer to any question.

Spot the number of times you fall short each hour. Don't get annoyed when you do: there will be many! Nevertheless, the intention is the main thing and if you continue the practice you will find the fail rate drops off as you get more sensitive to the technique.

Beware: when you get good at this, it becomes very easy to set yourself up in judgement of others. Remember, they are not playing the game!

REQUESTS

Along with conscious agreements, I believe that conscious requests are important elements of any relationship, whether at home or at work.

There are two elements to a conscious request: the request itself, and the response, which may take any one of three forms. *It is critical that the requester is prepared to accept all three responses, or the request ceases to be a request and becomes a demand.* That way lies a world of pain.

The request must be made in a calm, measured fashion, focusing on the change that's wanted and the positive outcome that will arise from it. So, for example: "My request is that you put your dirty clothes in the laundry basket and not on the floor, so that I don't have to pick them up myself." Or: "I request that you turn down the music you play at your desk so that I can concentrate on my work."

The three possible responses are: "I agree," "I refuse," and "I'll think about it," or words to those effects.

In the event of the second response, there may be a counter-offer from the person receiving the request (in the second example, this might be "OK I'll turn it down in the mornings but I need it in the afternoons to be creative.") or a negotiation ("I'll turn the music down if you'll stop letting your papers expand onto my desk.") Nevertheless, it is important that the requester is prepared to accept a negative answer or the request will not be a clean one.

In the event of the third response, a time limit for the thinking must be agreed to by both parties so that it doesn't become a *de facto* refusal.

Clearly such a system needs an agreement between all parties if it is to work well, so you might want to re-read the section on Integrity earlier in this chapter. Agreements and requests go hand in hand and form the backbone of a conscious relationship. One aspect of the agreement between parties that sets up the request system may be that, if negotiation fails after a negative answer to a request, then both parties undertake to accept arbitration of some kind from a pre-defined third party.

This may all sound a little legalistic, but agreeing to make and receive clean requests is a wonderful way to make sure that communication is clear and explicit in any relationship, and that needs are expressed and met, not suppressed.

STORYTELLING

Sir Ken Robinson's wonderful 2006 TED talk is the most watched of all time for good reason. Not only does it encapsulate an insightful Big Idea that changes the viewer's perspective instantly; it also contains one great story after another, all told with Sir Ken's irresistible charm and wit. Here is the transcript from the TED website of my favourite of his stories, which is very short and very funny:

> I heard a great story recently — I love telling it — of a little girl who was in a drawing lesson. She was six, and she was at the back, drawing, and the teacher said this girl hardly ever paid attention, and in this drawing lesson, she did. The teacher was

fascinated. She went over to her, and she said, "What are you drawing?" And the girl said, "I'm drawing a picture of God." And the teacher said, "But nobody knows what God looks like." And the girl said, "They will in a minute."

This story, which takes about 20 seconds to tell, delivers an important part of Sir Ken's message—that children are born with plenty of naive, self-confident creativity but that our education system crushes it out of them. Humourous stories like this one can be an excellent way to illustrate or communicate important points, so long as the humour is natural, not forced, and you are comfortable with being funny.

Human stories, particularly ones from your own experience, can act as powerful metaphors or concrete examples of your points, making your arguments or ideas easier for people to understand than if they were simply expressed as abstracts. I had the pleasure of collaborating with the internationally acclaimed author and storyteller Jon Ronson on his 2012 TED talk 'Strange answers to the psychopath test'. I commissioned and then played all the musical samples and sound effects during this talk, while my friend Evan Grant did the same with some powerful visual animations. It was a new and captivating form of fireside tale, where sound and vision enhanced Jon's storytelling to spellbinding effect. It was made all the more powerful by the fact that every word was true and had really happened.

Jon is an expert storyteller, so I interviewed him to discover what he believes the secrets of effective storytelling are. Check the panel for an excerpt from the interview and instructions on accessing the full interview in audio and written form online.

Stories don't have to come from your own life, as Sir Ken's example above shows. You can appropriate them from friends, books or myths and legends, or you can make them up from scratch.

There are certain storylines that clearly resonate with all human beings. Researchers from the University of Vermont and the University of Adelaide used sophisticated software to generate 'emotional arcs' for 1,737 works of fiction. The computer was looking for the frequency of words ranked as happy (the top 10 were laughter, happiness, love, happy, laughed, laugh, laughing, excellent, laughs, and joy) and unhappy (top 10: terrorist, suicide, rape, terrorism, murder, death, cancer, killed, kill, and die). When they analysed the data, they found they could classify six archetypical story arcs:

1. Rags to Riches (rise)

2. Riches to Rags (fall)

3. Man in a Hole (fall then rise)

4. Icarus (rise then fall)

5. Cinderella (rise then fall then rise)

6. Oedipus (fall then rise then fall)

'Rags to Riches' accounted for one fifth of all the books, but the most popular with readers (as measured by downloads from Project Gutenberg) were 'Oedipus', 'Man in a Hole' and 'Cinderella'.

Many books nest several of these archetypes together to create more complex arcs, but if you're seeking a storytelling framework to hang your own stories on, the simple archetypes form a useful starting point. Inspirational stories need to end with a rise; cautionary tales may end with a fall.

In sum, if you want to seize and hold people's attention, become a good storyteller.

Tip: You can use a story to prove a point or as an illustrative metaphor. Where possible, use stories from your own life: it feels authentic and gives your listeners an extra connection with you. Stories don't have to be long or complicated. The story I told on the TED stage about my mother, illustrating one of the seven deadly sins, was true, took only a few seconds to relate and illustrated the point very powerfully.

Storytelling: Jon Ronson

This is an excerpt from the transcript of a conversation with Jon Ronson. For the full transcript, and the audio recording, visit www.howtobeheardbook.com and use the password **conscious.**

Jon Ronson is an award-winning writer and documentary maker. He is the author of many bestselling books, including *Frank: The True Story that Inspired the Movie, Lost at Sea: The Jon Ronson Mysteries, The Psychopath Test, The Men Who Stare at Goats* and *Them: Adventures with Extremists.* His first fictional screenplay, *Frank,* co-written with Peter Straughan, starred Michael Fassbender. He lives in London and New York City. In the US, he is a contributor to National Public Radio's *All Things Considered* and *This American Life.*

Julian Treasure: What makes a great story?

Jon Ronson: Ira Glass who does *This American Life* always talks about his anecdotes as being great stories. You know, I got out of bed, and I opened the door, and I walked down the corridor. You can hook people that way, just in a kind of unfolding anecdote, you know it's going to lead somewhere and even if it doesn't, you still kind of feel intense.

Julian Treasure: Because you want to know what's coming next, I guess.

Jon Ronson: Sometimes it's just as simple as that. I'm sort of thinking about the process of writing and for me the process of writing is not easy. Nothing comes easy. I will never agree to do something where I have to deliver a piece of writing within like a day or a couple of days. It takes me a long, long time to get a story right. So what am I doing during that long period of time? I suppose the main thing I'm doing is structuring a story so that the narrative comes first but then the nuances and the meaning and everything else just sort of drifts gently out of the narrative.

Julian Treasure: So ultimately there's a point to make, there's a kind of arc of the whole story, which goes to a point, like a metaphor or something like that?

Jon Ronson: Yeah but it doesn't necessarily come in that order. Sometimes it just starts with me wanting to solve a mystery. You know what? Actually Julian, I would say pretty much all the time that's how it starts. There's something about the world that I don't understand and it's mysterious to me and I want to try and solve that mystery. I think every story I do starts with that. There's other writers, like you for instance Julian, I would say is somebody who has their kind of topic that they're expert in and they find different ways of exploring that same topic over and over again. You did that with sound, right?

Julian Treasure: Yes.

Jon Ronson: Then you know, the writer Ben Goldacre who's a doctor, he'll do it with medicine and pseudo-science. He'll take the same topic over and over again. I can't do that for some reason, I think the reason is that when I embark on a journey, I need to have to answer a question that I don't know the answer to, that's like the wind behind my sails.

Julian Treasure: That's a great tip for anybody starting a story, isn't it? To pose a question that's going to engage people, and then to discover the answer. I guess discovery, a process of finding out what's next and what's the answer and what's true, that's all part of the engagement of the story.

Jon Ronson: Yeah and it's got to be authentic. I can't pose a pretend question to myself, which I kind of secretly do know the answer to. The answer will show through and the reader will see that I'm trying to cheat them. So it has to be a real mystery. I guess, you know, once in a while, it hasn't happened that often but it's happened a couple of times in my life that I've thought if I go on this journey, I have no idea what's going to happen, but I know it's going to be interesting, it's going to be strange and mysterious and exciting and it will tell us something about the way the world works... I think the most important thing is to tell a story about something that you're passionate about, whether that means something from your own life or whether it's, like with me, a mystery that you really passionately want to solve. I think enthusiasm and passion is the most important thing by far.

Julian Treasure: You've brought up three words in my mind that really combine to create great story, which are respect for the subject matter and for the audience, curiosity, which you always have and passion. It sounds to me, if you can mould those three things into a story, you're onto a winner.

SPEAKING AIDS

In formal speaking, whether it's on a stage, a platform or in a conference room, you will almost certainly want to prepare what you say. Very few people have the skill to stand up and deliver a brilliant speech off the cuff; most of us need to know what we're going to say, which means planning and structure. But having a clear 'right' version of a speech immediately raises the spectre of doing it 'wrong', which is where most people's fear of public speaking comes from—in particular, the fear that one will forget one's lines.

Some people can deliver a great speech from memory, and we will review techniques for doing this at the end of this section. However, this is a high-risk strategy because there is no backup plan: if the memory fails, or a link in the chain is broken, the worst case scenario immediately ensues.

By way of reassurance, I have seen this happen to too many people over the years, and it's never as bad as the fear would have you believe. Even on the TED stage, people dry up and get stuck sometimes. You never see it on the website because the kind TED editors simply cut out those parts and make the speech look as seamless and polished as possible. What happens live is always the same thing. The speaker stops, becomes flustered, shows physical signs of stress and embarrassment, and then stutters an apology. The audience, far from being the feared stern-faced bank of judges, inevitably breaks out into a sympathetic and encouraging round of applause while the speaker regathers and finds the next link in their chain. It's rare that you will be in front of a genuinely hostile audience, unless you practice stand-up comedy or get involved in politics. People are generally kind and they usually want to hear what you have to say.

Nevertheless, drying on stage is not a pleasant experience, so let's examine some aids that may help you to stay in contact with your material, or to amplify your message with congruent visuals.

SCRIPT

In his TED talk on texting, John McWhorter makes a very illuminating distinction between spoken and written language and the actual practices of speaking and writing.

Obviously, we can speak spoken language and read written language. It becomes more interesting when we consider the cross-fertilisation of the language and the delivery methods. It is now possible to write speaking: this is what texting is, and why it has few rules. It is also possible to speak writing, as people used to do in the days before video, Twitter and soundbites, and to some extent still do today. Speeches were carefully written and then read out verbatim, and people would patiently sit for hours and listen as the speaker read out the writing. When done well, this can be very powerful. I saw Bono give his TED talk about world poverty in Long Beach in 2013. I was sitting very near the stage, and he was standing on a spur out into the audience, so I had to turn around and look at his back. What I could see, but most of the audience could not, was the big screen right at the back of the hall that was showing his speech on a teleprompter, word for word. His skill as a speaker was such that you would never know he was reading every word of the speech. Watch it on video and you will see how this can be done by an expert. Contrast this with a speech at the same TED conference that really disappointed me. I love Jared Diamond's book *Guns, Germs and Steel*, and was eagerly anticipating his talk. But a lectern was brought out (very rare at TED) and he stood behind it and read the talk from pieces of paper. As a result, it felt lifeless, static, fixed and far from engaging or inspiring.

For most people, reading writing usually sounds very different from speaking: writing has grammar, syntax, capital letters and punctuation—none of which we really think about when we're speaking, typically in successions of disjointed, uncompleted sentences with little or no formal structure. We have all sat and suffered as someone stiffly and awkwardly reads every word of a scripted speech, gripping a lectern and looking down almost the whole time. With no lectern, holding sheets of paper has a further disadvantage in that the paper amplifies any nervous tremors in your hands, making the shakes plain for all to see.

In general, then, I advise against reading a scripted piece of writing unless you really are an expert and you can use a professional autocue with a clear panel in front of you or a screen behind the audience, so that you can look at the people you are speaking to, rather than down at your material.

CUE CARDS

Hand-held cue cards can give you all the security of a script and yet allow you to speak naturally and maintain eye contact with audience almost all the time. They contain bullet points so that you know where you are and what's coming next, but when you start speaking, the words flow and seem authentic because you are generating them in the moment. For that reason, they are frequently used by professionals in many environments: you will often see them used by TV compères or interviewers, or MCs at major ceremonies. A great example from TED is Alain de Botton's brilliant 2009 talk on success and failure, for which he used just a few small cue cards.

Typically cue cards are simply standard index cards, though if you have a sizeable budget you can get them printed with a logo on the back for the audience to see. Use one side only. Write one heading on each card in large letters. If your handwriting is not crystal clear, it's best to use capitals; it's risky to assume the lighting will be perfect when you speak. Add any key bullet points that will help you remember all the points under this topic.

Cue cards can contain a lot more than the outline of your talk in bullet form. You can use colour codes, write yourself little stage directions and cues so that you remember any theatrics, emphasis the important things, and give yourself reminders to counter your stylistic weaknesses.

In the example shown, the speaker tends to look very serious and gabble at pace, so every cue card has the instructions to slow down and smile. On this particular card, there is a significant moment that requires pausing for effect and then punching the air, so the stage directions are there.

Slow down!

Cue cards

One chunk of content per card

One side only

Large font, CAPS CAN HELP

Cues too

Pause for effect

Punch the air   Smile!

If you prefer technology to old fashioned pens and cards, you can find apps that will turn your phone or tablet into a cue card deck.

SLIDES

This is my preferred aid. I've spoken with slides ever since the days of acetates and overhead projectors, and I embraced Microsoft PowerPoint and then Apple Keynote as they arrived to make more and more possible. Now there are numerous alternatives, from free packages that do a basic job, often perfectly well, to sophisticated tools like Prezi, where you create a large canvas and zoom about.

Whatever you choose, I can offer you some guidelines for using slides.

First, don't start with them. Use the techniques described earlier in this chapter to create your content, and design the slides when you know what you want to say. You can then think of them as enhancers, not the meat of the talk. The main course is you speaking, not what's on the screen.

Please avoid creating slides with bullet points or, even worse, all the words you are about to say. This is a very old fashioned technique and it has gone out of fashion for two very good reasons. First, the moment you show such a slide, people read ahead much faster than you can talk so that by the time you get to the bottom, they are faced with the spectacle of someone reading out what they already know. The speaker is redundant for much of the talk if this is the process! Second, this system tempts the speaker to turn around and start reading off the screen, presenting his or her back to the audience and almost becoming an audience member in the process. In my opinion, turning your back on the audience is simply rude.

I believe in using powerful images to amplify what I'm saying, or to create harmonics that give added richness to the words. I might add one word per slide, and then I use presenter notes to remind me if there's something significant I really want to remember to say on that topic. I get all my images from iStock (by Getty Images) or Shutterstock, paying for appropriate licences in each case, and crediting them either on each slide or at the start or finish. The search engines in both these massive collections of millions of images are excellent, and it's fun to see what engaging or even startling images you can find to illustrate your point. Simple, powerful images generally work best.

For inspiration in creating your own beautiful, powerful slides, I strongly recommend Garr Reynolds's terrific book *Presentation Zen*; there is also a website of the same name that contains many examples of powerful slide-based presentations. Reynolds makes a very important distinction between slides, which are designed to illustrate a talk, and a lead-behind, which may contain the whole presentation in written form with plenty of detail and references. The attempt to merge the two is what he dubs a 'slideument'—a nasty hybrid that does neither one thing nor the other. I used to get frequent requests to send my slides before speaking so that the organiser could produce a leave-behind. I always declined, explaining that my slides were simply pictures, maybe with one word on each, so the slides only made sense with my embedded sounds playing and me talking. I'm glad to say that those requests have ceased, so maybe we can draw a veil over the age of the bullet slide.

Aim to give your slides an identity—some styling that's consistent. I do this by using a single font family, Berthold Akzidenz Grotesk, mainly in Super weight. You might choose to use a consistent style of picture or illustration, or colour palette, or colour or texture of background.

Try not to get too word-heavy on the screen. The words need to come from your mouth, not your slides. Ideally the slides will support, express, amplify and extend what you say, adding impact and memorable moments. Avoid the flashier transitions; choose one or two that suit you and use them consistently. I tend to use a cube transition for a new topic, and a subtle dissolve transition when inside that topic.

There will be more to say about technology in Chapter Seven, where we explore the arcane world of stagecraft.

FLIP CHARTS

I still see these in meeting rooms, so let me give you some brief tips for using them effectively.

Always use large block capitals. Practice, so that you can write clearly—and horizontally. It's strange but true that almost everyone who is unpracticed in using flip charts creates lines of text that tail down as they go from left to right on the sheet, which is not a good look.

You can use colours to indicate different types of content, such as key points to remember, actions, quotes from the audience, or graphic illustrations.

Don't talk while you write, again because that would mean speaking with your back to the audience. Talk, then turn and write in silence, then turn and talk, and so on.

A very good use of flip charts on longer sessions like major trainings lasting one or more days is to post the charts around the walls at the end of each session or day, and then have people review them as they come in for the next. It's good use of the early part of the 1111 technique for improving recall: review the material after one hour, one day, one week and one month and you will make the neural pathways much more solid, improving your recall dramatically.

MEMORY

I would never dare to embark on a long talk using just my memory, because I know all too well how fallible it can be. However, there are people who can do that brilliantly. Most of them use permanent hooks onto which they hang the structure of the talk and any key facts. These hooks may be a set of learned words, or they may take the form of a device called a memory palace—an imaginary building that you construct and visualise vividly and repeatedly until it's fixed in your mind, with all its rooms and a route you always take through them. The trick is then to associate the topics and facts you want to remember with the rooms or with items in the rooms. For example, if you wanted to speak this section of this book, you might visualise the front door as a script, then the tiles of the hallway as cue cards, then the TV in the living room showing slides, and so on.

There are many books on using your memory like this. I would simply caution that you must be sure and practiced before taking this course. Actors develop the ability to memorise lines for plays, and it may be that this tool is the natural one for you. But please use a foolproof system like a memory palace because if you try to memorise a long chain of content and you lose a link, you will be cast adrift and find yourself floundering in public.

By way of reassurance, as already noted, I have seen this happen several times, and the response is always the same: the audience starts clapping in an encouraging way, and the person eventually gets back on track. We'll discuss having backup plans in the final chapter of this book. Using memory is an ideal candidate for having a backup, just in case.

PRACTICE

If you have to speak to a group or on a stage, especially if this is going to happen more than once, my number one piece of advice is to practice the skill of public speaking. I'm not surprised that so many people fear the microphone and the stage. I would be extremely nervous if asked to bungee jump or ski a diamond run, simply because I have never done it and I lack the experience, the knowledge, and the tricks of the trade to make sure it will go well. The idea of it not going well is scary indeed in both these cases!

I've always liked the famous comment attributed to the extraordinary golfer Gary Player, a man of iron will and titanic discipline who was still doing 1,300 sit ups a day at the age of 80. He holed a shot out of a bunker, and a spectator said: "That was lucky!" Player rejoined: "The more I practice, the luckier I get!"

Just as with any skill, the more you speak in public, the better you will be at it, and the more confident you will feel. If this is something you need to do in your life, take it seriously and devote some time and energy to practicing.

There are many opportunities to do this: Toastmasters, for one. This is a global organisation whose sole purpose is to help people develop speaking skills; it has a process, and mentors to take you through the various stages in their system. In any major city, you will probably fine multiple groups you can try. Toastmasters is a superb resource, and a great way of meeting interesting, like-minded people while you develop your public speaking skills. My only slight quibble with the organisation is that I find their finished product just a little too close to a performance, where virtuosity displaces authenticity. Nevertheless, there is nothing wrong with learning to be a virtuoso, because you can then give a talk that's brilliantly delivered as well as authentic and from the heart.

If Toastmasters isn't for you, then you could try local 'meet up' groups, readily findable with a quick web search on 'public speaking meet up'. In many cities, there will be such groups of people who are keen to practice public speaking among themselves—less structured than Toastmasters but probably just as committed. Or you could rally some friends who also want to learn public speaking, and create your own group, coaching one another and forming a ready-made audience for regular sessions.

Practice may not make perfect, but it will absolutely create radical improvement and bring those nerves under control, even to the point where you can start to enjoy the whole experience. This is all even more valid when you have a coach, which is our last topic in this chapter on great content.

COACHING

Every world champion has a coach. There is one simple reason for this: you cannot see you own game. These people become champions because of their dedication to the principle that improvement is the point: there is no destination for them, just an endless pursuit of that extra one percent. They achieve continuous improvement with the help of coaches—people who can see what might be possible to improve, and who can devise programmes and exercises to deliver it.

If you are serious about public speaking, you might consider seeking out a professional coach, whether a specialist in platform skills or a drama or singing coach to work with your voice—a subject we'll be turning to in the next few pages. But you can also get great results by making an agreement to coach in a pair. You can give each other sandwich feedback, which involves praise, criticism and praise. The praise is the bread; the criticism the meat in the sandwich. So, the first element will pick out something that was well done; the second might be positively expressed as: "What you could work on is…", or "Your stretch might be…"; the final element is a positive summary, emphasising another good aspect.

If you can't find anyone to coach you, don't despair: you can coach yourself up to a point by using a recording. Make a little analogue of a stage or theatre in your home: maybe the couch is the audience and the TV behind you your screen. Set up a video camera and record yourself speaking. As you watch back, you will be able to see any little issues you might want to fix and get a really good 'third party' perspective on your content and delivery. Take notes and work on one thing at a time. Compare your content, structure and delivery to master speakers, from TED and elsewhere. Be brutally honest with yourself and you will improve.

Chapter Six

Your vocal toolbox

The medium is the message

– Marshall McLuhan

People often ask me which is more important—great content, or great delivery? Some scriptwriters and speaking coaches place content ahead of delivery, asserting that brilliant material will survive poor delivery, while even the best delivery will not keep people engaged in poor content. Others say the exact opposite!

If I were forced to choose between the two, I agree with TED curator Chris Anderson who says in my interview with him: "The only rule that we're absolutely insistent on is that someone has something worth saying. Without that you can have all the performance in the world and it's not only worthless; it's deeply annoying."

Nevertheless, it's better to have both! I believe that content and delivery are two of the three legs on which powerful communication rests: any memorable speech must have both. The third, equally important leg is you—your authentic personality, your honesty, integrity and love all combining to make you a generator of great content *and* great delivery.

In the last chapter, we investigated what to say in detail, so I hope you now have plenty of tools to plan and structure superb content. Now, let's consider the way that you say it—not just in public speaking but in everything you say, all the time. We're going to do that by opening your vocal toolbox, something that most people don't know they have.

The human voice is an amazing, complex instrument—the one instrument that we all play. Sadly, not many people take lessons or practice the skill of speaking: there are relatively few virtuosi of the voice. This has surely been exacerbated by the culture of celebrity. We set singers and actors on pedestals, convince ourselves that they are special, and believe that we could never be like them. Have you ever said (or heard said) "I can't sing"? If you said that in any tribal society, today or throughout human history, people would look at you very strangely and say: "But everyone sings!" Only recently have we delegated singing to specialists and resigned from it en masse, sentencing our voices to express only a fraction of their true power.

This is not a book about singing, but I do recommend that you try taking some singing lessons or join a vocal or choral group. Not only will you become more conscious of your voice and its potential, but also you might surprise yourself and love it. My brother, completely musically untutored, joined a community choir here in Orkney some years ago and now sings great choral pieces like Handel's *Messiah* in impressive venues with world-renowned orchestras and conductors. Singing has become a great source of joy and passion for him; maybe it will for you, too. And don't forget the research showing that human beings gain many health and emotional benefits from making music— possibly including growing fresh neurons, given the recent research on musical training and brain development.

Whether you sing or not, it is possible to develop your speaking voice and become a master of this wonderful instrument. That is the subject of this chapter.

Exercise: Your vocal inventory

Before we start rummaging in your vocal toolbox, I suggest that you take a step back and review your current vocal assets and liabilities by taking a dispassionate inventory. What are the strengths of your voice? And what are the weaknesses? In order to get clear and complete in this exercise, try recording yourself speaking in various ways. You may have different ways of speaking for specific situations (for example, my mother had a very well-defined telephone voice which she would never use in face to face conversation) and the sound of your voice will be greatly affected by your emotional state.

You can record yourself at fair quality on most smartphones with built-in voice memo apps; or, for better quality and more features like transcribing to text or sharing with other apps, you can get a specialist app like Just Press Record (iOS) or RecForge (Android); or if you have an interest in recording high quality audio you can get a digital audio recorder like a Zoom—I still use an old Zoom H2 for its great combination of quality and simplicity.

Once you have a range of recordings of yourself speaking, listen back on good headphones, taking notes in the two columns (one for your vocal assets, one for liabilities). You can also ask friends or family members to help you by giving you their feedback in those two columns. This will help you to identify what it is that you want to work on to move your voice up to where you would like it to be.

POSTURE, STANCE AND GESTURES

Posture

Your voice starts with your posture, especially the angle of your neck, because your vocal cords are physically altered when you move your head forward, backward or side to side. In order to understand the profound way your voice changes with neck angle, try this simple experiment: sit or stand up straight and say your name. Now extend your chin forward as far as you can, stretching your neck out like a tortoise and say your name again. Can you hear the strain as you stretch your vocal cords? Now, without looking down, move your head back so your chin is tucked in and you are pressing the back of your head as far back as you can, and say your name again. Do you hear the compression as you squash your vocal cords?

These postures are but extreme versions of things most people do every day. Sitting at a desk and stretching the neck forward while speaking on the phone is a milder version of that first posture you just assumed. And we spend so much time looking down at screens and mobile devices that 'text neck' (a milder version of the second posture) is becoming an epidemic. With repetition, these postures become habitual and then physically embedded, and the natural voice becomes strained or compressed.

If your head is vertically above your shoulders, your vocal cords are relaxed and fully functional and your voice can give of its best. The first exercise below will help you to achieve this ideal neck posture.

Now let's consider the rest of your posture. Body language is very articulate, and yours will affect the way you are received when you speak. Your stance or sitting position speak volumes about how you are being in a conversation; in front of a group or on a stage, it communicates your state and attitude to the audience, and can also be distracting if it's unusual or beset by unnecessary movement. In general (and this is very general), leaning forward and maintaining eye contact (intermittently when speaking, more constantly when listening) indicate engagement; leaning back and avoiding eye contact indicate disengagement, or even boredom, anger or disdain. At the same time, postures that make your body smaller (such as crossing your arms or legs, hunching, stooping or drawing limbs in) indicate lack of power or certainty; postures that make you larger, colloquially known as power poses (such as raising both arms in triumphant pose), speak of strength and confidence.

Body language is important not only for what it communicates to others: it also affects how you feel and speak. It is a rare individual indeed who can delivery powerfully when supine, or slumped in a low-power posture. Following Amy Cuddy's TED talk, research by dozens of labs has confirmed that power poses do make people feel stronger and more confident.

Stance

If you need to speak in front of an audience, I suggest that you develop a neutral stance that can act as your home base. This is your castle, the place from which you can sally forth gloriously with expansive movement or gestures, and to which you safely return every time; a solid, impressive foundation that looks and feels powerful and established. Many times after speaking, I have been told: "You look so grounded!" That is all due to my neutral stance. It took time for me to develop and establish it; the exercise below tells you exactly how to generate one of your own.

Gestures

I love speaking on stage, partly because it heightens my own consciousness. I tell the delegates at all my seminars what I'm going to tell you now: **be conscious of everything, all the time**. Actually, the whole of this conversation about developing conscious listening and powerful speaking skills is rooted in a bigger challenge: that of being a conscious human being. Whether you prefer to think of it as mindfulness, awareness or consciousness, this state is not easy to maintain in the modern world, where so much sets out to distract or anaesthetise us, from TV, mobile music and social media to sugar, carbohydrates and alcohol—all great in moderation but potentially seductive consciousness-destroyers when taken in excess.

One significant aspect of developing consciousness in your speaking (and, to a lesser degree, in your listening) is to make your gestures intentional, bringing them from the realm of unconscious or habitual into the domain of your awareness. There are two good reasons for doing this. First, you can make sure that your gestures are congruent, which means they affirm what you are saying, expressing the same thing in a second way rather than giving a conflicting message.

Gestures are powerful. Great actors learn to express their character through iconic, characteristic gestures, as well as the voice and facial expressions. These gestures are not accidental. The actor Michael Chekhov (nephew of the great playwright) developed a system that is used today by many leading actors on stage and screen, from Anthony Hopkins to Johnny Depp. It contains five archetypal gestures: pushing, pulling, lifting, throwing, and tearing, each of which can be performed in six directions (up, down, left, right, forwards, backwards) and with infinite variations in quality, expressed as adverbs. These express the six 'statements of action' or basic motivations that are at the heart of every character: I Want - I Reject; I Give - I Take; I Hold My Ground - I Yield. You can imagine how they work: if a character wants power, their typical gestures might involve pushing down (on everyone else, metaphorically).

Now, I don't suggest that you start acting in real life (remember HAIL), but this technical clarity can be very helpful if you're planning how to put across a point of view or a whole talk as powerfully as possible. We can fall into the habit of using a gesture, or a small set of gestures, all the time, regardless of the sense of what we are saying. Often, a habitual gesture like this can undermine our delivery by communicating the exact opposite!

Tip: The only way to check your own gesturing habits is to video yourself giving a talk. Make it a long session, so pick a subject you really know, like your life history or your favourite hobby. Set up the camera to record you full length, press record and off you go. As you watch the video, ask yourself these questions: are the gestures congruent? Do I use gesture enough, or too much? Are the gestures too small, or too large? Are there any habitual gestures that work against what I'm saying?

Many gestures are regional or even local, and the repertoire changes over time. The classic Italian hand gesture of fingertips together with thumb and hand waved up and down (meaning "what???") is useless in Berlin or Singapore. Street gangs have their own hand gestures as signs of membership. Shakespeare's audiences knew that when Abraham enquired: "Do you bite your thumb at us, sir?" of Sampson in Romeo and Juliet, he was speaking of a grossly offensive gesture; today nobody would turn a hair if you walked down the street biting your thumb.

However, some gestures are globally recognised. One or both arms in the air for triumph; head in hands for despair; blowing a kiss; a clenched fist; the now-ubiquitous fist-bump... these are many more that are widely known and used.

The renowned family therapist and author Virginia Satir suggested that humans have a set of coping stances when the balance between self, other and context is lost. These tend to be accompanied by iconic, universally recognisable gestures:

blaming - often indicated by pointing or stabbing fingers;

placating - both hands open, palms upwards, as if to beg, or to reassure that one is carrying no threat;

computing - one hand strokes the chin, possibly with the other arm crossed underneath;

distracting - wild or irrelevant gestures that change the subject or distract attention (magicians and pickpockets are very good at this!);

loving/hating - thumping an invisible table, big open gestures.

Tip: Be careful if any of these iconic gestures become habits. I have seen entire talks given with the placator gesture constantly being used. This is a weak gesture unless you really are appealing for help, and when used incongruently, it severely undermines content. If you tend to wave your hands in front of you while speaking (there is nothing wrong with that per se; it can help illustrate cadence and emphasis), then make sure your hands are vertical, not horizontal with palms up. You will see many politicians speaking in exactly this way, with two hands in front, moving to emphasise each point, but always vertical, never open-handed.

To be authentic, your gesturing must reflect your character. You may be wildly expressive, or very controlled and understated. Either way, make sure that your gestures are congruent and authentic, and most of all make them conscious and intentional, and you will dramatically increase the power of your communication.

Exercise: Posture and stance

1. Neck posture

Stand with your back to a wall and see if the back of your head touches the wall. If it doesn't, you have forward neck posture and your neck muscles have probably weakened.

Here's how to adjust, in a one-minute exercise that you can do many times a day. Stand with your back to the wall and touch the back of your head to the wall. Do not achieve this by tilting your head back and increasing the curve of your neck: visualise a string attached to the top of your head and then pull it from above to lengthen your neck. As the back of your neck gets longer, you chin tucks in and down somewhat toward the back of your neck, while the back of your head makes contact with the wall. This is correct neck and head posture. Stand like this for one minute. It may be quite hard at first if your neck muscles have become weak. Repeat often, and you will strengthen those muscles and correct your neck posture.

While we're at it, let me give you some neck and shoulder stretches that will help to adjust and strengthen those muscles, whilst also relieving tension.

Front to back

Stand up straight. Breathing deeply, in through the nose and out through the mouth, slowly move your head to its fullest extension forward on your neck, leading with the chin, and hold for a count of ten. Now move your head back to its fullest compression, with your chin tucked in and hold for a count of ten. Repeat three times.

Side to side

Stand up straight. Breathing deeply, in through the nose and out through the mouth, slowly tilt your head as you aim to bring an ear toward a shoulder. Be careful not to raise the shoulder: only the head moves. When you reach your limit, hold for ten, feeling the stretch on the other side. Move slowly back and then repeat on the other side. Repeat the sequence three times.

2. Stance

This is to help you cultivate your neutral stance, whether on stage or in conversation.

Stand facing a full-length mirror with your hands loose at your sides and examine your posture. First notice: are there any asymmetries in the vertical plane—in other words, is your left side the perfect mirror image of the right? Note any differences. Now look at the lines of your eyes, shoulders, hips and hands. Are those lines parallel to the floor or tilted? Again, take a note. Now turn sideways and check your vertical alignment. Is everything stacked vertically (shoulders, elbows, hips, knees), or are there curves? (You may find it easier and more accurate to get a friend to take some pictures of you from the front and the side and then review them at your leisure.)

Here is how I build my neutral stance.

Stand with your feet about shoulder-width apart for males, slightly narrower than that for females. Check that your feet are parallel and pointing straight forward. It looks timid to have your toes angled inwards, and inelegant or even brash to have them angled outwards.

Now stack everything vertically. Your knees are firm but not locked (unless you have problems with nervous tremors in one or both legs). Feel that you are just slightly flexed, ready to spring. Your hips are above your knees and square on. Now look up and draw your spine up to its full height. Imagine a string attached to the top of your head, and feel as if you are dangling from it. Let your shoulders fall downwards and backwards, and feel your neck extend. Feel the relaxation in your arms and hands, which are hanging comfortably by your sides, with thumbs to the front. Feel the strength in the core muscles of your abdomen, and then gently tense the powerful gluteus maximums muscles in your backside. That feeling of a strong core is where you need to be. Finally, whilst still maintaining the feeling of dangling from that string attached to your head, visualise roots going down from your feet deep into the ground. That is the feeling of groundedness that so many people spot when I'm speaking.

Explore the tension between the feeling of lightness from the string, and solidity from the roots. You can maintain both with practice. Without shifting your feet at all, move around a little: this is not a waxwork posture but a place to be comfortable, relaxed and ready to move.

If you have long been standing out of alignment, it may feel like hard work to get into the ideal neutral stance (which, incidentally, is also just good, healthy posture that will slow down the ageing process by not putting unnatural load onto parts of your body). Just as it takes time to grow a six-pack or lose weight, it takes time to develop perfect posture. Be patient and do a little every day and you will move in the right direction. Practice standing and adopting this posture over and over and it will become natural and easy.

BREATH

Breath is life, and our voice is nothing but breath: it's no surprise that exercise and wellbeing systems like yoga rest entirely on breathing. Not for nothing do singers and actors practice so intently on breathing well: as we discovered in Chapter Three, your voice is simply breath, and breathing well is fundamental to speaking well. Breath is the fuel for your voice. More fuel gives more power.

Most people breathe like birds, taking little, light breaths to the top of their lungs. I wonder when you last took a big, deep breath and really expanded your rib cage. Unless you have a breathing practice from yoga or another discipline, the answer is probably days ago! The breathing exercises below are from my fiancée, fitness and wellbeing expert Jane Majendie, who is a multiple world champion at the martial art of Tang Soo Do and also a master of yoga. I commend them to you. Breath is life.

Exercise: Breathing

You probably haven't taken a really deep breath all day today, so start now with a good, deep breath through your nose, counting to 10 as you inhale. Didn't get to 10? You will if you keep at it! Now add an equally long exhale through your mouth in a whistling position. Do this three times.

Next, put your hands lightly on your stomach and change the exhale to a hiss for another three breaths, still aiming for 10 on your in breath through your nose. See how long you can make your hissing out breath… aim to get to 10, then more, as you feel the control from your diaphragm. Feel your hands lifting as your stomach expands on the in breath, then falling as it contracts on the out breath. This starts to get you into the habit of breathing into your diaphragm, not just to the top of your lungs. It may help you to visualise a long tube from your mouth down to your tailbone. As you breathe in, feel the breath going right down to the bottom of the tube as your stomach extends, and then force it out from the bottom upwards as your stomach contracts again.

Finally, again with your hands on your stomach, do a set of three deep in-breaths, again through the nose, with the out-breaths puffed in staccato bursts, as if you were blowing out a set of candles. Feel the puffs originating in your stomach muscles. (This is also a good exercise if you want to strengthen your abs.)

Do these exercises, particularly the second one, on rising and then as often as you reasonably can during the day, and you will retrain your breathing. Your voice will benefit greatly.

REGISTER

Human voices have four registers, or parts of the overall range. These are a little like gears on a bike or a car, and it takes serious training to be able to move seamlessly from one to another. For maximum power in speaking, it helps to understand the registers so that you can consciously choose the most effective one for the receiver and context at hand.

Whistle

The whistle (or flute) register is unlikely to be of much use to you because it occupies the very highest notes a human voice can produce, roughly spanning an octave upwards from C6 (two octaves above middle C). These high, piercing sounds are produced by resonating the back of the vocal cords, and are in general possible only for female singers. Singers like Mariah Carey use this register in performance; a good recorded example is the 1975 hit *Lovin' You* by Minnie Ripperton. For you and me, this register is of academic interest only.

Falsetto

The next register down is more recognisable: many successful male singers have used falsetto with great success, from Frankie Valli in the Four Seasons in the 1960s, to the Bee Gees in the 1970s, to Coldplay's Chris Martin today. Falsetto tends to be a purer sound than the natural voice, as it has less overtones; for that reason, it's also less characteristic of an individual. For males in speech, falsetto is a gear change up into an unnatural, slightly comical speaking range: think of the Monty Python team pretending to be women. However, for many females, particularly the older generation, it becomes a soft, unthreatening place to speak from, well out of the harsher traffic lanes of most speech. In Japan, speaking in a high falsetto has long been a female cultural imperative in order not to challenge male authority, though this is at last changing in line with social attitudes.

You will move naturally into falsetto from time to time, for example to express astonishment ("Whaaaaaaat?" starting high and going higher is probably in your falsetto register), approbation ("Woo-hoo" will often be belted out in falsetto) or some other strong emotion, differentiating this communication from your regular voice in order to make it stand out. But, as far as our mission to achieve powerful speaking is concerned, falsetto is generally to be avoided—so, once again, we move on.

Modal

The modal register is where most people speak from. It's the natural speaking voice, where the vocal cords are at maximum efficiency. Where your vocal register begins and ends is an important defining factor of your voice: when we describe someone as a soprano or a baritone, we're saying that their modal register is higher or lower.

I would like to distinguish four separate speaking voices within this register. That's two more than the common distinctions from singing coaches. You may have come across the terms 'head voice' and 'chest voice', especially if you've ever taken any singing lessons. I am going to add 'nasal voice' and 'throat voice'.

In fact, your voice is always produced by your larynx, which is in your throat, but you can change your tone and timbre significantly by altering many elements of the complex process that produces your characteristic sound. Following the work of Professor David Abercrombie at Edinburgh University, academics distinguish 'vocal settings', which are regional styles of speaking that overlay someone's accent and suggest where they are from. These include things like pace, emphasis and intonation, as well as the timbre or quality of the voice itself, and they need to be altered if one wishes to speak a foreign language like a local.

My distinctions of four voices combine the quality aspect of vocal settings with my own experience of voices from around the world to produce a practical classification of the modal register that's accessible to you and me through the idea of speaking from a specific place—nose, head, throat or chest. This is purely a practical tool, not an attempt at a scientific classification. There is debate, for example, about whether you physically can resonate your voice in your chest (logically, this would involve sending air downwards from your larynx when you speak, which is impossible), but I know in practice that I can change the depth and quality of my voice by *focusing* on resonating in my chest. These four voices may in part be metaphors, but they work!

So, let's step over all the scientific and pedagogical debates about this complex area and simply deal with the practical question of taking control of your voice. We'll consider the four voices in turn; meanwhile, you can consider which is your own home turf. You will probably use all four to greater or lesser degree, but for most people one will be dominant at any time. Leaving aside medical conditions, speaking primarily in one of these voices is partly genetic or cultural, and partly down to individual choice or upbringing; also, situations may dictate moving from one to another—for example, nervousness tends to move people up from chest to head.

The important thing is that, in my experience, it is possible to train most people to move consciously from one to another. We'll work on that in the exercise that follows.

Nasal voice: For everyone, the nose resonates to generate three sounds (ng, m and n, as in the word 'morning'). The nasal voice sends many more sounds to resonate in the noise, giving it a high, bright, thin and slightly harsh feel. It is widely used in Latin countries, and, famously, in New York City, as well as other locations. To check if you are using nasal voice, touch a finger very lightly to the side of your nose and say "Morning". You will feel slight vibration in your nose. Now say "He loves food." If you felt any vibration at all, you are using a nasal voice.

Head voice: This is the speaking voice most people use most of the time. It requires relatively little effort, resonating efficiently in the cavities of the pharynx, mouth and nose. It is light and bright in tone and pleasing in the main, and it's where singers (apart from basses) generate their voices from.

Throat voice: Common among males from the Indian subcontinent, this can sound hoarse and breathy, though in singing it can soar into magnificence, as with the astounding Qawwali singing of Nusrat Fateh Ali Khan.

Chest voice: This is the deepest and richest of the four voices, most naturally (but far from exclusively) found in those of sub-Saharan African descent: think of James Earl Jones or Morgan Freeman. Actors train to speak from here, and there are many examples of widely-admired chest voices in that profession, from Sean Connery and Sir Ian McKellen to Orson Welles and Vin Diesel.

So, where do you typically speak from? If you want to deliver powerfully, become conscious of the place you feel your voice is coming from, and practice moving it as appropriate. In most cases, the maximum power and authority come from the chest voice, so that one is definitely worth learning.

Vocal fry

There is one last register we need to consider. Vocal fry is a lazy, croaky sound from the throat, made by relaxing the vocal cords and letting air pop through them. It is particularly prevalent among young American females, and research suggests that it is increasing in popularity, possibly due to popular TV programmes that feature it. I advise against using it for two reasons. First, studies indicate that it is negatively received, being associated with being less trustworthy, less competent, less attractive and less educated—so not helpful in a job interview, for example. Second, it is a sad waste of the wonderful instrument we have all been given. Our voices have enormous compass, and it seems tragic to choose not to deploy the richness, tonality and harmonics that are available to us all. Please try not to use this register if you want to be heard.

Exercise: Moving voice

If you have any trouble with these exercises, there may be some physiological or other reason affecting your voice, in which case please seek professional advice, either from your doctor or from a qualified voice coach.

In all these cases, it will pay to record yourself doing the exercise and listen back afterwards.

If your home base is in the falsetto register, take a deep breath and sing a comfortable note, then move it down like an elevator smoothly descending until your feel a break in your voice. Below that is your modal register. Explore it. Sing some notes there, each time taking a deep breath. Now read some text and listen to the difference in your voice. This is where your power lies. Practice, and you can stay here.

If your natural home base is in the modal register (nasal, head, throat or chest voice), then your task is to practice moving from one voice to another. It takes practice to do this without sounding comical—in my workshops, people exploring chest voice for the first time tend to sound very unnatural and they always end up laughing! Be persistent in your practice and you will develop proficiency and consciousness.

The method is simple: start speaking, either repeating something meaningless like the 'one-two' used by live sound engineers, or reading some text. Now visualise your voice coming from your nose, then your head, then your throat, and finally your chest. Feel the resonance and vibration in each location, and listen to the difference as you move your voice from one place to the next. In particular, when you move down to chest voice, feel your whole chest resonating and experience the greater depth and lower tone that result. This exercise will develop your ability to place your voice appropriately for every occasion, and especially to deploy the chest voice when you want to speak powerfully.

You can also play with delivering different emotions, from surprise to joy to sadness to anger, and explore which voice (or even register) you naturally use. Then try different content and intentions, for example humour, authority, inspiration or affection, and again be conscious of where you naturally deliver these from. This practice will raise your consciousness of your range of voices, helping you to be more aware of where you speak from and modulate as required.

If your home base is the vocal fry register, you need to move to modal if you want to be well received (unless you happen to be in a social circle where vocal fry is the norm and it would be socially alienating to speak normally). Use the breathing exercises earlier in this book, because vocal fry tends to result from using very little breath when speaking. Take a deep breath before each sentence and focus on hearing your full, rich voice, with no pops or croaks. Also concentrate on making the last word of your sentences as strong as the first, because vocal fry tends to be strongest at that point.

PACE

Pace, speech rate, is simply about how many words a minute you output. Some people speak fewer than 100 words a minute, which feels very slow. Auctioneers and racing commentators may reach up to breakneck speeds of up to 400 words a minute. Although natural pace varies from language to language, most conversation will be between 100 and 200 words per minute; spoken English is mainly in the upper part of that range.

You will have a natural pace to your speaking, and it's important to become conscious of that par pace. If it's too slow, your listener or audience will struggle to stay engaged. If it's too fast, you will risk losing people as they can't keep up. Many people who are not used to speaking on a stage let nerves drive their pace up and the effect is gabble. Even the shortest talk can be nicely paced: for proof, look at some of the shortest TED talks.

This is one aspect of speaking where it's important to be aware of the listening you are speaking into. Many times, I have spoken on stages to non-English speaking audiences. Either people will be listening and translating in their heads, or they have a headset on and hard-working translators at the back of the hall are simultaneously translating my words. Either way, it is ineffective, if not downright rude, to speak too fast. I moderate my natural speed, making sure to enunciate clearly and give everyone time to process and understand.

It's also very powerful to vary your pace while you speak. A burst of fast pace indicates excitement; one of slow pace, emphasis and significance. Speech delivered at constant pace tend to lack light and shade, and can be less engaging as a result.

Exercise: Pace variation

Start with the simple concept that your voice has three gears: fast, medium and slow.

Pick a passage to read – it can be anything from a magazine or newspaper to a novel. Read it a few times so you know it quite well. Read it naturally. Now mark sections that you can read fast (for excitement) or slowly (for emphasis) and read it again.

Repeat this exercise as often as you like to get the feeling of varying your pace, and see if you want to add a couple of extra gears to give yourself even more variability.

PITCH

Pitch refers to how high or low your speech is.

In simple physical terms, the process of our voice starts when air is directed through our larynx, which contains the ligaments of our vocal cords or folds. Men's cords are 17-25 mm long, while women's are 12.5-17.5 mm, which is why men's voices are deeper and women's higher. As we force air past these cords they vibrate, and we modulate this vibration with attached muscles. This creates a fundamental tone of around 100 Hz on average for men and 200 Hz for women.

Within your modal register, you have possibly a range of up to two octaves to play with. You will naturally modulate your voice within this range depending on your level of excitement or agitation. Try saying "Where did you leave my keys?" in your regular voice. Now raise the pitch, keeping the pace exactly the same. And again, raising the pitch even higher. You see how pitch alone can indicate excitement?

The main reason for moving your voice down into chest register is to lower the pitch, because people associate deep voices with authority. Research shows that we vote for politicians with deeper voices (other things being equal). The association is probably based on the fact that larger things are potentially more important or dangerous than small, and that larger animals make deeper sounds: lions have much deeper voices than cats, which in turn are deeper than mice. As a result, higher voices tend to sound more timid and less authoritative.

To optimise your pitch before you undertake any significant speaking, I strongly suggest you do the warm-up exercises in Chapter Seven—or at least the last vocal warm-up, called the Siren.

Now let's look at the complex variation in pitch called intonation, or prosody.

PROSODY

Prosody is the major way we communicate sense, emphasis and emotion, and thus hugely important in powerful speaking. It includes intonation (the sing-song variation in pitch that we employ while speaking), as well as rhythm, emphasis and to some degree pace and timbre too. Lack of prosody results in a speaking voice that sounds literally monotonous (mono-tone being one note).

Prosody is probably older than language itself. It may have started with 'motherese'—infant directed speech which is typically inflected in an exaggerated way. We tend to speak in this way to babies and dogs, and even to old people or foreigners if we think we are not being understood.

As with so many aspects of speaking, prosody varies from culture to culture, and it's important to be sensitive to this when spotting the listening you are speaking into, and speaking in a way that people will

257

receive. Scandinavians tend to employ a restrained prosody that sounds almost bored to other cultures, while Latins (especially Italians) speak with unrestrained prosody, often all at once! When I visit Greece, I often mistake conversations between people for arguments because of the different local prosody.

Repetitive or forced prosodies tend to lose potency in speaking. A good example of this is up-talk, or high rising terminal (HRT), where the speaker raises his or her pitch on the last syllable of a statement, as if it were a question? (I'm sure you can imagine this habit now.) West-Coast USA and the Antipodes are typically accused of starting this trend in the last few decades, although there are long-established dialects (such as Northern Irish or the Scottish northern isles dialect I hear spoken at my home in Orkney) where this way of speaking is typical. When it's not part of a regional dialect, HRT carries the same issues as vocal fry. It's used much more often by females than by males, and it is associated with uncertainty, because it effectively embeds a checking question— the unspoken "Is that ok with you?" It also robs the speaker of the richness and variation of unrestricted prosody, which inevitably results in less power in speaking.

Exercise: Prosody

To assess and then improve your prosody, record yourself reading some pages from a novel or some stories from a news source.

Start by neutralising prosody to see what happens without it. Read the passage in a flat monotone, with no stresses or pace variations. Listen back. It sounds robotic and completely uninteresting, doesn't it?

Now read the passage in your normal voice. As you listen back this time, score yourself out of 10 for your natural prosody: to what degree are your intonation, rhythm and stresses making the content more powerful and interesting?

If you detect that your prosody is on the restrained side, scoring yourself at less than 5, reread the passage, exaggerating your prosody to 10, as if you were reading it to a small child. Practice this until you feel you have extended your range and can naturally turn yourself up to a natural 6 or 7.

A fun exercise that we do in my workshops is to express emotions or communicate concepts to someone with no words at all, much as the prehistoric proto-hum postulated by Steven Mithen might have sounded. You can do this on your own or have fun swapping these with a friend.

Making sounds, but with no words, express the following:
- sadness
- joy
- anger
- surprise

Now some more complex tasks:
- ask to be given something that you can see
- say sorry
- say you feel ill.

To work on stress, try saying the sentences below, while stressing the words in bold and seeing the difference it makes to the sense.

I'm going to run to work today.
I'm ***going*** to run to work today.
I'm going to ***run*** to work today.
I'm going to run to ***work*** today.
I'm going to run to work ***today.***

Simple stress can dramatically alter meaning.

TIMBRE

Timbre is the feel of a voice, expressed in words that describe tactile concepts. Most people tend to prefer voices that could be described just as you would a delicious cup of hot chocolate: rich, warm, sweet and smooth. If that's not you, don't despair: you may be able to amend some simple lifestyle changes and improve, and if that doesn't work you can transform your timbre with professional help.

Lifestyle

To work effectively, your vocal cords need clean air and lubrication, not to mention a healthy body around them.

Smoke damages your voice, so avoid it; if you're the one smoking, please stop. That's a whole other book, I know—the one I recommend from personal experience 20 years ago is *Allen Carr's Easy Way to Stop Smoking*.

Drinking enough water is important to maintain that lubrication. Make sure you're drinking the recommended amount for your weight and size every day. Before any important talk or speaking engagement it's a good idea to sip lukewarm water or herbal tea, possibly with some honey melted into it. Alcohol and caffeinated drinks are probably not good for timbre (more research is required)—but can be fine in moderation as long as you're drinking enough water, and as long as you don't overindulge before speaking: a heavy night before an important talk is a bad idea for many reasons, not least that it will dry out your vocal cords the morning after.

Milk and dairy products tend to thicken mucous, creating a phlegmatic sensation at the back of the throat for some people. If that's you, try low fat versions or cut down your intake, especially before speaking.

Finally, salty foods also tend to dry out the vocal cords, so many singers try to avoid them in excess. This rings true intuitively; would you really want to eat a bag of salty snacks just before an important speech?

A balanced, healthy diet will also be nothing but beneficial to your voice, as will some exercise, particularly if it benefits your posture (remember the section earlier in this chapter).

Professional help

If none of the above helps, search for local voice or singing coaches on the Internet, choose a few that feel good to you and book a try-out session with each of them. Choose the one you feel the best chemistry with, and work with that person for at least six sessions. They will transform your understanding of your voice and help you to reshape your timbre.

If you can't afford lessons or you live in a remote place, there's always the Internet. YouTube features many vocal coaches offering free advice and lessons.

VOLUME

There's a new word that has been coined to describe people who are not careful with their volume: sodcasting. This is inflicting your sound on other people, for whom it is simply irritating noise. The word was invented to describe young people playing loud, distorted music on mobile phone loudspeakers on buses or trains, but it equally describes vocal behaviour I have seen many times. One of the best examples was in a quiet airport lounge, full of people working. One man was pacing up and down, having a conversation on his phone, using ear bud headphones. He seemed to believe that the phone's microphone wouldn't do a good enough job, because he was speaking at something just below a bellow. It was amazing that he was oblivious of the rolling eyes and furious glares that followed him as he paced the length of the lounge. This was white collar sodcasting!

I have encountered uncontrolled volume in many places, but especially in large cities like New York, where I have many times been unable to focus on what someone walking next to me on a sidewalk is saying, because of the intrusive noise of a guy walking several paces behind, speaking with the volume turned up to 11.

Being conscious of volume is another vital aspect of speaking. Just as you have a range of tones available in your normal voice, you also have a range of volume you typically operate in. This can vary widely from one person to another: for every person like that New York sodcaster, there is someone who speaks in a tiny voice that is barely audible. I have trained people in workshops whose natural level is so quiet they are literally incapable of public speaking. Even when focused on the issue, they start loud enough to hear and then decrescendo gradually as they speak, retreating into the dark.

Unless there's medical issue, every person is equipped to create vocal sounds that go from a tiny whisper to a massive shout. The loudest shout in the *Guinness Book of Records* at the time of writing is a staggering 121.7 dB by Northern Ireland teacher Annalisa Wray; this is around one trillion times as powerful as the quietest whisper you could hear! Your shout may never be quite that powerful, but it is important to develop the upper end of your range for good reasons. You may have to speak in a noisy place, or to many people in a large room with no sound reinforcement system; also, it gives you great power to be able to vary your volume at will throughout a talk, creating yet more light and shade to keep people engaged. A shout can startle a sleepy audience, while a whisper can paradoxically create great emphasis as people instinctively lean forward to listen carefully.

The exercise below is great fun in my workshops. Try it and work on creating more and more headroom in the range of your vocal volume.

Exercise: Volume

When we do this in my seminars I conduct the group. You will be both performer and conductor now. I suggest you do this in a quiet place away from other as it may disturb people!

Stand up. Place your arm out in from of you, horizontal to the floor. This is your speaking volume—call it 5 out of 10. You can move your arm down to point at the floor, which is your quietest whisper (1 out of 10), or up to point at the ceiling, which is your loudest shout. At the top you can aim for 11 out of 10!

Start saying the word rhubarb repeatedly. (This is the word extras used to say in films to create impression of background conversation.) Move your arm down and up and adjust your volume accordingly; practice smooth changes and try to extend the top end of your range every time you get up there.

SPACE

Not the final frontier, but our old friend silence. Most people fear silence when speaking in public; many find it uncomfortable even in small groups or one to one. Make it your friend. I have demonstrated many times on stage that your audience will stay with you for much longer than you might think if you pause and say nothing: you can extend a silence for many seconds without the audience becoming frustrated. If you learn to use silence well, you will have an advantage over many speakers who feel the need to gabble or to fill space with '…um…', '…er…' or '…ah…'. Being at one with silence takes away the need to make those noises, giving you more authority.

Doing the silence practice from Chapter Four will help you to befriend silence. It can sometimes say as much as many words.

Chapter Seven

Stagecraft

The human brain starts working
the moment you are born and never
stops until you stand up to speak in public.

– George Jessel

This book has been about the art (and the science) of speaking and listening in every situation, from social and family to business and professional. However, most of the people who've trained with me over the years have come because they are faced with the task of speaking in public—something that many people find intimidating or even scary. The old adage that people fear public speaking more than death is an urban myth (I spent some time looking it up a few years ago), but there is no doubt that standing in front of a microphone and a large group of expectant people creates fear in most people, and in some that fear is extreme.

That's why I am devoting the whole of this last chapter to the skills of platform speaking, revealing all the secrets of that dark art that I have learned over many years of giving talks in many different locations all over the world, from offices, classrooms and lecture halls to huge auditoria and the stage of TED; I've also watched thousands of talks by others, ranging from life-changing experiences I will never forget to complete disasters. I have learned many lessons along the way about how to make public speaking as successful as possible, and it is these I want to share with you now. I call it stagecraft.

We'll follow the whole journey from the moment you know you have a speech to give, right through to your response to appreciation when you finish. Every step of the way, there are mistakes that many people make and little nuggets of knowledge that can help you avoid them. Stagecraft is mastering the art of public speaking, accumulating all these little nuggets and practicing them until they become second nature to you.

When you learn stagecraft, excessive nerves will be a thing of the past. So many of the demons that plague the imaginations of infrequent public speakers (and frequent speakers who have never bothered to learn stagecraft) are avoidable with care and wisdom.

When I fly home to Orkney I am always reassured as I see the pilot doing the visual pre-flight inspection, walking around the plane and carefully checking all the elements that can be visually assessed. They almost never find anything—but the important word there is almost. They don't skimp on the job or do the inspection half asleep because the consequences of one error could be catastrophic.

Stagecraft is like that. Much of it will be routine and unexciting, but if it isn't done, the result can be very messy indeed. Do it automatically and you will make maximum impact with talks that go smoothly and well.

So, let's learn some stagecraft.

VENUE

Sometimes you get to choose your venue; sometimes it is chosen for you. We'll consider both cases.

Your choice

When you are choosing your own venue, there are many factors to consider. Below is a comprehensive checklist for you. To answer all the questions and ensure success, you will absolutely need to visit the venue and check them all in person before you commit to it.

Is the location convenient to reach for the people you are inviting?

If people will be using public transport, is the journey from the nearest stop(s) easy and safe in all weathers?

If people will be driving, is there ample easy, free parking?

If you're renting a room in a hotel or other facility, is the brand appropriate for you to be associated with? Is their quote comprehensive, including all extras, and within your budget?

How easy, and how long, is the journey from the front door to your room? Is it well signposted? (If not, make sure you bring your own signage.)

Are there any issues for people with special needs?

If you are offering refreshments, what's the quality of the catering at this venue?

Are hotel rooms the right standard? If you are doing a multi-day event, you will likely be using a hotel and block-booking rooms, in which case ask to see some typical rooms to make sure that your delegates are going to have a good experience. They will hold you responsible for everything!

What audience layouts can the venue offer? You may want to choose any one of the following, each of which has its own advantages and disadvantages.

Theatre/auditorium style. Theatres, cinemas and large, custom-built corporate presentation spaces are generally excellent for large audiences: everyone can see due to the rake of the seats, and the rooms are custom designed for speech intelligibility. Although similar in layout, academic lecture halls are often far less satisfactory, combining uncomfortable seating for the audience with poor acoustics and inflexible equipment. The latter springs from the old-fashioned, entrenched academic paradigm of lecturing from a fixed lectern. All the electrical and electronic connections are in that one place and very often they cannot be extended to allow a presenter to move out from behind the battlements of the lectern and connect openly with the audience.

Classroom style. This means rows of desks, each typically seating two people. It's a fairly dense way of seating people, so it works well if space is limited and if you want people to be able to write while you speak.

U-shape. You speak at the open end of a U of seats or desks. This allows you to connect face to face with everyone, and stops people from hiding or disconnecting (which is very possible in the back rows when a room is laid out classroom style). You can walk down the centre of the U for dramatic impact, and all the delegates can see one another, which is very useful if your session is interactive or participative.

Boardroom style. Typical in business presentations, this works fine as long as you don't have a full table with the top seats facing away from you! These rooms often have a plasma, LCD or LED screen on the wall for slides or graphics, but the associated sound system can be very variable in quality. There is often a Crestron or AMX control system; if the interface has not been well designed, you may have trouble getting the result you want because these systems are often closed, with only the most basic controls made available to users. Many times, I have wanted to alter the mix between a microphone and the sound from my Mac, to be told that all the levels are fixed. Equally often, I encounter underpowered amplifiers outputting puny volume levels through small ceiling speakers. This won't bother you if you don't use sound but, in my experience, it still is worth getting access to boardrooms or corporate meeting rooms in plenty of time to make sure you can interface with any tech that you might need to use, even if it's just the lights or HVAC.

Cabaret style. This is a very good layout if you have exercises that involve breaking the group into smaller teams. Tables seating 12 are ideal, with four seats left vacant (the ones that would have their backs to you) so you can have eight people on each table. That's very flexible - you can have them work in pairs, or in fours, or as a table of eight.

Circle. This really only works well for very interactive workshops, where you are not so much presenting as facilitating group work. It's hard to communicate equally and maintain contact in the round, whether you stand in the centre and have to keep turning, or sit in the circle and have people immediately to your left and right, which is why this really only works for a softer, more democratic style of work.

Over and above these criteria, what I look for is the right attitude in the people I meet when I am choosing a venue. The critical factor is care. This must emanate from everyone you meet, from the event booking person to the receptionist, the chef and the support staff around the meeting room. I would never use a facility where the people don't care enough, even if it saved a lot of money.

Someone else's venue

You may get asked to speak as part of someone else's event, in which case you have no say in the venue and you are probably not responsible for asking people to attend which means that most of the questions above are unnecessary. However, you can do two crucial things.

First, state your requirements very clearly to the organiser, ask questions about the layout and facilities as far as they impact on what you plan to do, and/or research these things online: many venues post pictures which will give you a great feeling for what to expect. You may need a dressing room with a mirror and good light, or a seat in the front row for the rest of the event if the content interests you, or have specific dietary requirements. Bands state all this as 'tour riders' in their contracts with venues, some of which have become legend for their diva-ishness. My favourite is Iggy Pop's requirement to have a Bob Hope impersonator at every gig. I doubt you'll need anything quite so esoteric, but whatever you do really need, make sure you specify it and agree on it with the organiser in advance.

Each time I take on a speaking assignment, we email the organiser a clear list of technical requirements and ideally communicate directly with the Audio/Video (AV) team leader to make sure all is understood. For me, this involves having my Mac on stage in front of me so that I can see Presenter View; having a good sound system; and video projection being able to handle 16:9 aspect ratio. Most importantly, we stipulate a sound and vision check to an empty room as long before as is practical. Usually the AV people are there the night before, setting everything up, so that's a perfect time to do a sound and vision check. Once you know everything can and does work, the pressure is off and you can do final setup in a coffee break with confidence—though, even having done all that, I have had experiences where the gremlins have fun trashing the perfect process of the night before for no known reason!

I can testify from bitter experience that, despite being so specific and clear, it sometimes happens that the requirements don't get through to the people who actually need to know. Many times, I have arrived at a venue and had to explain to the clearly un-briefed AV team that I want to use my own Mac, producing a lengthy negotiation because the message from my technical requirements email never got through to them and the necessary cables have not been laid. That's where the second crucial thing that you can do comes in. This is to get to the venue early (I generally prefer the day before) and reconnoitre the facilities for yourself. I have seen people turn up just minutes before they are due to speak only to discover that some critical facility is missing. It's unwise to make assumptions, much safer to check the reality in good time.

I have spoken in hundreds of venues and encountered many and varied problems. Some are simple, but others take time to fix, which means that agreeing to set up in the coffee break just before you speak is a very high-risk strategy. Generally, the more complex the venue, the more important it is to do all this as early as possible. I spoke a few years ago at the futuristic BMW Welt in Munich, and was only allowed to access the room an hour before the speech. Their leading edge, highly complex video projection system took against my Mac, producing a juddering image that immediately induced a feeling of motion sickness. The technical people diagnosed that a filter of some kind was needed, and had to send out for it. It finally arrived about 30 seconds before I stood up to speak. That kind of stress is best avoided!

In a multi-speaker event, there are some other vital questions to ask.

Is there a dress code? The world is pretty informal now, but from time to time you may speak at events that require something other than the norm, which tends to be 'smart casual' or 'business casual'. It may be a themed event, or a black-tie dinner, for example. On the other hand, you may have your own style as part of your identity and be unwilling to depart from it. Remember the exercises on your identity we did in the section on Authenticity? You can add clothing and other style choices to that identity if you want to establish yourself as a brand or an iconic figure, or if you simply want to be true to who you really feel you are. My father wore a tie even at weekends: it was part of his identity. Some presenters rock up in a t-shirt and jeans, regardless of what everyone in the audience is wearing. Nevertheless, I do advise asking this question of the organiser, so that you know the lie of the land and are making a conscious decision.

Will someone introduce you? If the answer is yes, make sure to meet the person and check what they're going to say, as their information may be incomplete, out of date or even incorrect. Remember their name so you can shake hands as you walk on and they walk off, and say: "Thanks Jim!" as you prepare to start; it makes everything feel seamless and friendly to the audience.

Will there be any walk-on audio or video? In which case, how long is it? It's very eggy (as the acting profession say) to stride onstage and then have to wait 30 seconds while a video or a piece of music finishes.

Where do you come onstage from and where do you go off to? There are few things more awkward that someone ending a speech and then looking uncertainly around, clearly not knowing which way to leave.

Where on the stage is lit well, and where not? Where is it ok for you to move to? This is particularly important if the event is being filmed. If they have a lectern on stage, do you have to use it? I prefer not to stand behind anything, so I often get them to rotate the lectern so that I can see my Mac on it as I stand at the centre of the stage.

Will there be Q&A? If so, who will choose the questioners—you or an MC? Will there be mic runners, which will mean waiting for a mic to arrive before taking a question.

Is there simultaneous translation? In which case, go and introduce yourself to the translators and run through any jargon or unusual words you may use so they are prepared. They will really appreciate that, and work harder for you. I always try to go back and thank them afterwards, because they do an amazing job.

Using the Internet

Sometimes it's not possible to be there in person. It may be too expensive in time and money to travel a long distance, or you may want to broadcast a talk simultaneously to many people in different locations. I've done both of these many times, using Skype, Skype for Business and webcasting services like GoToMeeting and Zoom. Here are the lessons I've learned.

Get to know the tool. It is asking for trouble to agree to speak via a tool you've never used before without proper preparation. They are all different. Some have serious quality limitations, either for audio or for video, which you will need to take into account in preparing your material. Some allow you to share a screen and speak simultaneously, possibly with 'picture in picture' so the audience can see you as well as your slides. Very few allow you to send computer audio at the same time as speaking; the only one I'm aware of that does this at the moment is Zoom.us. If screen sharing is clunky or laggy, you might decide not to use slides at all, or at least not to broadcast them while you use them simply to help guide you through the content; the audience would see only your face as you speak.

Make sure you have a good pair of Bluetooth headphones and if possible use a high quality external mic. Using your laptop speakers and mic will probably not give a good result for people at the other end. I use Sennheiser MM 450-X headphones, which are small, light, unobtrusive and very good quality. You could use something even smaller, like Apple AirPods. A Zoom audio recorder like the H2 I recommended in Chapter Six will double as a high-quality USB microphone, and with a small stand can sit just out of short on a desk in front of you and produce a much better sound than your laptop would.

Think carefully about the room you're going to use. Avoid a room with very live acoustics; these will make it hard for people to understand you, even if you do use an external mic; go for a room that sounds as acoustically dead as possible, which means it needs plenty of soft surfaces to absorb sound and stop those reflections from confusing the signal. Also think about the background. Most of the conferencing apps will allow you to preview what your own camera is seeing, which gives you a chance to make sure that everything behind you is appropriate and not distracting, and to frame the shot nicely to include your head and shoulders squarely in the centre of the shot.

Practice as near to the real thing as possible with friends or colleagues until you are confident that what's being received at the other end is as good as it can be. As you do this, you can tailor your material to the limitations of the tool you're using. I have done boardroom presentations to rooms full of people on other continents where the audio was coming from a small PC loudspeaker on the table. Knowing that, I chose not to deploy my usual high-quality audio: it would have sounded thin, distorted and probably distracting. Clarity is everything: your task is to get the ball over the net with whatever equipment you are given. Don't attempt to squeeze the full glory of your presentation through a medium that won't do it justice. Be humble and adaptable and remember it's not about you, and you will achieve a good result even with some of the more basic tools that are commonly used.

Those are some hard-won tips that I hope will see you in good stead whether you book your own venue, speak at someone else's or give a virtual talk.

TIME

Scheduling an event

If you are scheduling your own event, it's generally a good idea to avoid peak holiday times (in most countries that's August, when, for example, the whole of France goes on vacation), public holidays and rush hours.

If your event is in the personal development area, weekends usually work best: choose Saturday for a one-day event; Friday and Saturday for a two-day event (so that people can decompress and absorb on the Sunday before going back to work); or Friday, Saturday and Sunday for a three-day event.

If you're aiming at the business market, then Friday from 10 am to 4 pm works very well: people love getting home for an early weekend. In order, the next best days are Wednesday, Thursday and Tuesday. Monday is a bad choice because people get back to work after the weekend and become very conscious of their task list; if you choose Monday you are likely to get many last-minute cancellations. Breakfasts can also work very well for shorter business-oriented events.

Timing your content

If you are the event organiser, you have some flexibility here. Whether you are speaking for 20 minutes or eight hours, what's vital is to agree to the timing with the audience, making a contract with them. In my seminars and workshops, I lay out the schedule and ask all the participants if they agree to be present for the whole thing—and if anyone has to leave punctually at the end for transport or other reasons, just in case anything delays the proceedings and we have to overrun.

If you are not the organiser, it is critical to be clear beforehand about timings, and to stick to them.

For business presentations, I always agree to meeting start AND finish times. It is amazing how many people think that meetings need only a start time! Having agreed to the start and length, I can then ask at the beginning if everyone is ok for the whole meeting. Sometimes people must leave early, in which case you know in time to edit your content accordingly. For example, if a key decision-maker can stay for only 15 minutes, you can agree with everyone at the start that you'll do a short summary of the whole thing in 10 minutes and leave five minutes for discussion, then go into the details after the person has left the meeting.

Being accurate in your timing requires that you know how long your material takes to deliver, and that you have a structure with waypoints against which you can check your progress. The first of these requires rehearsal, of which more in a little while. Not knowing your talk's length because you haven't bothered to practice is a major error; in my opinion, it is also downright rude. This is a pitfall that can come from pride, or at least overconfidence. I remember once at TED seeing a CEO who was a highly practiced public speaker be rather humiliated. He had been given a six-minute slot and rather arrogantly chose to busk it. He either failed to look at the clock or assumed that TED would turn a blind eye if he overran (which they almost never do!) so by the end of his six minutes he had barely started to deliver his point. At that point, he was asked to summarise the rest of his talk in one minute and move off so the next person could speak. He was quite flustered; it was a little like seeing a balloon deflate. I have lost count of the number of times I have seen people at multi-speaker events play fast and loose with their scheduled time, and sadly many organisers are not as tight as TED about it. The record for late running in my experience was a marketing conference in Istanbul, which was an hour behind schedule after just two speakers! You can't control the organisers or the other speakers, so your job is simply to be on time yourself whenever it finally gets to be your turn.

Structure and waypoints can be managed in two ways. For most talks, you can use a countdown clock. I have one on my Mac in Keynote's Presenter View; PowerPoint offers the same function, as do most presentation packages. TED has long used a countdown clock at the speaker's feet, ticking down from the talk's agreed length to zero. Many organisers now emulate this practice with a screen on stage that counts down, or something similar (at one venue I remember there was someone in the front row holding an iPad with a countdown clock on it!). You can work perfectly well off a clock long as you have a rough idea of your key waypoints: by minute six I must have completed this much, and so on.

More complex tracking for longer content like a seminar requires something I call a *syntax*, defined as 'a connected or orderly system: a harmonious arrangement of parts or elements'. This breaks long content into bite-sized chunks, each timed and practiced, so that you can plan accurately. To create a syntax, I use a simple spreadsheet with five columns. The first describes the chunk of content; the second the duration of that chunk in minutes; the third the start time (copy the end time of the previous chunk); the fourth the end time (using a formula to add the duration to the start time); the fifth any notes required, for example describing props or exercises. My one-day seminars break down into four 90-minute units with breaks in between, so each unit has its own syntax spreadsheet where the total duration must be 90 minutes. Designing content at this level of rigour and detail is tremendous for ensuring that you deliver completely and efficiently. You can keep a printed copy of the syntax in front of you as you speak; or you can build the cumulative timings into your slide package or your index cards; or you can have someone work with you to signal how you are tracking against the schedule (more on this in the section on Team that's coming next).

TEAM

For anything more than a small presentation, there is usually a need for a team. If you're speaking at someone else's event, this will be organised for you, and your job is simply to be pleasant, clear, professional and appreciative. You never know when you will meet people again, so it's not only good manners but also good business to leave them feeling positive about their experience of working with you.

I always make a special point of saying hello to the AV person or crew, because they can make or break my talks, given the amount of sound that I use. I chat them through any issues or possible hiccups so that they are fully briefed and happy to help: for example, if I am starting with a black slide it's vital to tell them—without knowing that, they would switch to my presentation and probably panic when they see nothing on screen.

For large events, there is usually a producer or stage manager; there may be a host or MC; there may even be make-up and hair (the latter being not so vital in my case!). Treat them all well, and they will usually return the favour by giving you their best effort.

If you are running your own event, you will decide on your team. You may need one or more meeter/greeters, particularly if you are asking people to fill in any paperwork when they arrive, or giving them name badges. You may want to have a 'room captain'—someone who oversees the 'Zen' of the room, making sure that everything is just so, and is reset completely in every break.

That same person may be able to be your second, sitting at the back of the room and thus able to signal to you privately over the heads of the participants. These signals might be cards held up with the number of minutes remaining (a manual version of the countdown clock), a hurry-up sign if you're running behind, or just an encouraging thumbs-up when you do something particularly well. Your second may also bring notes up to you when required, for example when someone's car needs to be moved or the venue announces that there will be a fire alarm test.

The composition of the team is up to you. Large events need large teams and lots of planning, which ideally means a team leader with good experience of every aspect of your event; this might be a professional from an event management organisation, who can assemble the whole team for you. Your team may include one or more AV people, who will usually come with the venue's house AV system, or from an AV hire company that you engage yourself. If you're doing the latter, do make sure you get direct testimonials from former clients about the quality of the kit and the service, ideally by speaking to them yourself. If you can draw from a community of people who believe in what you're saying, it may be possible to get most of your support team by enrolling volunteers; this is typically what happens at political, charitable or self-improvement events.

For events with sizeable support teams, you will probably want to create team t-shirts or badges so that the team members are east to identify.

Depending on local laws, you may also need formal risk assessment documentation, health and safety guidelines, approval from regulatory authorities and so on.

THE ROOM

We've dealt with how to select a venue, so now let's chunk down and consider what you need in the room itself.

Whichever of the layouts discussed in the venue section you choose to go with, you also need to consider the following.

Do you need a podium or stage? Generally, this is unnecessary for small groups, but once you go above about 30 it is definitely worth considering. It ensures that everyone can see you, and you them. It adds a little authority and gravitas to the event, as it's clearly more formal than standing on the floor.

Do you want a lectern? As I've already said, that's not my style, though there are plenty of very good speakers in history who have used lecterns and been highly effective. This was possibly more relevant in the age of oratory, when people would sit patiently and listen while someone read writing for an hour or more. As we've already covered, it takes a lot of skill to make reading writing interesting. Also, a lectern covers up much of your body, forming a barrier between you and the audience and restricting your nonverbal communication. I think many people also associate lecterns with lectures. If your material is academic or proclamatory, then this may be the best style of delivery for you. If you and the material are equally important elements of the talk, then I advise not having a lectern.

In your room, how flexible is the lighting? (This is particularly important if you're using a projector and screen; I have often been in rooms where it's impossible to switch off powerful lights that flood the screen and wash out the projection, without switching off all the lights in the room!)

Is the room well ventilated, and can you control the temperature? People get very sleepy if there's not enough oxygen in the air, or if a room is too warm. I like to have the temperature at no more than 20 degrees Centigrade (68 degrees Fahrenheit), and always advise people to bring layers of clothing. Of course, if people feel too cold I will turn up the heat a little, but in my experience, anything over 22C (72F) is liable to make people drowsy, regardless of how fascinating the speaker may be.

Does the room have the tech you need? We'll be dealing with technology in more detail next; for now, you must ensure that, if you need a screen or projector, or sound, or flip charts, or any other facility, it will be there and will work without problems. I advise testing this in advance of booking; check out the room and connect up whatever you need to make sure that you won't encounter some major unforeseen issue on the day when you arrive to set up. Simple things, like checking there are enough power sockets for you and your delegates and, if necessary, ordering gang plugs or extension cables, can save a lot of stress and trouble when done in advance.

Do you want a set? You might want to dress the stage, or the front of the room where you will be standing. If you have any products of your own or of others with relevance to your content, such as books or discs (slightly old-fashioned now, admittedly), then you might want a table displaying them. Flowers always look fresh and attractive, too. Will you need a seat or stool? What about a table for your computer if you're using one?

How will you dress the delegate seating? If you use tables, most hotels will cover them in black cloth, which looks great. You will almost certainly want to have water on every table, and probably also pens and paper, which is usually part of the package when you rent a room from a professional conference facility, or may even be your own branded stock. What about some sweets? You can make a statement with cool brands of mint or other fun sweets on every table. Whatever you put out, your team or the support staff from the venue will need to replenish and reset it all in every break so that the room looks perfect every time people come back in—no used cups or glasses, no scraps of paper, no half-empty water bottles. It's amazing how people's energy falls away when the room starts to look lived in and messy.

TECH

Of course, technology is not essential for a good talk or presentation. Some of my favourite TED talks have used the minimum amount of tech (just a microphone) for example Alain de Botton's brilliant 2009 talk about success or Bryan Stevenson's barnstorming 2012 talk about injustice. If you are speaking to a small group, you won't even need a mic and you can pass on to the next section.

However, many talks and presentations these days do use technology so here are some tips from my long experience. I started using tech to add visual impact before laptops were invented—an overhead projector which projected images from acetate sheets. I used to lug this unwieldy piece of kit around for new business presentations. It was worth it; simply because they were different, the projected acetates were more memorable than the printed books that the opposition were using.

As soon as presentation software came out, I used it. In the early days, PowerPoint with bullet points ruled, but as we discovered in Chapter Five in the section on slides, this is no longer the norm, and for good reason. We've discovered how to use dramatic pictures and graphics to back up the speaker, amplifying the message and making the talk more memorable as a result. Doubling up by having the same thing on screen that's coming out of the speaker's mouth is actually distracting! When I see someone still using that technique, I remember Pythagoras and his conviction that the eyes can detract from what the ears are receiving, hence the screen he erected to stop first-year students from being distracted by seeing the teacher.

For many years now, I've used Apple Keynote. I still have and prefer the iWork09 version, the one before Apple inexplicably dumbed the program down in version 6. I'm sure PowerPoint can achieve the same results, but as a Mac user Keynote is natural and over the years I've developed some skill with it. When you stay with one tool and master it, it's amazing what you can achieve with it. Take a look at Larry Lessig's 2013 TED talk about US politics for a good example of how diverse and impactful Keynote can look.

Most presentation apps allow you to activate Presenter View. This is indispensable, because it shows you the slide that's on the screen behind you now, alongside the one that's coming next, so you stay one step ahead and never get lost. You can also show your own countdown clock and your presenter notes, which can be very valuable if there are many details or specifics relating to a topic and if your memory is not flawless.

Most large venues will have a 'comfort monitor' on the front of the stage, set up to show what's on the screen behind you so that you don't have to turn around and present your back to the audience. That's a good thing, though you do have to remember not to point at it when you want to indicate something on a slide, because the audience won't be able to see what you're pointing at!

In my experience, the comfort monitor can show presenter view only if you send your presentation to the organiser and they run it on one of their own computers—and even then, it often is not possible. If you do adopt this course, please check they have the same version of the software, and all the required fonts, or things can get very messy. I like to keep things simple by using my own computer onstage, feeding

HDMI or VGA (I always carry a Mac/VGA adapter) to the main screen, and audio separately from the headphone jack to the sound system— the latter because I like to ride audio from my remote control; this is impossible if it goes through HDMI, because that fixes the output level. This setup means I see presenter view on my own screen, which ideally is on a low table in front of me.

I always use 16:9 aspect ratio, which is becoming standard now; an excellent app called SwitchResX gives me great control over output resolutions and aspect ratios. Many times, I have found that venue video systems initially stretch or squash my slides, and it can take some time and fiddling, with the help of the AV crew, to get everything looking as intended. More reasons to get there early!

If you're going to use slides, you will need a remote control or you will be stuck behind your laptop, operating the slides from the keyboard. I use a Keyspan Pr-Pro3 remote from Tripp Lite. It's plug and play, like most of these devices, requiring only that you plug a USB dongle into your laptop. Crucially for me, it manages audio volume as well as slide forward and back; it also has a laser pointer and a mini-mouse, along with a very useful 100-foot range. There are many excellent remotes on the market, so take some time and find the one that best fits your needs.

If you have rented the venue yourself, you will want to check the projector alignment and focus when you arrive if you want your slides to fill the screen and be perfectly sharp. Often this means clambering onto a chair or table as these devices are usually suspended from the ceiling. If you're lucky there will be a remote control or, better still, a house technician who can do this for you.

The other piece of tech you are likely to encounter if you speak to anything other than small groups is a microphone. If you get a say, always request wireless. There are three common varieties: lavalier, headset and hand held.

The 'lav', or tie-clip, is the one you see on television chat shows. It has a small capsule and a spring-loaded clip that can fasten it to a lapel or shirt. It can be fitted pointing downwards to avoid plosives—the unpleasant popping sound that happens when you say a hard t, p or b sound and the mic gets hit by the resulting sudden blast of air. Around sternum level is generally the best placement, but bear in mind that this requires the right sort of clothing, with an edge that the clip can fasten onto. The cable will ideally go inside your clothing, so getting mic'd and de-mic'd can be a little awkward. The main issue with lavs is that head movement dramatically affects the sound, whether side to side (taking you effectively off-mic) or up and down, when you can suddenly boom as your mouth gets much closer to the mic; also, they can suffer badly from clothing rubbing them if they are not carefully mounted.

With a headset mic, the small capsule is held in a light headset, which is normally flesh-coloured to be as unobtrusive as possible. The cable will be taped behind your neck for security, then run down the back of your jacket, shirt or blouse. The advantage over lavs is that the sound is much more consistent, regardless of head movement. However, there can be two noise issues with headset mics: beard or bristles rubbing on the mic if it's too close to the face; or earrings rattling or banging on the boom arm. The first can be fixed with correct setup. The second can't, which means that if you are going to use a headset mic and you wear earrings, you must avoid long, dangling ones.

For either of these mics, the cable runs down to a small radio pack that typically clips on the back of a belt, or goes in a pocket, and transmits the signal to the receiver at the sound mixing desk. It is important to consider what you're going to wear if you're going to be mic'd in this way: it's not very elegant if the radio pack has to be taped to your back because there's nowhere to hide it.

Make sure the sound engineer has muted your mic once you are rigged. We don't want any *Naked Gun* bathroom moments! You may also be able to switch off your radio pack to be extra safe.

The third alternative is a hand-held mic. These generally produce the best quality, because they have the largest capsule (though an expensive headset or lav will probably sound better than a cheap hand-held). The cost is that it takes a hand to hold one. If you like to gesticulate a lot, that may be a crucial drawback. On the other hand, if you feel awkward and don't know what to do with your hands, this can be a blessing in disguise. It certainly hasn't bothered some of the world's greatest, most expressive singers.

If you are going to use a hand-held, you will need to know some mic technique. I have seen many people fail badly by not understanding the basics. Here they are:

Hold the mic so that the capsule is just in front of your chin (not under it), with the mic pointing directly at your mouth; this will typically mean the mic is angled up. For speaking, a good distance from the capsule to your mouth is around the width of four fingers, which is easy to test by using your free hand. Here's a picture of me speaking at a conference in Brazil that gives a good indication of ideal mic position.

Don't move off mic. If you move your head, follow it with the mic, or your words will fade and be lost.

Don't gesticulate with your mic hand! Be always conscious of that gap from mic to mouth and keep it consistent. By the same token, don't go unconscious and let your hand drop.

If you want to get sophisticated, you can explore the proximity effect: the closer you are, the more warmth and bass there will be in your voice, and the more intimate (and yet louder) the sound will be. That can be fun for a 'secret' aside, or just to change the timbre of your delivery for a moment, though you have to be careful not to 'pop' the mic with plosives from that close, and the sound can feel rather overbearing, so it's not something to do consistently. The inverse works too: get further away from the capsule, and your voice will seem more distant and high-pitched. If you're going to shout for any reason, it's kind to move the mic away so you don't shock people. If you watch expert singers carefully, you'll see them moving the mic away at some moments, closer at others. Play with mic distance and its effects, and you'll discover if the near or far positions might be useful to you in your performance.

A final tip on hand-helds: I always check the battery level myself. Professional sound people will almost certainly have inserted fresh batteries that will last many hours, but once or twice there has been an error and I have had to ask for fresh ones. Holding a dying mic is not fun when you're in front of an audience.

If you do a lot of speaking, you may want to buy your own mic or mics. The world leader is Shure, who will be known to any musician for their iconic SM58, still the go-to vocal mic for most singers. They make great lavs, headsets and radio hand-helds (including the two radio versions of the great SM58). I have also had excellent results from Audio-Technica headsets and hand-helds. This is all very much down to personal taste, so you might also wish to check out other leading names like Sennheiser, Behringer and Sony.

CHECK

Whatever tech you choose to use, please make sure you agree or set a time to do a full tech check as we've already discussed, ideally in the empty room with the full AV team (if there is one) present, in plenty of time to manage any problems that may arise.

This is critical. Without it you will be at risk of an epic fail.

BACKUP

If you've read Daniel Kahneman's excellent book *Thinking Fast and Slow*, you'll know that human beings are very poor when it comes to risk assessment, or indeed evaluating the consequences of any choices. We tend to focus on any certain costs, while ignoring unlikely ones even if they might be disastrous, and this results in behaviour that often verges on brinkmanship. If there is a doomsday scenario, even a highly unlikely one, it pays to take precautions against it, because the cost of *not* preparing may be catastrophic, while the cost of preparing is probably very small. It's the old umbrella argument: the cost of carrying one and not needing it is quite small, while the cost of not carrying one and needing it can be a soaking—and yet so often we choose to leave it at home.

For speaking, what this means is considering the high-cost possibilities and having a backup plan wherever possible. Let's explore some scenarios.

If you're using your own computer, what if it dies on you? If there will be other compatible machines at the venue, then you may be able to survive this by carrying a copy of your presentation (and anything else that's critical, like required fonts) on a USB stick. I always do this as a matter of course. If there are no other computers to use, what can you deliver without the slides? What would that look like, and what materials could you prepare that would allow you to carry on, at least in part? Perhaps a printed copy of your slides or your syntax would give you enough waypoints to be able to busk most, if not all, of your talk. If so, bring one along.

If the whole venue goes dead, what then? This happens even to the best-organised conferences. At TEDGlobal in Oxford in 2010, the power grid of the venerable Oxford Playhouse collapsed under the weight of the massive AV and stage lighting rig: fuses blew and the whole theatre went dark and silent. Just as in 2008, when Robin Williams memorably saved the day at Monterrey, there was salvation at hand in the talented audience. Opera singer and entrepreneur Genevieve Thiers gave a solo performance, with no sound system required, that brought the house down; comedian Max Jobrani followed up with a great informal set ("Whoa. For a minute, we didn't have any technology here. We were just ... ED."). Finally, TED Fellow and poet Ivie Okoawo performed a poem. Redeemers of catastrophic failure are often more memorable than the original event itself. In the UK, millions of people still remember the occasion when Wimbledon was rained off in 1996 and Sir Cliff Richard entertained the crowd for 20 minutes with *a cappella* songs, starting with *Singin' In The Rain.* I doubt they remember who won the tournament that year.

Could you be the one who puts your hand up and saves the day if there's a show-stopping disaster? You could be, if you prepare something.

At a more mundane level, it's not too hard to make sure you have backups for the things that often let you down. Carry spare batteries for everything. If you travel, carry two international power adapters, not just one. Carry extension leads for anything you may need to extend. You might even carry a gang-plug if you have several items to power and you are not sure how many sockets there will be.

In summary, review all your equipment. If anything is mission-critical, carry two of it, or if that's impossible or too expensive, have a plan to manage it failing. Work through all the scenarios you can and wherever possible plan for them. You just might be the one to save the day

PROPS

Props can be highly impactful. Take a look at Jill Bolte Taylor's famous 2008 TED talk if you want proof of this: she brings on stage a real human brain, which certainly made people sit up and pay attention! A rather simpler prop, and yet equally effective in deepening the impact of the talk, was the bag full of books that Susan Cain brought on stage in her powerful 2012 talk about the import role of introverts.

However, props can also be clunky, distracting and even annoying if badly deployed. Here are some guidelines for prop use.

Be sure that the prop is relevant. Just as with slides, the objective is to amplify what you're talking about, not distract or confuse. The brain that Jill Bolte Taylor used was completely relevant, because her whole talk was about what happened to her brain on the day of her stroke.

Practice so that you are expert in using the prop. Clunky, fumbling prop management or design will result in your effort falling flat, leaving people feeling that you tried to be too clever, and failed. I still chuckle whenever I think of the scene from the brilliant 'rockumentary' comedy film *Spinal Tap* where the bass player Derek Smalls is trapped in a plastic chrysalis that fails to open. Don't let that happen to you!

Be sparing unless your whole style is prop-centred. In general, less is more: too many props can easily become distracting.

Have backup plans in case props break or fail, or are unavailable for any reason, like simply forgetting to bring them.

REHEARSE

"Give me six hours to chop down a tree and I will spend the first four sharpening the axe."

– Abraham Lincoln

We're nine sections into this chapter on stagecraft and we are nowhere near the stage yet! If you're starting to sense that most of the secrets of successful platform speaking are in preparation, you're quite right. Just as with almost every skilled human activity, preparation is the critical area to focus on. Sports stars have started summarising this very well: when congratulated on breaking a world record or winning a major tournament, or asked if they were nervous, they often say something like this: "We prepared really well, so all I had to do was execute."

Possibly the most important part of your preparation is to rehearse. Earlier in the book we discussed practice, which is more general. It's great to practice the skill of public speaking so that you become more comfortable and expert at the activity in general. Rehearsal is more focused: it happens when you have a specific talk to give. You've created your content, the date is set, your aids and logistics are in train—so what you need now is to rehearse to the max.

What I mean by that is both quantitative and qualitative: put simply, it's giving your talk in real time, full size, enough times to become completely proficient.

I have coached many people out of a habit of rehearsing small, which involves skipping through the content, or sitting, mumbling the words and giving tiny versions of gestures. Every time you rehearse something, you strengthen synaptic pathways that reinforce whatever you are repeating and make it easier to reproduce it; the same applies to muscle memory.

If you are going to deliver standing, rehearse standing. If you are going to use slides, rehearse with your TV as the main screen behind you. If you plan to use a big, expansive gesture, rehearse exactly that gesture every time, not a watered-down version of it.

Even after years of speaking in public, my first talk at TED on the four effects of sound was an intimidating prospect. This is not your average audience: as you look out from the TED stage, you see people like Jeff Bezos, Larry Page and Peter Gabriel looking back at you. I rehearsed, and how! My daughter Alice knew the talk backwards by the time I left to deliver, because she had been my audience throughout the rehearsals. The result was that when I walked on stage, I had no concern about forgetting the material or the basics of delivery: I could enjoy the experience and be creative, a little like playing jazz when you know the tune really well.

Rehearsal also makes sure that you know your timings. These days I am very accurate at estimating my timings in slides per minute, but that only comes with years of familiarity and will be entirely individual. For a new talk, rehearsing for real is the only way to be definitive about how long you will take.

WARM UP

At last the big day has dawned. You're fully prepared; you've done your tech check and all is well, and now it's the final run-up to delivery. There's just one more thing to do before you walk on stage: warm up. Just as an engine needs a little warming before being opened up to full throttle, so do you. For this you will need a quiet space, ideally away from people (but that entirely depends on how self-conscious you are!). I have done my warm-ups in hotel corridors, remote backstage corners, bathrooms, dressing rooms, and even outside in a quiet street. Anywhere will do, just as long as you feel comfortable.

First, your body. If you have a gentle stretching routine, do it now. Make sure you feel as limber and relaxed as possible. At the very least, shake off your arms and legs and maybe do some forward and backward shoulder rotations to dissipate tension. Make sure your neck is loose and you are neither stretching nor compressing your vocal cords.

Now you can take a leaf out of Professor Amy Cuddy's book (or rather her TED talk, which at the time of writing is the second-most viewed of all time) and do a power pose to warm up your body chemistry. Cuddy and other researchers have established that striking power poses creates a feeling of increased strength and capability, probably by causing a release of testosterone. For a confidence boost, an easy and immediately effective power pose is to raise both your arms triumphantly and dramatically above your head as if you had just won an Olympic gold medal, and hold for several seconds. You may want to find a quiet place to do this!

Finally, you can warm up your voice. Below are my recommended vocal warm-up exercises, which take very little time to do and get you ready to speak at your best. You can also find them in a short audio file on this book's website.

Chest Raise your arms above your head whilst taking a deep in-breath, and then sigh the breath out as you lower your arms. Repeat until you feel your ribs have moved and your lungs are awake.

Lips First, do what you did as a small child when cold: a nice, expressive b-r-r-r-r-r, letting the lips move freely. Second, repeat several times the sound BO (say it like the word bop, without the final p), exaggerating the way your lips move. You may now find your lips feel much more alive and vital.

Tongue Again we have two exercises. First, repeat several times the sound LA, exaggerating the way your tongue moves, flicking it right from the back of your palette to the front of your mouth. Second, roll an R for as long as you can. It took me weeks to learn how to do this, and I'm glad I persisted because this one is like champagne for the tongue. I hope by now your whole mouth is feeling fully alert and ready for speaking!

Voice If I can do only one exercise for some reason, this is the one I will always go to. It's called the Siren, and it really gets your voice ready to give of its best. It's like a sine wave, moving from the highest your voice will go to the lowest, with the sound WEEE at the top and AWWW at the bottom. As your WEEE-AWWW-WEEE-AWWW sound swoops from high to low, be conscious of any discontinuities. They will smooth out and disappear as you continue with the exercise. After this, you may find your voice has lowered in pitch a tone or two, and you will have access to your full range at a moment's notice.

Doing all of this warm-up takes no more than two or three minutes, so there is no excuse for missing it. Really, it's worth doing this before any important speaking, not just a talk on a stage. Whether you're planning to propose marriage, ask for a raise, or run a meeting for your team, you owe it to yourself to make sure your voice is fully ready.

BESS

At last you are walking on stage, fully prepared and warmed up. Before you deliver your first word, I suggest a little routine that will create just the right connection with your audience. It's called BESS—another useful little acronym.

Breathe

We covered the importance of the breath in Chapter Six. Taking a big, deep breath as you walk on counters any nerves you might be feeling, and gives you all the fuel you need for a rich, confident first word.

Expand

This refers not to your voice, but to your vision. Some people will tell you to focus on one person at a time in the audience and have individual conversations with each of them. I disagree. Yes, it is essential to maintain eye contact with your audience, but, for me, the conversation is not with one person at a time, but with all of them at once.

You can do this by expanding your awareness, which means moving from foveal vision to peripheral. Foveal vision is a very narrow field of view where you perceive detail and colour most clearly; it's what you're using right now as you read these words. Most people unconsciously start to frown a little when concentrating in foveal vision; the eyebrows tend to draw together a little, the forehead tenses and the eyes squint slightly.

By contrast, peripheral vision is everything outside the narrow foveal corridor. It becomes less clear and detailed as you move to the edges of your field of view, which for most people are well past 90 degrees on each side. Peripheral vision's job is to give you an impression of the whole situation, which is exactly what we need when speaking to a large group or an audience. By being in peripheral vision, I can sense the listening in the entire audience; I can see the whole room, even if it contains thousands of people; I can sense centres of positive (or negative) response as I am speaking. One other advantage, for me at least, is that moving into peripheral vision tends to uncompress the facial muscles, smoothing away a frown and opening up the face. The eyebrows move apart; the eyes widen; the forehead relaxes; you might even find yourself smiling!

Try it now. Hold up your hands, fingers pointing upwards and palms forwards, to either side of your face. Start wiggling your fingers gently and slowly move your hands back until you can't see the wiggling anymore; when you reach that point, reverse until the wiggling fingers are just visible on both sides. Now pick a spot on the wall in front of you and focus on it in foveal vision. Gradually transfer the focus of all your awareness away from the spot on the wall and onto your wiggling fingers at the edges of your visual field. Did you feel your face relax? Can you now see the whole room at once? Practice this transition into peripheral vision until it becomes natural to you. Mastering this transition will be very useful; it's the E of BESS. As you walk to your spot and breathe in, simultaneously expand into peripheral vision and become aware of the listening in the room.

Stance

We dealt with stance in detail in Chapter Six. If you've done those exercises, you will know how to adopt a strong, grounded, upright, relaxed and powerful stance the moment you reach your mark.

Smile

It's amazing what a smile will do. As you take a moment to look around at the audience, smiling shows that you're happy to be there, as well as making a connection. It doesn't have to be a big, cheesy grin and it certainly starts to look slightly odd if you hold it for too long. Whatever's in character and authentically you, lasting a second or two, will do the trick nicely. Of course, this is not appropriate for every talk: if your subject matter is painful or very serious, a more sombre expression will be required. But if your material is anywhere from neutral to uplifting, enjoy the gift you're about to give, and connect happily with your audience for a moment. They'll enjoy it.

The whole BESS process ideally flows as you walk on, with all four things pretty much happening at the same time, taking just a few seconds from start to finish. With repetition, it will become automatic and seamless for you to do this. As with most aspects of speaking and listening, practice and consciousness are the keys. Please work with a coach or a video camera until you are fluid, natural and can inject your own personality into this process.

STAGE ANCHORING

You may want to use your stage or set for different messages, or to represent a process or a timeline. If you do this, it's important not to confuse your audience by being inconsistent. I'll borrow a third concept from NLP (alongside the chunking and clean language ideas we have already discussed) to explain how you can do this with clarity. The concept is **anchoring**. In my work with The Sound Agency I often talk about the power of music, which, like much of sound, affects our emotions largely through association, as we discussed way back in Chapter One. Anchoring is in effect simply managed association, where you give areas of the stage or props some meaning.

Let's consider the two dimensions of the stage; front-back and left-right. On the front-back axis, most of the time you will want to be roughly central, or slightly forward of central. It would be rather intimidating to deliver an entire talk from the very front of the stage—though if you want to get more intimate, for example in giving a 'secret' aside, then you might move further forward to do that. As already mentioned, if the stage is professionally lit, I suggest you ask the lighting people or the director where it is best-lit and what your range of movement is. This also applies if you're being filmed, either for recording or for large screens live. I think it's part of being professional to be aware of the camera(s) and their limitations. I have often seen people moving so fast, or so unpredictably, that they spend much of their talk at least partly off-camera as the poor operators frantically try to catch up with them.

On the left-right axis, the same criteria apply about light and cameras, but there is more to consider: the dimensions of time (past to future) and transformation (problem to solution, good to bad, old to new). Think about time for a moment. If I ask you to visualise time as a line in your mind's eye, where would you put the past? And the future? Most people in the West have time running from left to right. Did you? This is probably to do with our way of reading and writing, where the flow is from left to right. By contrast, Arabs and Hebrew speakers tend to have the past on the right, while Mandarin speakers have the past high up and the future low down on a vertical timeline. Understanding your audience's timeline visualisation can be very important if you want to be clear and easy to understand.

If, like me, you will be speaking almost exclusively in English to people who read from left to right, please bear in mind that you and the audience are facing in opposite directions. This means that, as they look at the stage, their timeline goes from past on your *right* to future on your *left*. You will make people rather uncomfortable if you retain your natural timeline and talk about the future with a gesture to your right (which will be their left). I am so used to this now that I've essentially reversed my own timeline, and instinctively indicate to the right when I talk about past and the left when I talk about future.

The same applies for good-bad, problem-solution, broken-fixed or any other emotionally weighted continuum. I suggest that you anchor them all the same way for yourself so that you don't confuse people. To your right will be past, bad, problem, old, broken, illness, darkness, difficulty and so on. To your left will be future, good, solution, new, fixed, health, light, ease and so on. I find that this consistency helps: it feels rather strange to the audience if you talk about a problem with a left-hand gesture when you have just indicated the future with the same hand, though of course the specifics of what you anchor, where, are entirely up to you.

This anchoring isn't confined to gestures: you can move gradually from one side of the stage (your right) to the other (your left) if you're delivering a speech that starts with a problem and ends with the solution, or if you are presenting something you want people to buy. You can anchor props or particular places on stage, too. For example, we covered the importance of storytelling in Chapter Five: if you tell a lot of stories, you might do what I do in my longer seminars, and have a storytelling stool. After a while, people forge the association between the chair and the stories, so the moment I sit in the stool I can sense people leaning forward slightly and metaphorically curling up in anticipation of another tale.

The most important thing is to be consistent in your anchoring. People will make associations, and it's part of your job to make sure that they are clear, accurate and congruent with what you're trying to communicate, and not confusing, messy or distracting.

COMMON ERRORS

Let's end with a few of the mistakes I have seen people make most often. I hope this short list helps you to step over the pitfalls and deliver brilliantly.

Speaking to the screen

As we've noted, this becomes tempting if you use bullets, and especially if you don't have a comfort monitor. The answer? If you're going to use slides, *always* have a comfort monitor or Presenter View in front of you. If you need to gesture to the screen, do it without turning around; at worst, half-turn so you can point with one hand whilst keeping eye contact with the audience. Turning your back on your audience is simply rude.

Not looking at the audience

This is incredibly common. Some people habitually stare over the heads of the audience as they speak; some like to read writing from a lectern and simply forget to look up; others can't get their eyes off the floor. All three habits are very disconcerting for the audience, who start wondering if they've done something to offend the speaker! Please use video to check your eye contact. It is dramatically emasculating for a speaker to fail to look at the people he or she is speaking to. If you have any one of these habits, it is critical to train yourself out of it by using video, friends and if need be a professional coach.

Lack of variation

It's all too easy to get into a rhythm when speaking. This becomes a form of self-hypnosis, where one goes into one's comfort zone and loses full consciousness. The cadences start to repeat; the volume level gets fixed within narrow margins; the pace becomes easy and uniform, like a long-distance run. That may be comfortable for the speaker, but it will send the audience into a trance-like state not far from sleep (and possibly real sleep in some cases!). A talk delivered without variation is like a billiard ball: uniform, featureless and entirely unmemorable. We need valleys to create mountains and darkness to have light; a good talk will have tensions in it, contours and colours that make it memorable. Make sure you stay conscious every second. Intentionally vary your pace, volume, prosody, pitch and body language. Use silence to great effect. Prepare these changes if need be, and make notes to remind yourself of delivery variation, not to go to sleep and let the talk become automatic.

Tics

Many people have characteristic habits when speaking. On stage or in front of a group, these may become accentuated or obvious, in which case they qualify as a speaking tic. This can be verbal or physical. Common verbal tics include "You know what I mean?", "Um", "Ah", "Er", and any oft-repeated word. The latter is hard to break: sometimes words lodge in our brains and become what the audio branding community call 'earworms'—things that rattle round in our heads like an annoying piece of music, and spill out unconsciously, often much to our own annoyance. The word 'just' can be like that for me: often, after training people on the importance of avoiding it I find it tripping out of my mouth every other sentence. It sometimes seems to have a mind of its own! Many times in my life, hyperbole has infected my speech— everything suddenly becomes 'fantastic' for a few days, for example, or I find myself indicating approval with a mindless phrase like "Good

good!" Slightly annoying in normal life, these things can be devastating on stage as the audience starts counting your usage.

Physical tics can be even more distracting. They may include swaying from side to side, alternating leaning on one hip then the other, little continuous walks around and around, or regularly walking from one place to another for no particular reason. They all share the same negative property: they distract from what you are saying.

Check in regularly using video or friends' eyes to make sure you haven't developed any annoying or distracting tics. Remember the joy of being completely conscious when you're speaking (and listening). Tics are a great indication that you're going to sleep again.

Overtime

We discussed this at length earlier in this chapter, but I make no apology for mentioning it again. If this is someone else's event, going over is simply rude, not only to your host but also to the person due to speak after you. Use your Presenter View clock if the venue doesn't give you one. If it's your event, make sure you have feedback from a clock or supporter. If you are going to go overtime for some unavoidable reason, stop and ask permission the moment you realise it. You may find people are fine with a few more minutes, but it's arrogant to make that assumption without asking.

Rushing off

The most common thing I adjust when I'm training people is their tendency to dive off stage the moment their last word is delivered. If the audience is going to applaud, stand and take it! Many of us feel uncomfortable being affirmed like this, especially if we don't encounter an audience very often. It is rude to rush off when people are trying to say thank you. It's polite to honour their affirmation, without of course going over the top and looking arrogant or milking the approbation. Simply stand and look happy; nod if you like; sometimes I have clapped the audience back if they've been particularly responsive. Don't overstay your welcome: usually a few seconds of nodding and smiling is enough, and the applause will fade as you disappear from view, job done.

In closing

CONSCIOUSNESS

As we reach the end of this journey through speaking and listening, you won't be surprised to find this word again; it's cropped up many times throughout this book.

Powerful speaking and listening both require you to be fully conscious. We do people a disservice when we listen without complete attention; just in the same way, most of the bad talks I've seen in my life have been delivered by people who went unconscious about what they were doing, or failed to prepare consciously. Whether you're standing in front of one person, a room of eight people or an auditorium of 800, you own it to them (and to yourself) to be fully conscious. That includes how you stand, where you look, the expressions on your face, your gestures, your words and your use of all the tools in your vocal toolbox.

It's a wonderful practice to elevate your level of awareness, becoming completely mindful of what you are doing. We spend so much of our time half asleep, being seduced and anaesthetised by screens and other distractions, that opportunities to break those shackles and be fully conscious, far from being things to fear and dread, are in fact precious chances to experience living at a new level. I strongly recommend that you practice the art of public speaking for this reason if no other, because it's in the crucible of that activity that you will feel most scrutinised, which will push you to make the extra effort to be fully conscious.

I sincerely hope that the exercises throughout the book, and your practice of public speaking, will in this way elevate your natural level of mindfulness in both speaking and listening.

I believe that speaking and listening consciously and effectively will transform your outcomes in life—and it is also the only way we can achieve greater understanding in the world. Both of these are prizes worth striving for. I wish you well in achieving them.

Author Bio

Julian Treasure is an author and international speaker on sound, speaking and listening. His five TED talks have been viewed an estimated 50 million times, including one in the top 10 TED talks of all time. Julian is founder of The Sound Agency, which has been proving that good sound is good business worldwide since 2003.

THANK YOU FOR READING.

In writing *How to be Heard*, Julian Treasure did his very best to produce the most accurate, well-written and mistake-free book. Yet, as with all things human (and certainly with books), mistakes are inevitable. Despite Julian's and the publisher's best efforts at proofreading and editing, some number of errors will emerge as the book is read by more and more people.

We ask for your help in producing a more perfect book by sending us any errors you discover at errata@mango.bz. We will strive to correct these errors in future editions of this book. Thank you in advance for your help.

CPSIA information can be obtained
at www.ICGtesting.com
Printed in the USA
JSHW031119261121
20787JS00002B/2

9 781633 536715